More words of praise for
LISTENING FOR THE SOUL

Deeply rooted in the Christian tradition of pastoral ministry, Jean Stairs' work invites us to a dynamic and creative reconsideration of pastoral care and spirituality in the Protestant ethos. Listening for the Soul *is not only the title, but the touchstone theme for Stairs's reflections in each of these important chapters. Particularly challenging is the conversation on the distinctions and relationships between Protestant pastoral care and Catholic spiritual direction. This book will appeal to all who minister in Christ's name who are interested in a fresh, exciting "read." The excellent suggestions for exercises at the end of each chapter add a welcome practicality to the text.*
    —Caroline Dawson, IBVM, Spiritual Director and Theologian

The subject matter of this book is invaluable to the field of pastoral care. Stairs focuses on soul care as an integral dimension of pastoral care, encouraging caregivers to find ways to elicit and support stories of religious experience. She offers several practical strategies and case examples throughout the text of how to help people to use their faith perspectives to find meaning in their life experiences. She explores soul care at individual, family, and congregational levels, spending considerable time on how to offer soul care to children. She also offers an excellent chapter on the importance of spiritual practices for caregivers for the sake of their own spiritual health and their credibility in offering soul care. Pastoral theology needs to take the issues raised in this text with the utmost seriousness.
    —Christie Neuger, United Theological Seminary

In Listening for the Soul: Pastoral Care and Spiritual Direction, *Jean Stairs explores the unique relationship between spirituality and Protestant Christianity, arguing that spiritual growth is the ultimate aim of pastoral care. Specifically addressing the difficulties that Protestants have with spiritual discipline and practice, Stairs draws on a wide range of traditions to offer a rationale and practices that root pastoral care in contemplation. In so doing, she untangles a particularly knotty problem in pastoral care: she demonstrates how care for others and care for oneself can become complementary, rather than competitive, aspects of the Christian lifestyle. She addresses practices often associated with spirituality, such as hospitality, Sabbath-keeping, and simplicity, but also pursues an uncommon and overlooked arena for spirituality: soul work with children.* Listening for the Soul *is a substantive and nourishing treat for those persons committed to religious leadership and the practices of pastoral care and spirituality, for persons who are simply curious about the way that the established Protestant tradition addresses spirituality, and for the many skeptics who doubt that Protestants have anything at all to contribute to the wide-spread popularity of a lifestyle rooted in "spirituality."*
    —Pamela D. Couture, Colgate Rochester Divinity School/Crozer Theology Seminary

For Wayne,
whose soul-listening is full of truth and grace,
making all the difference in my life.

LISTENING FOR THE SOUL

pastoral care
and
spiritual Direction

Jean stairs

fortress press   minneapolis

LISTENING FOR THE SOUL
Pastoral Care and Spiritual Direction

Scripture quotations from the New Revised Standard Version of the Bible are copyright ©1989 by the Division of Christian Education of the National Council of Churches of Christ in the United States of America and are used by permission.

Excerpt from *Psalms of Lament* ©1995 Ann Weems. Used by permission of Westminster John Knox.
Excerpt from "Journey of the Magi." Copyright ©1927. Used by permission of Faber and Faber and Harcourt.

Cover design: Marti Naughton
Cover art: "Friends" by Jan Zrzavy. Reproduced by permission of Art Resource, New York
Author photo: Frame and Photo Centre, Kingston, Ontario
Interior design: Julie Odland

Library of Congress Cataloging-in-Publication Data
Stairs, Jean (   )
       Listening for the soul : pastoral care and spiritual direction / Jean Stairs.
          p.   cm.
       Includes bibliographical references.
       ISBN 0-8006-3239-7 (alk. paper)
       1. Spiritual direction.   2. Pastoral theology.   3. Spiritual life—United Methodist Church (U.S.)   I. Title.
BX8349.S67 S73   2000
253.5'.3—dc21   00-035465
                                                                                            CIP

The paper used in this publication meets the minimum requirements for American National Standard for Information Services—Permanence of Paper for Printed Library Materials, ANSI Z329.48-1984. ♾ ™

Manufactured in the U.S.A.   AF1-3183
          06   07   08   09   6   7   8   9   10

CONTENTS

⊷≡◉⇌⊷

INTRODUCTION
Listening for the soul Again

❖══◐◑══❖

Look on my right hand and see—
there is no one who takes notice of me;
no refuge remains to me;
no one cares for me.

I cry to you, O Lord;
I say, "You are my refuge,
my portion in the land of the living."

I stretch out my hands to you;
my soul thirsts for you like a parched land.

Psalms 142:4-5; 143:6

THOSE OF US WHO ARE PRIVILEGED TO CARRY OUT the ministry of pastoral care are becoming increasingly aware that we have neglected to listen for the soul. What North American mainline Protestant churches once understood to be central in pastoral care is now marginal in pastoral practice. Because we have neglected to foster *soulfulness* (soul fullness),[1] the church and the world alike cry out like the psalmist of old: "No one cares for me. . . . My soul thirsts for you like a parched land." A jarring dichotomy exists between society's pervasive longing for meaningful spirituality and the faltering pastoral responses of Protestant churches.

The public Quest for soulfulness

The world is crying out for the church to be more like the church, to represent the space and place where holiness, meaning, and God can be found, experienced, understood, and reimagined. Yet even at the beginning of a new century, for many, the traditional patterns of religious life remain too patriarchal, inadequate, and even obsolete. For others, the church seems too much in appearance like the world—too busy, too tired, too involved, too demanding, too unstable, too spiritually impoverished, too leadership deprived.

I

At the same time that such strong and ambivalent feelings are being expressed about the church, people remain interested in spiritual matters. Spirituality is newsworthy and remains marketable. Pollsters report on religious trends and affiliations. Popular television programs from *Touched by an Angel* to *NYPD Blue* regularly address spiritual matters. Also, the increased plurality of North American society and the visible presence of Eastern religions have heightened our consciousness of spiritual traditions and the spiritual life. People are consistently providing evidence that there is a deep-seated craving for religious sensibilities and rituals. Even taking into account the sentimentality triggered by the Christmas holiday season, the notable increase in attendance at Christmas Eve services can be partly attributed to the fact that people want to connect in some way with the holy mystery of the Christmas event. Some men and women openly confess the need to feel more spiritually connected and alive. These needs are frequently demonstrated through pursuits that seek to merge the psychological, medical, and spiritual paradigms. Zealous interest in Yoga, Tai Chi, massage, meditation, and relaxation therapies, and chiropractic, homeopathic, and naturopathic care indicates that ours is a time of intense personal and social yearning for spiritual wholeness.

In such a climate, it is not surprising that enrollment levels for university and college religious studies courses have soared. People are devising personal spiritual belief systems and seeking with renewed vigor places and practices that put them in touch with spiritual values. Most bookstores contain entire sections on New Age spirituality, women's and men's spiritualities, and alternative health. The number of books (including this one!) published in the last few years with the word *soul* in their titles is staggering. We gorge on books, hoping to digest clues for fixing our bodies, our businesses, our relationships, our addictions, and now even our souls. No longer are retreat centers the sole/soul enterprise of the church. All sorts of healing, inner renewal, and spirituality centers are springing up in a secular context, advertised as getaway places from the stresses of work and our technological addictions. Alternative and holistic approaches to caring for body, mind, and soul are rapidly finding their way into an eager consumer-driven market. Attending to the soul, in all its emptiness and fullness, has now become a trendy and profitable enterprise. When our hunger is so intense, it seems that we will eat anything put before us that promises nourishment.

Many pastoral caregivers are acutely aware that people are desperately seeking to make connections with holiness, the mystery of life, and the divine force of creation. The reordering of priorities brought about by a decrease in financial resources, changes in employment and work patterns, and external stresses placed upon personal time commitments has led to a lack of balance in life. Many people simply are overextended and unable to discern what leads to a balanced life and what leads to burnout and long-term disability, the new dis-eases of our time. The fact of change has produced increased anxiety and turned up the volume of noise in our souls. So, too, the ever-widening gap between the haves and the have-nots and a growing discomfort with the idolatrous nature of consumerism have evoked in many a quest for simplicity and a renewed spiritual life.

Protestant churches are now scrambling to respond to this renewed interest in matters of the soul, but it is clear that they are ill equipped to do so. Indeed, they are almost frantic in their quest to catch up with the public's emphasis upon matters of the soul, and they fear that inaction may indeed hasten the demise of the church's capacity to address spiritual matters and care for the soul. The church fears that its failure to attend to the soul has contributed to destructive patterns of disconnection with God, others, ourselves, and the earth.

While the public's interest in soul matters is surging, Protestant churches continue to flounder in their response to this phenomenon. Why is this so?

A cautionary and confused response

The main reason Protestant churches are giving uncertain and mixed responses to this public quest for the soul is because of a historic tendency within Protestant life to exercise caution toward some of the ways care for the soul has been offered and structured. Unlike the Roman Catholic, Orthodox, and Anglican communities, which sustained formal structures for spiritual direction as a one-to-one means of caring for the soul, Protestants generally resisted this approach for reasons that are theological and distinctly Protestant in nature. For many Protestants, the notion that one human being can advise another human being on intimate matters of the soul is perceived as contrary to the Protestant principles of *scripture alone* or *Christ alone*. The fear of sacerdotalism, and the thought that any individual spiritual director might assume the role of prime mediator, displacing the unique role held by Jesus, may partly explain Protestant preferences toward group experiences of faith-sharing and weekly prayer meetings. For Protestants, the word *director* suggested too much control and authoritarianism, contrary to theological notions of the priesthood of all believers and lay empowerment. Instead, Protestants have developed a pattern of mutual care, making no distinction in this regard between clergy and laypeople, and seeing spiritual direction as a function of the entire community.

Many Protestant laypeople simply remain unaware of the classic tradition of spiritual direction and the resources available for individuals who wish to participate in it. Even though placing soul care in the hands of the entire faith community is consistent with the historical tendencies of Protestants, many individuals do expect to grow spiritually through their clergy and no longer entrust the care of their souls to the faith community. The problem is that, in many cases, the community is no longer caring for the soul. Too many congregations have lost their sense of purpose, forgotten it, or never learned about a spirituality that motivates care for the soul. They have grown comfortable with their neglect as a way of dealing with their discomfort. Too many Protestants still carry a confused and cautionary stance toward words once used to describe the spiritual life. Our picture of a pietistic Christian is painted with the broad brushstrokes of "a saccharin sentimentality" or a vision of a "delicate, easily shocked conscience of moral rigidity."[2]

Another more modern reason Protestants remain guarded about formal spiritual direction is their historic enchantment and ongoing relationship with the field of psychology.[3] With the dawn of new psychological theories and advancements in medical science, the boundaries etched between pastoral care and spiritual direction became more pronounced. For the most part, Roman Catholics and the Eastern Church preserved the tradition of formal spiritual guidance and accepted counseling as complementary to it. Protestants, however, increasingly viewed counseling as having the strongest possibility for alleviating individual and in-depth pain. For Catholics, care of the soul remained a sacred art for spiritual directors, while Protestants increasingly identified *care* of the soul with *cure* of the soul administered by therapeutic specialists. Cure of the soul became associated with the tasks of fixing, adjusting, or making healthy. The restoration of the soul became increasingly less spiritual and more therapeutic.

The result was confusion, not about the need to be responsible for the soul's well-being, but about the nature of that well-being, and who, or what, more effectively promoted it. Motivated by a desire to stay relevant, Protestant clergy flocked to training centers and opportunities to become certified in counseling methods that incorporated psychological theories and principles. They genuinely desired to appreciate the wisdom of human science and to embrace appropriately the clinical language and the approach of psychology within the practice of pastoral care. The clinical pastoral education movement grew in strength and became an institutionally valid form of training within theological preparation for ministry. Some clergy left the church to set up private practices. Others attempted to integrate their newfound understanding and techniques into their pastoral practice within the church, relying less upon overt spiritual language and more upon psychological language. The confusion between the world of psychology and the realm of the spirit continued to be felt in the decades of the seventies and eighties when the pop psychology, self-help, and self-actualization movements began to lose their appeal. In spite of having invested good money in analysis and therapeutic resources, which did lead to increased self-understanding and healthier behaviors for many, the fundamental questions of meaning, purpose, and life vocation still lingered.[4] Yet the popularization of psychological language had shaped the way Protestants understood care of the soul, and the problem-solving therapeutic model now integrally influenced it.

Protestant clergy and their parishioners now find themselves enmeshed in behavioral patterns and practices that mirror these struggles of the past decades. Ministers once occupied a study, usually at home, a place where daily prayers, scriptural meditation, and reflection on the movements of God's spirit were not only routine, but also clearly expected by the public and the people of God. Now, many clergy have begun simply "keeping office hours." Too many churches today remain captive to the therapeutic and professionalized model of pastoral care, and they find themselves unequipped to listen for the truth that speaks from the deep, often hidden places of the soul. It seems that historically conditioned Protestant reluctance to adopt individualized methods of soul care (such as spiritual direction) and Protestants' increased reliance upon professionalized (often therapeutically oriented) delivery modes for pastoral care have contributed immeasurably to the dislocation of the soul as central to pastoral care.

Nevertheless, many Protestants have an observable renewed desire to listen for the soul again and to reclaim the distinct contribution that soulful pastoral care can make to individuals and faith communities. Many pastoral caregivers, theological schools, and congregations are trying to move care for the soul from what has become its marginalized position back to its historic central place in pastoral care.[5] Some of these pastoral strategies are intentionally helpful and serve to point us in new directions. Others may unintentionally mislead us in our attempts to relocate listening for the soul to its historic center in pastoral care. As we consider the growing desire and movement among Protestants to attend to the soul, it will be important to ask why some responses contribute to the task of reclamation and why others may pose danger.

The protestant Desire to Listen for the soul Again

The Desire Revealed in Pastoral Caregivers

Increasingly, many Protestant pastoral caregivers are turning toward spiritual direction as a means of dealing with their own spiritual hunger and to strengthen their pastoral practice so that it attends to soul matters. This attraction to spiritual direction has led to a growing tendency for pastoral caregivers to make referrals to professional spiritual directors. Spiritual needs once addressed freely within the context of a congregation's pastoral care ministry are now frequently being taken to contractual external sources, usually those representing Roman Catholic traditions of spirituality.

Another consequence of this turn toward spiritual direction is that Protestant clergy and laity are increasingly enrolling in spiritual direction courses and programs. Usually the intention here is to become a specialist trained in the ministry of spiritual direction in order to practice spiritual direction in congregational pastoral care or to freelance as a spiritual director. Interest in such training has resulted in spiritual direction training programs springing up all over the continent and with diverse criteria and standards. The number of Protestant spiritual directors now available in peripheral, often independent offices and locations increased remarkably in the 1990s. One merely has to type in the words *spiritual direction, spirituality*, or *soul* on a World Wide Web search and the resulting locations number in the thousands.

As spiritual direction is becoming increasingly specialized and professionalized, retreat centers are also experiencing unprecedented growth. The intense spiritual hunger of most Protestant parishioners and clergy has clearly been the main reason that the number of spirituality workshops being offered and marketed, by and for both churches and the general public, has undergone a substantial increase.

This impulse on the part of pastoral caregivers toward personal spiritual development and the desire to be equipped to respond to soul matters is a healthy sign that the reclamation process for soulful pastoral care is underway. Opportunities to deepen our understanding of classic and contemporary spiritual disciplines and traditions and to have experiences that strengthen our spiritual lives and those of our faith communities help to bring soul matters from marginalized places and memory. But as long as educational opportunities are absent within the Protestant context, or fail to present adequately the Protestant heritage in terms of how it has dealt with the soul, then pastoral caregivers and parishioners will turn to secular, popular, or other denominational opportunities that may either mislead us or be misappropriated by us.

For example, the practice of spiritual direction itself can be misappropriated. In recovering pastoral care so that it truly listens for the soul, one must explore how aspects of spiritual direction can be integrated into a congregational ministry of pastoral care. It is especially important to emphasize that soulful pastoral care includes much more than an appropriation of the specialized purpose of spiritual direction. Pastoral care is not spiritual direction. Rather, spiritual direction is one means for offering pastoral care. In all its various forms, pastoral care seeks first and foremost to attend to the soul. If Protestant churches merely co-opt the practice of spiritual direction, they will be in danger of continuing to propagate a more individualistic orientation to life in general and the spiritual life in particular. While the interior life is important, listening for the soul necessarily includes discerning and acting upon the increased vitality and stirring of God's spirit at work within us and others. Pastoral care that listens for the soul happens best within faith communities where listening is a mutual task and a gift for the sake of the world.

The Desire Revealed in Theological Education

Another sign of this growing desire to listen for the soul can be found in more and more Protestant seminaries and schools. It was once possible to assume that soul care and development happened in the church before a student pursued a degree in theological education. This can no longer be taken for granted. It is increasingly common for students to lack a formal or significant relationship with a church. Henri Nouwen recognized the dilemma years ago when he said that "we need to explore ways to introduce schooling in prayer into pastoral education."[6] Nouwen's earlier challenge is still before us, but there is now a growing desire and will to make care for the soul integral to the preparation of persons for leadership in the church.

Over the last decade, the clinical pastoral education movement has been challenged to include in its basic training courses (often a theological degree requirement) components that deal with the spiritual life, disciplines, sensitivities, and prayers of the pastoral caregiver and those to whom pastoral care is offered. Recent trends suggest that Protestant seminarians are giving strong voice to their desire to see courses, chaplains, or spiritual guides that can help address their spiritual lives and questions in more than a purely rationalistic way. They want to do more than *study* spirituality. They want to *practice* the presence of God and build the rhythms of such practices into their daily lives so that their pastoral care becomes grounded in an authentic sense of God's presence and action.

A quick survey of current Protestant theological school calendars reveals that several new courses are being offered in the area of spirituality, many of these linked (either purposefully or by default) to pastoral departments. That there is an increased emphasis on spiritual formation within theological education is also evident in the separate category of *Personal and Spiritual Formation* inserted under the heading "Program Content" within the recently revised accreditation standards for the Association of Theological Schools.[7]

This emerging awareness that spiritual formation is to be included in theological preparation for church leadership is a necessary step toward an integrated curriculum. Soul matters are integral to the development of spiritual capacities required for holistic leadership within a church and society suffering immeasurable fragmentation of body, mind, and soul. This move to strengthen the essentiality of spiritual formation also presents some dangers, however. We have yet to understand that listening for the soul is the central task of pastoral care. By creating specialized courses in spirituality, we may overlook the connections between soul matters and pastoral care offered through the diverse and public expressions of congregational life, including liturgy, biblical preaching, Christian education, and outreach. In addition, there is also the question of the relation of soul matters to biblical studies, historical and theological studies, and ethics. The danger here is that we reduce spiritual matters to those that pertain to the individual's interior search for meaning and wholeness, a concept and practice that stands quite outside the mainstream of Protestantism's historic experiences with the Christian spiritual life. However we choose to attend to soul matters in theological programs, Protestant schools will want to retain a focus upon living the spiritual life in a way that is consonant with our historic focus on the priesthood of all believers and the realization of that call to priesthood within the world God so loves.

The Desire Revealed in Congregations

The desire to focus with greater intention upon care for the soul is also evident within local Protestant congregations and their struggles to address soul matters within their mission and ministry. Some Protestant congregations are participating in denominational projects designed to strengthen congregational spirituality. A recent example of this is the "Project in Congregational Spirituality," a cooperative concern of Auburn and Princeton Theological Seminaries and the Christian Faith and Life Program Area of the Presbyterian Church U.S.A.[8] From 1997 to 1999, these three groups worked with teams from eight Presbyterian congregations in an effort to determine what best enables congregations to be spiritually centered and renewed.

Another route being taken by some Protestant churches is to follow the recommendations of church growth consultants and the burgeoning church growth literature that focuses upon methods for reaching the so-called seeker generation.[9] These methods generally tend to place more stress upon the importance of fostering affective spirituality and less upon the meaning system that informs the development of spirituality. Admittedly, a reductionist summary of this approach is: "Get people into the church, give them a sense of belonging, and they will gradually absorb the Christian spiritual life." To package a serious concern for the soul as a church growth strategy runs the risk of presenting a quick fix for a much deeper spiritual reality that includes connecting with transcendent and immanent divine mystery. This may be a reason many Protestant churches have been determined not to diminish or cast aside the role of preaching in favor of what some have called alternative or seeker worship. In our preaching, there remain meaningful opportunities to address spiritual and pastoral concerns that can connect people's lives with God and the ways God continues to participate in revelation, history, and creation. The sermon has always been central for Protestants as a source for communal spiritual instruction and guidance on soul matters.

Other congregations are testing ways of integrating historic spiritual disciplines and the practice of spiritual direction within the broad pastoral care ministry of the congregation. In these cases, the pastoral methods being tested are a direct response to local initiatives and available resources. Common to all of these experiments is the desire to be intentional about the spiritual development of individuals and the congregation and to resist placing responsibility for soul care exclusively in the hands of ministry personnel. Three such congregational stories can be found at www.augsburgfortress.org. These stories highlight the opportunities and challenges facing Protestant congregations as they seek to be intentional about listening for the soul.

What is promising about this emerging awareness within congregations is that soul matters, at least, are being located where they belong—within the faith community and as its central pastoral task. What remains a challenge for us in moving soul from the margins to the center of pastoral care is to do so in ways that neither demean the depth of commitment and time involved in soul-listening nor exclude the whole people of God from the process. Listening for the soul is certainly the primary task of pastoral caregivers, but it is also the privilege and responsibility of the entire faith community.

The Quest for soulful pastoral care

It is because so many Protestants are on a quest for soulful pastoral care that I have written this book. My aim is to set out a vision for *soulful pastoral care*. This vision will be enacted first and foremost within faith communities. The primary method for enacting the vision of soulful pastoral care is *listening for the soul*. It is time for Protestant churches to reclaim the soul as central to pastoral care and to practice soulful pastoral care. To listen for the soul again means helping people to connect with God, live in the image of God, and discern how best to participate in God's ongoing creative and redemptive work in communities and in the world.

Defining soulful pastoral care

Definitions are important. We need to be clear about what we mean when we talk about soul matters. By *soul,* I mean the spiritual essence of one's existence expressed through body, mind, or any other facet of one's being. Our souls are brought into living reality by the vital and dynamic force of being, the very breath and spirit of God. This force of being connects us to each other and the mysterious source of all. By *listening for the soul,* I mean being aware and open to the wondrous spirit of God and hearing the ways God invites and reveals on all levels of our being and human longing. Our *spirituality* is simply the way we express our belief in and experience of God in this world.

We practice *pastoral care* when we enable individuals, groups, and communities to find meaning and make connections between their life experiences and the God who is concerned for the whole of the created world.[10] What will make pastoral care truly *pastoral* and not merely any form of care is focusing upon the soul as the essential self in relationship to God. By *pastoral caregivers,* I do not distinguish between clergy and laity but refer to anyone who has made an intentional and accountable commitment to the ministry of pastoral care and is in a continual process of nurturing his or her capacities for offering effective pastoral care.

Soulful pastoral care is a pastoral care that is intentional—deeply committed—full of soul for listening for the soul. It will listen for the soul in an integrated way both within and beyond the faith community. Soulful pastoral care listens for the soul in all ages and circumstances of life. It will practice a variety of intentional methods for awakening individuals and communities to the depth of divine mystery. Soulful pastoral care seeks to uncover the presence of God in everyday events, but also affirms and enables our human capacities to cooperate with the creative work of God and to orient life God-ward.

There is no one way to practice soulful pastoral care. It will be enacted differently in our faith communities. The particularities of our context and the sorts of people and resources that are available to us will influence it. Whenever we are listening for the soul, seeking to deepen our own and other's relationships with God, and discerning and acting in response to our deepening awareness of God at work in our beings, our daily lives, and our world, then we are practicing soulful pastoral care.

contributing to the quest for soulful pastoral care

The quest for soulful pastoral care is one that is shared by pastoral care-givers, spiritual directors, theological institutions, faculty, theology students, pastoral counselors, laypeople, and congregations. My hope is that this book will be a helpful contribution to the quest for these various readers and that there will be insights applicable to the practices of pastoral care and spiritual direction, as well as to both Protestant and Roman Catholic faith communities. I hope that practicing spiritual directors will find it valuable in clarifying the distinctions between pastoral care and spiritual direction, and in the cautions it presents to those who misappropriate the practice of spiritual direction or too hastily make claims for competence as spiritual directors. I hope it will inspire congregations who want to explore ways and means for pastoral care to reclaim its spiritual centeredness. I hope that those whose souls yet need to be heard into speech will treasure this book.

This book is meant to be used, not just read. Each chapter contains methods for soulful pastoral care that can be tested in congregations and pastoral practice. Woven together, a pattern for soulful pastoral care emerges. Not every congregation will have the resources at any given time to practice all of the methods presented here. Any attempts to do so may merely repeat past patterns of frenzied pastoral activity that oppose soulful pastoral care. It is more important to embrace methods that seem most suited to the realities of particular congregations.

At the beginning and end of each chapter are spiritual exercises, reflection questions, and a means for increasing awareness of the soul in pastoral practice. In some instances, the book contains elements of actual pastoral situations. Since confidentiality is essential to effective pastoral practice, all case descriptions use fictitious names in order to preserve anonymity. The experiences and pastoral tools are offered as a way to help congregations, pastoral caregivers, and theology students to begin the practice of soulful pastoral care.

The exception to confidentiality is in the appendix. Since we have much to learn from listening to the souls of our brothers and sisters, these yet-to-be-finished stories of three Protestant North American congregations serve as examples that may lead to the birth of even more models that aim to provide soulful pastoral care. Each congregation represented in the book has given permission for the publication of its story and has approved its telling as it is found here.

Chapters 1, 2, and 3 elucidate the concept of listening for the soul. The first chapter takes a closer look at the essential role that listening has within pastoral care. Listening is probed as an act of intentionality, obedience, intimacy, receptivity, hospitality, focus, soul inquiry, and habit. How we listen for the holy in the ordinary rhythms of life is explored through actual pastoral situations and the provision of two methods for the pastoral practice of *soul inquiry*. The second chapter focuses upon the contemplative tradition as a basis for pastoral care that encourages soul listening as a way to come to a deeper awareness of God. It presents contemplation as both a preventative and restorative approach to our practice of pastoral care. The third chapter invites us to move from a crisis-oriented pastoral care to one that listens for the soul's rhythm of death and resurrection. Rather than intervene in crisis in order to manage it, we intervene in dying moments in order to interpret spiritual meaning that awakens the soul to new life. Interpretive methods for pastoral intervention are the communal practices of lament and discernment.

Chapters 4, 5, and 6 address specific dimensions of pastoral care within congregational life. Chapter 4 treats the spiritual lives of pastoral caregivers themselves and reminds us that our credibility as pastoral caregivers depends upon our willingness to sustain not only personal spiritual habits but also public spiritual practices. The spiritual practices of hospitality, keeping the sabbath, and simplicity are presented as means for enhancing the credibility and content of pastoral care. When spiritual practices are enacted in daily life, they can restore, liberate, and integrate self and others into community and into deeper relationship with God.

Chapter 5 focuses on the laity and their involvement in pastoral care. It emphasizes how laypeople can reclaim their rightful ministry of caring for the soul and providing spiritual guidance for one another. Including a lay ministry of soul companionship within soulful pastoral care helps people to take responsibility for soul listening, both their own and others, and to locate the presence and activity of God in their daily lives and work.

Chapter 6 considers the little ones among us and invites us to recognize, affirm, and respond to the soul longings of children between the ages of three and eleven. For the most part, Protestant congregations have expressed concern for children by ensuring their Christian identity and inclusion, responding to crises in children's lives, and making sure that children are familiar with the content of the faith. This chapter takes Protestant churches beyond caring intention and challenges our thinking and pastoral practice with regard to the spiritually alert soul of the young child. I propose three ways to entice children into the habit of listening for the voice of God in their souls—through participation in ritual, the experience of wonder, and spontaneous and silent prayer.

The final chapter, chapter 7, presents some challenges to the two practices of pastoral care and spiritual direction. The growing desire among Protestants to reclaim the spiritual centeredness of pastoral care requires careful examination of how the practices of pastoral care and spiritual direction need to remain distinct while at the same time challenged to develop a mutuality and ethical complementarity. These two practices diverge in purpose, method, and scope of opportunity, yet they can cooperate and move toward a greater complementarity so long as they share a vision of soulful, spirited and liberating communities of faith making all the difference in the world.

Before I began this book, I prayed that God would "be in my head, and in my understanding; in my heart, and in my thinking; in my mouth, and in my speaking."[11] As I began to write, I prayed that all the people and places I have met would shape and challenge the final form of this book. Listening for my own soul during the writing process included listening for the sounds of God's presence in my soul—a soul that is clearly shaped by my Canadian identity, my feminist convictions, my call to ordained ministry (first as a Baptist, then more recently as a minister of the United Church of Canada), my teaching as a professor of the Practice of Ministry, my personal experience with spiritual direction, my commitment to be in community with the people of my local congregation, my cherished friends and colleagues, both near and far, the challenging and constructive comments of my editor, Henry French, and my beloved soulmate and marital companion, Wayne. All of these people and places are wrapped up in my passion for the recovery of a pastoral care that listens for the soul. Because I have been so immeasurably blessed by the gifts offered to me through soul listening, it is my prayer that this book will move souls to offer that same gift to others through soulful pastoral practice within a faith community.

I
soul inquiry:
Evocative Listening for the soul

⊷══◉══⊷

The Lord GOD has given me
   the tongue of a teacher,
that I may know how to sustain
   the weary with a word.
Morning by morning he wakens—
   wakens my ear
   to listen as those who are taught.
The Lord GOD has opened my ear.

Isaiah 50:4-5a

O VER AND OVER AGAIN, I AM STRUCK by the transforming significance
and profound simplicity of the ministry of listening. Maybe that is why
Simone Weil once reflected upon attention as the only faculty of the soul
that gives us access to God.[1] God both wakens our ears so that we may listen
and opens our ears so that we may hear. Listening for the soul is the primary
and essential form our pastoral care takes when we are concerned with fostering spiritual depth in the lives of those within our faith communities and
neighborhoods. As we live our ordinary routines, experiencing moments of
difficulty, surprise, and play, we can develop in ourselves and others the
habit of listening for the soul. This includes listening for our own soul as we
also practice listening for the souls of others. It is about letting our ears be
awake and attentive to the voices of yearning, weariness, and supplication in
the form of words, holy screams for new life, or sighs too deep for words.

To listen seems like such an ordinary thing; perhaps we too readily
underestimate its extraordinary value as an approach to pastoral care. The
essential role it can play deserves a closer examination. What might it mean
if the people of God had open ears? We need to open our own ears to hear
what it means to listen for the soul, and in particular, to discover how we
might become habitual in practicing such listening. To enhance our own
practice of pastoral care, we need especially to learn from the types of listening done by spiritual directors.

Listening as an Act of Intentionality

I use the term *listening* deliberately. In many ways, to listen for the soul, both our own and those of others, is more central to life than anything else we do. Pastoral care has spoken historically of "curing the soul," then of "caring for the soul," and more recently of "minding the soul."[2] It seems to me that, unlike the notion of "listening," these approaches seek to avoid damage, find an end to trouble, provide protection by watching over and tending, eliminate disease, see to the safety or well-being of another, and encourage freedom from anxiety or worry. We use regularly such expressions as "plan with care," "handle with care," "leave in your care," "take care of," "not a care in the world," "minding the shop," "minding the baby," "minding the step," "minding one's P's and Q's," or "finding a cure." Clearly, we are concerned with both care and cure as ways of minding; I am not recommending we obliterate the positive dimensions of these approaches to the soul. Sometimes the first things we need to do are provide protection, help the individual recall what is important, and ensure hospitable conditions so that he or she feels safe to tune into the soul's own trembling voice.

I suggest that the term *listening* be used to describe an overarching framework for pastoral care in our current societal climate. People will still need physical and mental healing of ailments, and they will frequently need help in exploring ways to cope with their immediate problems or crises. But the underlying dimension of the soul, the core of our lives and its denial or cultivation, remains the primary ministry given to the church, and we do this ministry best through the intentional act of listening. If we listen only partially and are too quick to cure the soul, the soul may simply get on with daily living without addressing the deeper issue of how life should be lived now and in the future. The immediate pain may dissipate long enough for familiar routines to be restored and for daily functioning to return, but if the deeper gnawing in the interior life remains unaddressed, the soul's restlessness will be experienced yet again. Our hearts are restless, after all, until they find their perfect rest in God, not in a cure.

Listening for the soul is not a quick fix or a limited intervention. Nor is it haphazard. Cultivating the soul essentially requires attending, in deliberate, habitual, and sustaining ways, to every aspect of our lives and all levels on which we live life, both consciously and unconsciously. To listen is to wait with a posture of alertness, in anticipation of hearing something of the voice and presence of God, who longs for us to be whole and abundantly alive. But we do not listen in order to make God present. We open our ears as a way of responding to the presence of God, who is already and always present in our lives, with or without our recognition.

In placing such a prominent emphasis upon listening, it needs to be said that I am not describing a passive act, but a process that engages us actively in response to what is heard. Listening is about more than a well-honed skill (although certainly skill is involved). Undeniably, listening for the soul will involve those essential skills normally identified with the act of listening, such as expressing interest by caring behavior, using appropriate facial expressions and posture, posing open-ended questions, closely observing nonverbal clues, responding by paraphrasing, clarifying, supporting, prob-ing, understanding, confronting, evaluating, and recommending. Such responses and ways of listening have a necessary function in listening for the soul. To listen for the spiritual dimension in every human experience and life circumstance, however, requires listening with a definite spirit and intentionality. We are listening for more than what is consciously expressed. We are listening for the very voice, presence, or absence of God in the soul, the core of our lives where meaning is created.

Listening as an act of obedience

So what does it mean to listen with open ears for the soul of another? In Hebrew, to listen, *shema*, includes the meaning "to obey." Likewise in Greek, *hypakouein*, from which we derive our word *acoustics*, means "to lis-ten and to obey." Our English word *obey* is from the Latin *obedire* (and its root *audio*), meaning "to listen from beneath." Unfortunately, the rich value of obedience has become misunderstood and much maligned over the years. In traditional wedding vows, when partners promised "to love, honor, and obey," the promise of obedience did not mean unwavering submission so much as obedience to the promise to listen to and for the other.

To be truly obedient is to hear the other into speech, or to help the other to express what has remained hidden or beneath the surface. In 1987, theologian Nelle Morton first introduced the phrase "hearing into speech" as a way of understanding that what we hear may well have been known all along.[3] Who we are and what we are about inside, in our souls, is our own truth. In the presence of a receptive soul-listener who can help us put into words what lies implicit or dormant in our lives, we can bring truth into the light of consciousness and discover its meaning for our lives. Sam Keen and Anne Fox make a similar assertion when they write that "to be a person is to have a story to tell," but that "you can't tell who you are unless someone is listening."[4] We come to recognize and name things in our lives when we have a chance to express our thoughts to a person will-ing to listen.

In this sense, soul-listeners are about life-affirming acts. By hearing others into clarity and truth about their lives, others will know they exist and are valued children of God, with boundless potential to attend to what is meaningful in life and meaningful in God. The act of listening becomes God's own means of melding the divine cry with our own in those holy screams for new life. Listening validates our God-given existence and affirms that our frailty need not cripple us nor our glory be denied. In this sense, listening for the soul is a basic, life-forming, and transforming act, both for the listener and for the one being heard into speech.

Everyone knows the pain of not being listened to or heard. We shut down, withdraw, and distance ourselves because not to be heard feels too much like we do not exist. In a society so stressed and rushed, to be unheard is the plight of too many, including the very young, the old, the sick, the dying, and the distressed. In our obsession with timekeeping and staying on time, we can undervalue both the actual time it takes to listen and the act of listening itself. Few individuals, it seems, have the will, time, or patience to listen with a spirit of intentionality, except those we pay to listen—including even spiritual directors. The time is long overdue for the church to wake up to its calling, open its ears, and practice listening for those individual and corporate souls in the realm of our everyday pastoral practice.

Listening as an act of intimacy

In a sense, listening is the most intimate of acts, which may explain why such a simple ministry of attending to the soul becomes fraught with difficulty for us. When I say that listening is intimate, I do not mean to suggest simply physical or sexual intimacy, although intimate listening obviously includes these dimensions of our lives. By intimacy, I mean a closeness of spirit generated by sharing the full range of human emotions, thoughts, and experiences, including one's strengths, vulnerabilities, and deepest spiritual images, questions, prayers, laments, and concerns. Intimacy is willingness to self-disclose and cherish in mutuality our humanness and our common seeking of the God who seeks us. It is in this sense that soul-listening is profoundly and intensely intimate.

The intimacy involved in listening must not be equated with mere sociability or an exaggerated notion of vulnerability. As soul-listeners, we must sometimes resist invitations to keep things pleasant or to chat too much about ourselves, especially if doing so merely feeds our own ego needs, uses others to help us deal with our own pain, or simply is our way of keeping things on an even keel.[5] Soul-listening includes a certain mutuality. It is not based on a mere swapping of stories of our hurts and hopes, though it may be quite appropriate to ask what another wishes to know about us. Sharing experiences can deepen a sense of trust and remind us that we share many similarities as human beings. Listening for the soul is grounded in the deep awareness that each of us is a human being who needs other human beings in order to realize our fullest potential to live in the image of God.

It is possible for us to feel that it takes too much courage to be intimate in this way. To listen fully to another human being means that we need to be ready, willing, and able to hear that which may startle the teller, the listener, or both. Often people do not consciously know their own thoughts, experiences, feelings, questions, or concerns until they have had a chance to put them into words for attentive and receptive ears. We can find ourselves saying things to another that express feelings, convictions, or supplications we really didn't know we possessed at the core of our being. Such revelations may invoke an initial spirit of discomfort, but one need only recall that it is an awesome privilege to stand on the threshold of the inner soul and the outer world expressed by another.

Listening can also be described as intimate because it involves a kind of interaction that embraces more than speech. Listeners, perhaps more than tellers, must be comfortable with silence and the conversation that our bodies' language inevitably reveals. Too many of us feel vulnerable and uncomfortable in silence and with the ways our bodies can betray or disclose our innermost feelings. For instance, when both arms are drawn across the chest, the soul may well be expressing anger or a desire for protection. Yet even in such silent moments when bodily reactions are observed and sometimes named, a certain level of listening is taking place that contributes to our being heard.

Listening as an Act of Receptivity

Who we are as listeners and how receptive we are is every bit as important as what we listen for. Describing a listener is not easy. If I were to draw a picture of a soul-listener, the heart would be visible, the mouth would be small, and the ears disproportionately large! In fact, the listener would have three very large ears, two in order to hear the ordinary noises and speech of life and a third to hear what is being said beneath or beyond the obvious. Such an illustration, however, does not presume a figure of a certain age, nor one with all sensual and mental faculties intact. It would be erroneous to conclude, for instance, that the best listeners are those with the wisdom that can accompany graying hair; the aging process does not necessarily ensure the development of deeper spiritual understanding. Nor does mental health.

Jean Vanier and L'Arche communities around the world stand as testimony to the spiritual wisdom and guidance inherent in those who face developmental challenges in their daily lives.[6] Frequently, too, children make the very best listeners for adults, and lead the way toward a fuller recognition of God. Similarly, deaf persons listen to the souls of hearing and non-hearing persons in different but equally valid ways. Without wishing to romanticize poverty, it is also true that the have-nots can challenge others about their spiritual poverty and lack of relationship with a God who consistently demonstrates a preferential option for the poor.

Stated simply, good listeners are those who are willing to love and pray for the people who instinctively trust them. They find themselves naturally, almost accidentally, approached by others. Although most people can practice habits of listening for their own soul and develop the skills that accompany soul-listening, usually listeners are more called or found than created. If you find yourself wondering, "Am I able to do this? What makes this person think I can hear them?," then you are probably called to this pastoral care ministry of listening for souls. Persons who instinctively question their own motives are already practicing what it means to listen for the soul—in this case, their own.

Being natural, being oneself, is one of the most basic and enabling qualities we have as pastoral caregivers and human beings. Can we laugh or cry spontaneously when something that is shared with us warrants such a response? Laughter has a way of restoring perspective and our tears reflect the importance of empathy, compassion, and sometimes, shared emotion. Are we relaxed, at ease with ourselves and others? Can we acknowledge our own fallibility? Can we let long periods of silence happen without needing to break them? Are we in touch with our own life sufficiently so that it will not get in the way of our hearing the life of another? Do we have empathy for others? Are we able to speak freely about the meaning of a life rooted in God?

People are not going to feel heard by someone who is in a hurry, nor will they feel that they can approach someone who always seems to have too much going on in their lives. It takes some time to reveal story, life experience, or searching questions, and we need to be willing to let the spoken word and truth of a human life unfold in its own time. Those who favor a rhythm of pausing to pay attention to the ordinary, vernacular life will be more able themselves to value, accept, and confirm the pace and nature of the journey of another's soul. Soul-listeners know that sometimes we wait, often in silence, for a very long time for the soul to reveal itself fully. At other times, the soul speaks loudly, clearly, and immediately. Listeners are able to respect the variance of these rhythms and the time it takes for both inner and outer expression.

Listening happens best when we pause and take time to hear more deeply and reflect upon the depths we hear. Our souls simply cannot thrive in a fast-paced life without claiming some time to take things in, uncover what lies deeply within, and mull things over. If we are gulping things down without taking the time to chew on them well, then we won't know what we've just eaten, let alone what effect it will have on us. For this reason, listening for the soul requires ongoing attention and sustained habits of reflection. The process of listening is gradual in its regularity and devotion, since the deeper mysteries of our lives usually are not revealed instantly when we are in the midst of keeping pace with those swift routines of life. Occasionally we will experience an epiphanic moment in the midst of an event, but more often, soulful listening requires us to stop daily, purposefully observe our lives, consider what is happening to us, and name those things that are dying, persisting, changing, fermenting, or bursting forth with new life. In essence, good listeners choose to call a halt to expending frantic energy. They claim time to notice time. They give the gift of their presence to their own lives and the lives of others.

Listening for the soul is a lot easier when we have a sense of inner peace and can, at the very least, pray for the grace to be calm and focused on the other who is before us. In this sense, listening is about being truly present for the other. People are altogether too distracted themselves, perhaps anxious because they missed their bus or felt surges of road rage on the way. Their frenzied states need to be intentionally contrasted with the listeners who offer a non-anxious presence. If, as listeners, we have never really felt listened to ourselves, or currently are not being listened to in any disciplined way, then it will be increasingly difficult for others to experience any feeling of being heard by us. Just how important this is—for soul-listeners to be at home with their own souls even as they continue to journey themselves—is the subject of a later chapter.

Listening as an Act of Hospitality

As pastoral caregivers, we offer the best of ourselves to another, including a willingness to be generous of spirit and warmly hospitable. We offer meaningful space and time that is uncluttered and personal, but spacious and appropriately comforting. Telephone calls and public places like restaurants and coffee shops are, in some instances, the best we can do, and they can actually be highly effective vehicles for soul-listening. Such listening opportunities at least establish a contact that may seed enough trust to open up further doorways to the soul. Simple, open-ended questions or invitations on such occasions ("How are things going?" or "Tell me a little more about your situation") can provide significant openings for further, deeper level soul-listening to take place. But let us not be naive about the disadvantages of such contacts. When a waiter wants to go through the list of specials for the day and there are people at tables all around you, the environment can be less hospitable or meaningfully silent and more chaotic and intrusive. Distractions are just that—distractions. If we are serious about listening for the soul, then we eventually need to be free of possible interruptions, restrictive time limits, or conceivable violations to the ministry. Genuine listeners seek to become totally dedicated, focused, and attentive to the well-being of the ones before them waiting to be heard.

In essence, effective listeners are those who practice the familiar biblical notion of hospitality. In her book *Holy Listening*, Margaret Guenther devotes an entire chapter to the metaphorical exploration of "welcoming the stranger" as a way of understanding the ministry of spiritual direction.[7] The holy listener is one who serves as host, welcomes the other, and makes sure he or she feels comfortable and at home. If the listener does not feel safe, either in place or space, then the soul may remain a buried treasure. In this sense, physical place and emotional space have the potential to become spiritual space or sanctuary for the soul.

People more readily trust revealing their souls to another when they feel that the distance their souls are traveling will be acknowledged, especially since they are often very far from what is familiar or recognizable. Listeners need to be able to hear and wait with the feelings and issues that are wrapped up in times of confusion, doubt, or despair. Too often the horror and fragility of a human life, including anger and melancholy, are avoided, dismissed, rejected, or cajoled. That may be why theologian and spiritual director Alan Jones was moved to confess that "the thought of praying fills me, on occasion, with an undisguised dread, even disgust. Prayer invites me to stand still when all I want to do is run."[8] A good host will stand still and receive and honor the emotional space of the guest, whatever that may be. A sense of confidence that the host knows how to begin and end the time is often what enables trust in the host. It may be very painful to look into the depths of one's soul, and an hour may be enough before one needs to avert the eyes. Sometimes the spiritual exploration feels unbearable and the desire is to run. But aversion also can be interpreted as taking a healthy time-out in order to return to the uncomfortable invitation to pay attention and hear the soul's stabbing voice of distress. When it is the listener's responsibility to choose an appropriate moment to end the listening that has taken place, then the time together will not be experienced as perilous, rushed, rambling, or trivial, but as sheltering, meaningful, and optimized.

Listening as an Act of Focus

Listening for the soul generally requires us to focus our energy on being aware of, and with, the other person in the relationship, rather than worrying about what we will say or do next. Not many of us are unfamiliar with being with someone who glances at their watch, keeps their hands on the doorknob, or simply seems to be preoccupied with their own needs and thoughts. Too many opportunities for listening pass us by because we fail to suspend our own agenda, put on hold our concern about a future task, or be in touch with our own feelings and issues. The soul that longingly has drawn alongside us can depart feeling empty and depersonalized.

Besides our own lack of centeredness, several other things can get in the way of focusing in helpful ways on the other. For example, we may fall back into the curing mode and too readily come up with solutions that may be premature, unwelcome, or not required at all. Or we may resist relating in depth because of our own unaddressed blockages that prevent emotional or spiritual resonance. Also, it is altogether too common for people to describe their experiences in terms of others rather than themselves. We must be prepared to say things like, "I'd rather hear about how this is affecting you, not Martha," or "I sense you are feeling burdened about something. Do you want to tell me about it?" It is also possible that, as listeners, our bodies may communicate something we do not intend. Our hands and face can get in the way. If they are not relaxed, and if our hands are doing anything but resting comfortably in a receptive posture, then we surely will convey a sense of hurriedness and inattention.

What gets heard depends on us as listeners. Soulful listening is affected by who we are and by what we believe is there to be heard. Do we listen for reality as we would have it be or as it is? Are we listening to confirm what we already think, or are we open to being surprised by the grace of God revealed in others or the discovery of something new? We may hear another confirm our previously formed personal assessment that a troublesome, annoying, antagonistic church member is power-hungry and closed to change within the church. Evocative listening may create a reversal. We may discover that our annoying church member is actually in deep sorrow (due to multiple deaths in the extended family, for example) and is feeling abandoned by

God and the church. Our own receptivity to truth and meaning is a critical factor in the listening we do.

Of equal importance are the means we employ for paying attention to the holy in the ordinary lives of those who draw alongside us. Do we listen only for those things expressed on the surface, or do we listen for other forms and levels of dialogue that may be going on within a person? On one level, a conversation with a mother about her adult son's pending marital separation may be about her concern for the welfare of her son and her grandchild. On another level, it may be about her own understanding and experience of the unconditional love of God for her as a woman, mother, and grandmother.

Listening as an act of soul inquiry

Wakening our ears to God's voice requires our listening to take on a habit that I call *soul inquiry*. Keeping in mind that pastoral care aims to facilitate personal, communal, and systemic empowerment, it may seem that to affirm so strongly the method of deliberate soul inquiry and spiritual guidance is to return to patronizing forms of care that deny the one in pain may know better than the pastoral caregiver what needs attention. But by habitually listening for the soul, I am not suggesting a return to authoritarian patterns, nor encouraging a regression in our deep commitments to fostering human agency and autonomy. The practice of soul inquiry is not so much about taking away one's voice as it is about providing spiritual guidance sufficient to more truly find one's voice. We need to let go of the timidity we have developed over the years about raising questions and concerns regarding spiritual issues and the need for spiritual growth.

Practicing intentional spiritual inquiry undoubtedly may feel somewhat awkward at first, because it does stand in marked contrast to more recent and less directive approaches to pastoral care. Yet well-timed questions may open doorways for listening to the soul precisely because such questions invite people to awaken their own ears to what is happening with their faith and their image of God. In other words, I want to be clear that the practice of intentional soul inquiry need not be understood as an antithesis to self-directed learning and development. Any inquiry or guidance we offer can be seen as more *evocative* in nature than commanding or instructional. An evocative style seeks to draw out what is happening with others in terms of their relationship with God. It is more about creating conditions that allow God to stir the mind and heart than it is instructing about God and spiritual matters.

Although this evocative approach of intentional soul inquiry is much more directive and has the capacity to influence the focus of what is listened for, it fundamentally remains within the realm of practicing the spiritual discipline of basic humility. Simply put, we cannot know on behalf of others what their relation to God ultimately involves. By recalling that our listening requires humility, we remain open to surprise and to God's own direction through the spirit at work in the process of what is said and heard.

It is important to sound another cautionary note. A compassionate soul-listener will only practice such intentional inquiry if there is a basis for developing relational trust, and in the case of a genuine crisis, once the acute phases of that crisis have been dealt with. It can't be emphasized enough that it is only when we feel safe that we are able to breathe freely again, including taking in the very breath and spirit of God.

So just how do we assume this habit of soul inquiry? Like any other habit, it requires discipline, practice, and a willingness both to try and to learn from experience.

Listening as an Act of Habit

My pastoral care training included some classroom experience in skill development. My peers and I practiced listening skills in sessions that were called *reality-practice*. These listening skills included developing my ability to read a situation, note details about the person(s), the environment, and the conversation, and assess the issues at stake. These skills of observation and analysis remain extremely helpful to me in my desire to listen for the soul. Immediately following an encounter, I would ask myself the following questions to assist my analysis and discern what, if any, further pastoral response was required:

+ What just happened here?
+ Why did this person choose to talk about this event, memory, conflict, or concern?
+ What is most important to this person?
+ What did I hear?
+ What didn't I hear?
+ What, if anything, surprised me?
+ Who is God for this person?
+ How does all of this fit with the Christian story?

In essence, these questions enabled me to debrief my experience of listening and to prepare myself for further conversation. The questions also helped me to continue learning about my own practice of pastoral care and to discover what I could affirm and what needed ongoing development.

What is most notable about this listening method, integral to my own early pastoral practice, is that it was largely retrospective. Although it facilitated my listening for things that helped or hindered living a life in the image of God and in the spirit of God's freedom, I did not necessarily approach a conversation with a method that anticipated discovering the soul. To consider a more intentional approach meant I had to become more evaluative in the moment as well as after the fact, and ponder from the start the extent to which a life was centered in God and alive in the spirit. If it is not the primary task of our pastoral care to discern the spiritual health of others, then whose task will it be? Obviously I needed to begin the journey of finding out how to integrate pastoral care and spiritual direction so that I could be more intentional and habitual in reading the spiritual dimensions of an individual's life.

A moment of listening for the soul:
Hearing more Deeply

Here are fragments of a recent, ordinary, initial act of pastoral care in which the voice of the soul can be detected and the spiritual dimension noted:

Pete: Hello, Sara? This is Pete. Sorry I missed you when you returned my earlier phone call, but I slipped out to buy a soda.

Sara: I was glad to hear from you, Pete, and to know you've arrived. How are things going? Have you been in town long? Are you settling into the college?

Pete: I've been in class now for two weeks and am really enjoying my journalism courses. It feels right.

Sara: Glad to hear it. So . . . tell me about the residence . . .

Pete: Well, I'm living in residence and have a roommate. (*Here Pete speaks with a heavy, empty-sounding tone.*) I'm not sure how we'll get along. I don't like it much. It's my first time away from home, you know.

Sara: First times can be hard . . . disorienting.

Pete: My mom told me about your church and all. Where is it from here? I brought my bike with me. Can I get there by bicycle?

Sara: It would be a bit too far for you, I'm afraid, but I know some folks from the church who live near the college who would be delighted to give you a ride. Would you like me to call them?

Pete: That would be great. I think it's going to take a while for me to make some friends.

Sara: Well, I'd like to spend some time with you if you're willing. I could come out to the residence and we could go for a cappuccino or something.

Pete: That would be great.

Sara: I'd like to hear more about what it's like for you to be away from home. . . . Oh, by the way, I promised your mom that we'd have you over to the house for Thanksgiving dinner. You may find you have other plans by then, but if not, the invitation is a standing one.

Pete: I'd like that. And I'll look forward to getting together before Thanksgiving.

Sara: How about if I call you early next week and we can set up a time?

Pete: Okay. You can call anytime before 9:00 P.M. and after 8:00 A.M. I go to bed early because of rowing practice every morning at 5:00 A.M.

Sara: Wow. Sounds like something else I'd like to hear about.

Pete: Sure. Well, bye for now.

This contact, although brief, has initiated what could be an ongoing opportunity for Sara to listen for Pete's soul. They have begun a caring relationship, and Sara has initiated some important acts of pastoral care. At a basic level of care, Sara has ensured personal human contact (both immediate and in the near future), provided a means to respond to his desire to connect with a faith community, and extended a future invitation for a traditional holiday celebration, one normally spent with family. Such an occasion holds the potential for Pete's homesickness to be revealed. Further, Sara was able to communicate an authentic interest in his life and situation. Pete also has revealed something of his passions in his references to journalism and rowing. Why he has chosen these particular pursuits will be part of his "giving voice to that which he already knows."

Beyond these explicit revelations, Pete has dropped hints about his soul's deeper aches. He desires friendship and connectedness and sounds disappointed in the potential of his roommate to meet this need. That he revealed so quickly in the conversation that it was his first time away from home suggests the presence of feelings of separation, emotional distance, and loneliness. Pete's soul is experiencing loss and change. What *home* means to him is subject to the shifting tides of his new experiences. How and where Pete will find his soul's home in a time of transition may be themes that will emerge as Sara continues to listen intentionally, make spiritual inquiry, and invite spiritual exploration. It will be important for Sara to ask Pete's permission for such spiritual exploration: "I'd like to talk with you about how your faith is doing in the midst of this. How would you feel about exploring that with me?"

As Sara continues to listen with her third ear, she has the opportunity to hear into speech the call of God at work in Pete to come home to himself, his family (perhaps in new ways), his vocation, his faith community, and his God. Some examples of open-ended, intentional spiritual inquiries that may be used in such a follow-up encounter are: "How do you understand your feelings in the light of what's important to you in life?" "Where have you experienced God in this move?" "How does God seem to be present with you now in your life?" "How does being away from home affect your relationship with God?" "How is this changing your faith?" "What might God be asking you to say no or yes to?"

Sara might provide spiritual guidance by inviting Pete to recall and meditate upon when he has felt this way before. Sometimes it is helpful to begin with what we know. During those times in the past, how did he experience the grace of God? What enabled him to "keep on keeping on?" Sara might guide Pete toward recalling and meditating upon biblical stories that can ground his present experience in the lives of others who have gone before him. Such stories might provide a helpful interpretive lens and serve to widen his horizon of understanding about God. It is not the first time men or women have left home to find their own way in the world. The Garden of Eden presents a deep image of home that beckons us. Abraham and Sarah were called to risk a journey away from security to a new homeland that God would give them. Young Joseph discovered that his involuntary trip was used for good and that his understanding of family had changed. In all four gospels, Jesus' ministry is a series of journeys leading to the final journey to the cross and resurrection. These and other biblical images may resonate with Pete's experience of life's paradoxical rhythm of security and risk. The images provide models for keeping us open to experiences of grace along the journey and for discovering the balance between solitude and community, security and vocation.

Through such invitations and through drawing out Pete's meaning, Sara can be faithful to hearing Pete's ache and to waiting with him for the grace and presence of God to meet him there.

Listening for the Holy in the ordinary

In most cases, people seeking pastoral care do not present obvious and explicit spiritual and theological issues. Occasionally people may want help with their doubt or belief, especially in terms of their understanding of the nature of God. But for the majority of parishioners, the secular climate makes it difficult to describe their soul's deepest desires in spiritual language. As philosopher and Catholic theologian Thomas Moore observed: "Most of the time when we tell a story about our lives, we couch it in purely human terms. When was the last time you talked about monsters, angels, or demons when you were describing some strongly-felt experience?"[9] It is not most people's first inclination to look for God in their daily issues and concerns, and without someone attuned to listen on the wavelength of spiritual longings and to assist in the process of recognizing holiness, the spiritual dimension is missed.

Discovering the presence and activity of God in the ordinary joys, struggles, activities, and hopes of life is like the woman in the parable who sweeps into all the corners of her life until what has been present all along is found, recognized, and treasured. As elementary as it may sound, sometimes we just lack a broom and have neglected to search all the crevices or rooms in our soul. Whatever is found may be so new to us that we need help describing it, or it may be so covered with dust that we need help shaking it off and polishing what is there. As pastoral caregivers, what we are listening for and helping others listen for is the spiritual dimension in every human experience or circumstance, whether it is explicit, apparently hidden, or unfamiliar. This is not to eliminate giving care or attention to physical, social, or psychological needs, but to interweave them simultaneously with the core purpose of our pastoral care, which is to enable spiritual growth in wholeness throughout life.

In my experience, people can name the ways God is present if they are invited to do so. Without the purposeful invitation, however, the ways of the Spirit are generally not self-evident. Often they are subtle, unobtrusive, hidden in the midst of daily events and interactions. It takes practice to see and identify the grace of God in everyday life. So, listening for the soul means paying attention to the signs of God's voice and graceful activity and inviting others to become more aware of God speaking through such signs. "There is nothing—no thing, no person, no experience, no thought, no joy or pain—that cannot be harvested and used for nourishment on our journey to God."[10] When we recognize what is before our eyes, what is hidden becomes revealed to us.

Recently a young father described to me what it was like to rock his newborn girl in his arms. "I stared at her and stared at her in wonder, counting every toe and finger twice over. They were all there, so tiny and perfect. I watched her sleep, breathe, gurgle, rest. I imagined her at two, twelve, twenty. I imagined her in safe places and in places where she had to resist evil. As I cradled her in my arms, I felt this intense desire to utter a deep sigh of contentment—a guttural 'ah' . . . "

What a marvelous example this is of the soul being revealed in a brief time of listening! Here was gratitude for creation and appreciation of the mystery of life, birth, parenthood, and growth. Such an ordinary event likely would be described by most as a rocking chair moment cherished between father and daughter; in other words, a moment within the human, horizontal dimension. In contrast, it could be described as a God-rocking vertical moment spent within the spiritual dimension. Here was a moment in ordinary time where father and child were one with God, a God who basks in us taking the time to luxuriate in wonder, praise, and mystery. "How was God present in that moment?" Such a simple question posed by the listener (one frequently used by spiritual directors) might enable the person to name his or her own experience of the holy in the ordinary. This sense of wonder and transcendence illustrates how we can listen for the soul in life's seeming ordinariness.

There will be many events in the daily rhythms of our lives that present opportunities for us to listen for the soul. In a later chapter, we will explore the spiritual invitations present in both maturational stages and in moments of intense crisis. Usually such times invite us into what becomes a lifelong spiritual project of learning to live and die in the grace of God. Listening for the soul inevitably will involve us in seeing how the story of death and resurrection is at work in us every day as an invitation to become who God wants us to be.

I want to present two sets of spiritual questions that embrace a more evocative approach in listening for the soul. These are means for practicing intentional soul inquiry in our pastoral care and can be used in our ordinary day-to-day conversations. Spiritual directors will care about some of the same spiritual themes and soul matters as those posed by these questions. We need to remember, however, that their focuses in spiritual direction and in the guiding questions they pose may differ. Spiritual directors are more concerned with an individual's prayer life and current image and experience of God. In contrast, soul inquiry as a pastoral care habit will be concerned for the soul throughout all of life, including daily rhythms.

I offer these questions in an attempt to make the basic spiritual dialogue focal, that is, conscious and attended to. Of course, the questions of one's soul do not usually emerge as clearly as do questions such as these in a book on pastoral care and spiritual direction. But the listener who is paying attention will gradually learn to hear how each seeking soul is facing or evading the spiritual questions emerging from his or her own life. Keeping before us the kinds of spiritual questions and issues that can lie beneath the conscious level may help prevent us as listeners from getting lost or stuck in the surface self.

The questions are not meant to be used as a pseudo–instruction manual for ensuring that God-language is used in our conversations. Nor are they intended to become a grid for analyzing, predetermining, or restricting our listening and hearing. They are not intended to be used in their entirety or even, necessarily, sequentially. It also would not be wise to use these for spiritual interview sessions with congregants. I offer these questions merely as a technique for helping us as listeners to keep the soul prominent in our consciousness. This applies to both our own soul and those of others.

Because the spiritual dimension is too often buried or tacit, it may be beneficial for us to hear and practice some ways of phrasing our language to make said what is unsaid. Eventually, as with the development of most language skills, we move from concern about grammar and sentence structure to lived, spontaneous communication. Gradually, questions such as these will become instinctive, permeating both our discourse and our being, and enabling us to be present, receptive, and responsive to whatever of the soul emerges. We will find ourselves making a spiritual inquiry naturally. Similarly, we may refer easily to a biblical experience, story, or text in ways that orient the teller more deeply toward God and the meaning that emerges from such a connection.

The first set of questions is based on James Fowler's work in which he poses some basic life questions.[11] The second set is based on questions I have found helpful in listening for my own soul and the souls of others in my pastoral work. They are intended to serve only as guiding questions as we proceed in our daily lives to listen for the soul in others.

practicing soul inquiry: Basic Life Questions

Hardly new but still extremely relevant are the overarching questions about life posed by James Fowler in his influential book *Stages of Faith*. These basic life questions can be kept in the back of the mind when listening for the soul. They provide clues about what to listen for, and when employed can bring concealed dialogue into the open.

+ What are you spending and being spent for? What commands and receives your best time and energy?
+ What goals, dreams, or institutions are you pouring out your life for?

✦ As you live your life, what power or powers do you fear or dread? What
   power or powers do you rely on and trust?

✦ To what or to whom are you committed in life and death?

✦ With whom or with what group do you share your most sacred or private hopes for your life and for the lives of those you love?

✦ What are the most sacred and compelling hopes and purposes in your
   life?

These questions have the common undergirding theme of commitment
and aim to hear how a person may be facing or evading issues that are
emerging in his or her life. Spiritual director and author Carolyn Gratton
suggests that Fowler's questions are "not simply problem-oriented questions
that ask for advice on what one should do. They are mystery-oriented questions that flow from a heart that seeks a future for its love."[12] Our soul-listening will lead us to hear the dialogue going on within another. The dialogue
will not always be free or honest, since it is shaped within a culture that can
generate illusion. But the concealed dialogue is precious, and listening for
the soul compels us to hear the preciousness of the soul's own inner movements. Remember that the aim here is not to ask all of the questions at once,
indeed if ever, but to begin with whatever questions are emerging from the
lived experience of the person or persons with whom you are in conversation. The teller's own questions emerging from his or her life experience will
likely parallel one or more of those identified by Fowler as life's basic mysteries and absorptions.

Recalling for a moment the rather ordinary conversation that took place
between Pete and Sara, Fowler's questions that deal with human connectedness and vocational hopes or dreams may be most relevant at this time.
And there may come a time when Sara actually might use one or more of
these questions in her spiritual inquiry with Pete. More likely, however, Sara
will allow these questions to guide her own consciousness, framing her listening for spiritual themes and patterns that provide clues to Pete's ultimate
fears and to where he lodges his life commitments.

practicing soul inquiry: Discerning spiritual wholeness

Another method for practicing intentional inquiry is to pay attention to the
attitudes and practices of persons that encourage or block abundant living
in the spirit of God. Whether people realize it or not, they are following a
spiritual path of sorts in their daily patterns of loving, caring, working, and

living. This set of questions aims to increase our ability to notice what is invisible in, beneath, and around the visible. They aim to listen for the urges of the soul for a more harmonious, balanced approach to life, and to bring into consciousness how solitude, devotion, compassion, and service are integrated within the daily life. Any of the following questions can become a point of entry for listening for the soul's voice:

- What helps you to be aware of the basic wonder and mystery of life? How do you celebrate and respond to the basic good gift of life?
- When, where, and how do you find God?
- When you pray, whom are you conscious of praying to?
- What nurtures your relationship with God and keeps you growing?
- What daily practices do you use to help you to be aware of God's presence?
- What weighs you down and intrudes on your relationship with God?
- To whom or what are you deeply attracted? Why?
- What grace or truth from God would set you free and bring you inner peace?
- What are your priorities in life? How are they aligned with God's intention for you to love your neighbor as yourself?
- What is God calling you to? What are you being beckoned to be or do?
- What motivates you to say *yes* or to say *no*?
- How are your relationships honored and given quality time? Do you see them as a place to find holiness?
- What daily rhythms keep you healthy, imaginative, and playful?
- What gives you hope?

To achieve wholeness in life and to be centered in God, we must develop rhythms that foster deeper connectedness with God, self, neighbors, and the world. There ought to be a rhythmic alternation between engagement and disengagement, solitude and community, work and play, withdrawal and involvement, holding of a self and handing over of our self to God and others in love. An inquiry into the soul can be concerned about how these rhythms of life are being cultivated or denied, for the patterns of our lives testify to our soul's deepest commitments, and the soul is not satisfied until it comes home to God.

Evocative Listening: A Way Home

When we listen for the soul, we listen at several levels. As expressed earlier, we listen to uncover the spiritual dimensions of people's lives. These can be explicit and revealed in what is said. How people make meaning may also be hidden in the silent texts of their lives, including the body's own strange way of speaking. Listening to what is said certainly includes listening to whatever story is being remembered or told. But because listening for the soul is an intentional act, we listen foremost in order to hear the other into speech. We form a habit of soul inquiry and guide the telling so that the focus does not drift toward external realities but remains on the grist of the interior life of the one sitting before us. Such intentional listening is not passive but is evocative and actively responsive. It is all so that weary, troubled, or hungry souls may discover a place that is safe enough for them to name the truth of their lives. And there is no place like home in God.

--=◦⊂=--

Reflection Questions

1. Read and meditate upon Luke 1:39-45. How does this passage speak to you about listening for the soul?

2. Bring to mind an ordinary moment in your day. How would you describe it as holy?

3. What qualities and characteristics do you think are essential for a good soul-listener? If you were to draw your own picture of an intentional listener, what would it be like?

4. In this chapter, hospitality is presented as a metaphor for soul-listening. What other metaphors could describe this intentional practice?

5. What frightens you most about listening for the soul? What draws you most to this ministry?

--=◦⊂=--

Spiritual Exercises

1. Bring to mind someone who has crossed your path today as you went about your daily rhythms. Visualize that person once more. Focus your thoughts and picture yourself sitting in light. Picture the other person in the light. Hold the face in the mind's eye; then picture yourself holding that person in your heart. Place your hands in an "X" shape across your

chest. After a few minutes, exhale, dropping your hands and releasing this person in love into the arms of God.

2.   The next time you do a meaningful, menial, or routine chore, dedicate it to anyone who earns a living by regularly doing that same act. For example, as you mow the lawn, clean a toilet, set a table, pick vegetables in the garden, read a book, or teach your child to tie a shoelace, pray with special intention for the souls of immigrant workers, teachers, farmers, writers, and waiters.[13]

⊷⟞═◉═⟝⊶

practicing soul inquiry

In groups of three, identify one *listener*, one *teller*, and one *observer-reflector*. The teller has five minutes to share something, at the invitation and encouragement of the listener. The observer-reflector keeps time and then shares his or her observations on the following questions: "How was the soul revealed or hidden?" and "How was the listening attentive to the soul?" Rotate through each role until each person has had the opportunity to be a listener, a teller, and an observer-reflector. At the conclusion of the practice, reflect together on the experience of soul inquiry. What new insights have emerged?

ב
contemplative living:
a preventative and restorative approach

~⋙◉⋘~

Ho, everyone who thirsts,
   come to the waters;
and you that have no money,
   come, buy and eat!
Come, buy wine and milk
   without money and without price.
Why do you spend your money
   for that which is not bread,
   and your labor for that which does not satisfy?
Listen carefully to me, and eat what is good,
   and delight yourselves in rich food.
Incline your ear, and come to me;
   listen, so that you may live.

Isaiah 55:1-3a

THERE IS NO OTHER WAY FOR US TO KNOW GOD than through the experience of breathing, eating, working, living, and dying. Not long ago, on a Sunday afternoon outing, my eyes caught this expression on a church signboard: "At the end of life's road is God." Whether such an ambiguous statement is designed to evoke a reader's fear or hope is unclear. Either way, it seems to suggest that God is somehow disconnected from the journey of life, only to be experienced at its end. Sadly, too many congregants unwittingly adopt such a view of life, missing that the whole joyful and painful adventure of laboring and living is itself an experience of God.

Becoming more conscious of God is not so much about seeking a mystical, out of this world or end of life's road kind of religious experience, but rather developing a deeper awareness and appreciation of how our everyday experiences abound in the mystery and presence of God. The ordinary events of our experience should not be in the way or apart from the way to living in the presence of God, but the way to it. The writer of Acts reminds us that "in him we live and move and have our being" (Acts 17:28). Such intimate union with God in our earthly journey is meant to become conscious, savored, and interpreted. It is in the passionate embrace of life that "we come to know God the way a lover knows the beloved, or the friend knows the friend."[1] On the road of life we can be intentionally and knowingly engaged in the exploration of God who dwells within us.

The focus of this chapter is on ways to cultivate, in ourselves and others, a conscious, savored awareness of God who dwells within us and in our ordinary living. One of the primary ways we can cultivate a conscious awareness of God is through contemplation. Contemplation is both a lifestyle and a way of praying. In order to understand what it means to cultivate a contemplative life, we first need to explore the nature of contemplation and why it is so important to encourage it as a way of life for Protestant laity and clergy. Simply stated, contemplation is a way to listen carefully, incline our ears, and come to a deeper awareness of God. I will look at how contemplative prayer invites us to listen and respond to the more neglected intuitive faculty within us, and how such openness inevitably exposes us to the reality of ourselves, our world, and the truth that lies within and beyond us. Contemplative prayer can be a way to prepare ourselves for the pastoral care that we give, it can be used by the caregiver on behalf of those we encounter, and it can be taught and encouraged as a habit that contributes to personal and spiritual wholeness and systemic health and vision.

This chapter will then examine some of the biblical tradition so that it can inform us about pastoral strategies for fostering a contemplative lifestyle. Since prayer is central to developing a loving awareness of God, the remainder of the chapter will present some ways and times within our pastoral care that we can encourage daily contemplative habits, including the practice of *noisy contemplation*. Finally, I will suggest some contemplative ways of praying and fostering silence that can be practiced regularly.

A preventative and restorative Approach

Encouraging contemplative living and teaching contemplative prayer within congregations are acts of pastoral care. In effect, such pastoral care has the potential to be both preventative and restorative in nature. It is *preventative* because it lessens the likelihood of burnout for pastoral care practitioners, and it can significantly modify the range and type of requests received for pastoral services. By promoting a contemplative lifestyle, we may find that laypersons not only develop the means for their own daily self-care and spiritual growth, but also the resources and vision for offering pastoral care to others. As individuals adopt a contemplative lifestyle, they find themselves empowered to act in new and bold ways. If people are given tools for loving

God more dearly and seeing life more clearly, then they will be mobilized for daily acts of pastoral care toward self and others.

Encouraging contemplation as a dimension of congregational pastoral care is also *restorative*. Contemplative living contributes to spiritual wholeness by restoring balance, perspective, and mental, physical, and spiritual health. Contemplative living and praying embody a concern for the whole person and for the development of souls that experience a stronger integration of the sacred and secular, body and soul, heart and mind, and the inner and outer worlds. "It provides the necessary space in our crowded lives for the essential, but often neglected, 'activities of the whole, albeit, incomplete human person . . . for dreaming and desire, hunger and aspiration.'"[2] Fostering a contemplative lifestyle and teaching forms of contemplative prayer can enable laity to experience less fragmentation and more connectedness between their internal and external worlds, their relationship with God, and their daily actions. Many who practice contemplation observe that it restores their souls by helping them feel less isolated and more connected to the social and organic environment around them.

Living contemplatively has obvious personal benefits. Contemplative practice can enliven personal prayer and contribute to the health of an individual's body, mind, and soul. But just as important is the health of the corporate body, mind, and soul. If a significant proportion of a church's membership is practicing a contemplative lifestyle, then it is highly likely that the culture, vision, mission, and faith environment of the congregation itself will undergo significant change. The congregation may experience renewal by becoming more alert and able to notice its wider mission and context, thus becoming a valuable resource for local and global ministries of restorative justice. The self-knowledge that contemplation makes possible deepens our awareness of God's indwelling presence in our hearts. It makes us more conscious and responsible in our interactions with others.

To encourage contemplative living and to teach effectively about contemplative prayer, pastoral caregivers must themselves be familiar with the contemplative tradition and committed to the habitual practice of contemplative living and prayer. Such familiarity is essential to provide credibility as pastoral caregivers and to model the lifelong nature of contemplative practices and prayer. A contemplative lifestyle is a work in progress and always under construction. There are continual new discoveries about the frustrations and joys of practicing contemplative habits that need to be shared broadly and boldly among the members of the faith community. Obviously, pastoral caregivers practice contemplation to enrich their own lives and pastoral encounters; however, a natural beneficial outcome is that contemplative pastoral caregivers can and do contribute to the increased physical and spiritual health of systems, be they familial, congregational, denominational, or global in scope.

contemplative living as a pathway for the soul

In spite of the obvious individual and systemic benefits, within many local Protestant churches the spiritual practice of contemplative living remains a largely undervalued and underdeveloped source of healing and transformation. Medical clinics, psychotherapists, psychologists, and alternative health centers often appear to pay more attention to the promise of contemplative practice than do communities of faith. It is time for Protestant faith communities to claim the pastoral potential that resides in contemplative living. Contemplative living is a pathway for the soul to experience greater wholeness and a deeper connection to God.

Benefits to Contemplative Living

The advantages of contemplative habits are well documented. They include heightened self-awareness, an increased capacity to embrace reality, the discovery of truth, an openness to affirming the mystery of life, a shift of perception from seeing the "I" as the center and measure of all things to a development of humility, the transformation of consciousness, a deepened respect for balance in life, increased creativity, joy, and a sense of purpose, and various other physiological benefits.[3]

There is a substantial amount of research that indicates that contemplation can help reduce the heart rate, lower blood pressure, relax the muscles, and improve motor skills.[4] Contemplative practice can attend to insomnia, listlessness, and frenzy. It can quiet our mind and fears, center our consciousness, and increase our clarity of thought. The clarity that comes also increases our sensitivity to pain and suffering, deepens our capacity for empathic response to others, and strengthens our efficiency of action. We gain a different appreciation of time and space. Contemplative habits also can increase our basic awareness of bodily rhythms and patterns of breathing. As life speeds up, we can slow down. By becoming less scattered and stressed, we can become more energized, focused, and present to ourselves and others.

In essence, contemplation is a natural way to facilitate productivity, creativity, and a truer sense of purpose in our work. By giving greater consideration to a contemplative approach to life and to contemplative prayer as a vehicle for healing soul-deprivation and spiritual hunger, we can be brought into deeper self-understanding and authentic relationship with God and others. Contemplation allows us gradually to overcome our sense of separateness and experience true joy in community.

Common Misconceptions about Contemplative Living

Of course, it is easier to speak of contemplative practice than to practice contemplation. For many, the very word *contemplation* conjures up something remote and alien to the modern practices of life. The contemplative lifestyle, which includes the regular habit of deep and serene prayer, most commonly has been associated with the monastic tradition. Going off into the desert, either to retreat into splendid isolation or to wrestle with inner demons or angels, is to be expected of those deemed vocationally committed to seeking communion with God. We falsely assume that a contemplative life is not for most people. We mistakenly presume that contemplation is only for those interested in superior piety or for those set apart to pray in their towers or cloistered cells. A contemplative life seems at odds with our more task-oriented lives. Moreover, we are too quick to say that it takes a certain kind of personality, one suited to the intensity demanded by solitude and inner exploration.

Because we tend to associate contemplation primarily with introverted and intuitive personalities, extroverts and persons whose ways of knowing emerge primarily from rational thought and activity can seem impossibly mismatched to the more contemplative approach. It is a common misconception that contemplation is best suited to certain personality types. Although a contemplative lifestyle may seem foreign and less natural to the extroverted majority, it offers a different way to see, understand, and relate to reality. Such a difference, it seems to me, is most needful in our frenetic, harried time for the development of an integrated spirituality. The most extroverted, activist, and rationally minded among us can really benefit from trying on a more contemplative approach to daily living. So too can the rest of us, since our ways of knowing and living have generally suffered a severe imbalance over the years. Through cultivating contemplative living within the congregational context and in the lives of the laity, we may be able to restore balance and promote a more God-conscious, open, compassionate, connected, integrated approach to life.

It is important to acknowledge that in recent decades, much movement has occurred in dealing with misconceptions about contemplation, and much has been accomplished to nourish laity in contemplative forms of prayer. These have included retreats and renewal groups focusing on centering prayer and meditation. Yet there remains an immense gap between the monastic paradigm and the normative conditions of Protestant clergy and laity. The majority of the laity find it impossible to imitate the dominant monastic model and can too easily feel guilt if the path of inner unfolding is not chosen or practiced regularly. In contrast to those cloistered in an environment with minimum distractions, the laity spend most of their waking hours in noisy, active environments where attachments are difficult to set aside, even temporarily. Each day there is a long list of things to do with little time to do them. Just to keep up can be overwhelming. Of course the noise experienced by the laity is not merely external but also internal, including the sounds of conflicts, confusion, indecision, demands, ethical dilemmas, painful betrayals, failures, and broken relationships. Wayne Oates reminds us that it is the normal events of life that "create a noisy uproar in hearts that pant for silence."[5]

But contemplation is neither a marginal gift nor one that is reserved for only a handful of saints and mystics. A contemplative approach can be practiced by any who thirst and long to taste, touch, and see that God is good. The problem is that we have failed to see our noisy circumstances as locations that reflect essential sacredness, ripe with opportunities to develop our awareness of God. What is holy need not always be restricted to special times and places. Life in all its ordinary activity is itself sacred ground.

How do we foster a contemplative approach to life when sitting still, silence, and detachment continue to slip through the hands of the majority of the laity and clergy? It is important to acknowledge that contemplative living is not necessarily the best or only way for people to incline their ears to God. But the glaring lack of emphasis on contemplative living and practices in many, if not most, Protestant faith communities makes it more inviting and compelling now than at any other time.

A Compelling Time for Contemplative Living

It was Blaise Pascal who once intimated that all human evils derive from our inability to sit still in a room. Quieting down and focusing long enough to listen to the voice of God within us and within our noisy circumstances is perhaps one of the most important things we can do for ourselves and others at a time when we feel held against our will by the force of hurried living. It is the apparent incongruity with the whole direction of modern life that makes contemplation profoundly healing. No longer should contemplation be an optional item on a list of things to do, but it should be seen as the breath of life for us and others. Contemplative living is a path to wholeness that we can take on the road of life. It is compelling enough that it may well have fresh possibilities for leading our souls home.

Although some Protestants have discovered the contemplative path by seeking out friendships that emphasize it within particular faith traditions, the majority of Protestant laity and clergy remain unfamiliar with the contemplative tradition and its practices of prayer. Our pastoral care for active and working persons needs to embody some deliberate strategies to effect greater balance between the monastic paradigm and the dominant lifestyle of the laity, and to remove unfortunate lingering Protestant fears that contemplation will lead to becoming too Catholic or Eastern in our practice of the faith.

Minimally, we need to create specific opportunities within Protestant congregations to explore and experience the contemplative tradition, its meaning, and its contribution to the life of faith. We need opportunities to move toward seeing our ordinary noisy experiences and actions as locations for cultivating a capacity for contemplative, prayerful living. Small group structures can serve as safe places to learn and grow in the contemplative lifestyle. Individuals will benefit from opportunities to speak candidly with others whose joys and struggles in practicing daily contemplation may be similar. Small groups provide a means for mutual learning, sharing, and keeping accountable to the goal of living contemplatively.

Of course, small groups are not meant to replace but to complement our ongoing pastoral care to individuals. Our everyday pastoral practice with individuals remains a prime location for encouraging a contemplative lifestyle. If a relationship is troubled or a life circumstance shatters someone's routines or perspectives, a contemplative approach may lead to enlightenment, inner peace, and a deeper trust in self, others, and God.

cultivating contemplative Living

What is contemplation and how do we live contemplatively? To cultivate contemplative living in others and within our congregations, we must clearly articulate the meaning and purpose of contemplation, claim sources within our biblical tradition as examples of what it means to live contemplatively, and explore what it means for us to practice contemplation in our extremely noisy and busy world.

First and foremost, as we seek to cultivate contemplative living, our own understanding of contemplation needs to be clear. At the core of our souls, God, the source of all that is, can be found and known. Because God is on the *inside* of our spiritual thirst, hunger, and longing, contemplation is simply a way to be in touch with this God who already dwells in the inner core of our being. If our seeking for God always takes place on the *outside* of our souls (listening for God in external events, persons, and circumstances), we

overlook the ways that God may be expressing the gift of God's companionship with us in the very core of our being. If God is creating a longing and
thirst within us, then God is already on the inside of our longing.

Contemplative living is a way to attune ourselves to the conversation
already going on deep in our souls. This conversation parallels our human
relationships in significant ways. The vitality of any relationship depends on
the desires, intentions, commitments, freedoms, and frequencies of communication. Several years ago, Alan Jones suggested that "if we are created
to be in communion with God, if God is our lover, then we have to indulge
in the things that lovers do. The lover wishes always to be in the loved one's
presence, and to gaze and to hold."[6] In this sense, the basic name for such
loving regard is contemplation. We live contemplatively when we explore
and enjoy the gift of the companionship of God.

understanding contemplation as seeing and shaping reality

Exploring the presence of God from the inside of our souls leads us to see and
shape reality from a different perspective. Our vision gradually comes into
alignment with the desires of God being expressed in the core of our souls.
In this sense, contemplation is the central divine-human partnership action
that lets us see perceptively and lovingly the innermost reality and truth of
everything. It is an act of love, a gazing at and an entering into reality. As we
enter more deeply into reality, we find ourselves wanting to participate in the
shaping of reality. We become involved in respecting and responding to the
reality we see in ways that lead to the making of a new reality.

In a fast-paced world, contemplation is the still point that gives us the
opportunity to explore the interior landscape of our lives and to view the
exterior landscape of our lives differently. It enables us to look into the daily
reality of our souls, to find what gives meaning and purpose, to see God
there, to allow ourselves to be loved by God, and to love as God loves and to
see as God sees. In this sense all of our living and all of our actions emerge
from the heart of contemplation. Henri Nouwen clarified the integral relationship between contemplation and action with this definition: "To contemplate is to see and to minister is to make visible." He went on to say that
the contemplative life "is a life with a vision, and the life of ministry is the
life in which this vision is revealed to others."[7] Such an understanding is not
dissimilar to Karl Barth's classic affirmation that hands clasped in prayer are
the beginning of an uprising against the disorder of the world. When we see
all of reality—including that which sometimes we wish we did not see—

then we are able to participate more fully in the divine process of soul-restoration and world-healing.

Seeing from the Underside

Expanding upon Nouwen's definition, contemplation is what enables us to see clearly things from the *underside* of life. It involves the development of compassionate attention. When we see that reality is not just what appears on the top, or on the surface of things, but that it includes a perspective from below, then reality necessarily includes the outcast, the downcast, the oppressed, or those voices that otherwise go unheard. Sometimes, standing too close to a situation can blind and deafen us to what is really going on, while standing apart can provide the contemplative distance that allows us to truly see and hear.

Contemplation reveals truth that is hidden. It makes clear that which is clouded. People, circumstances, and things become less blurry, thick, and invulnerable. Contemplation pulls the blindfolds off our eyes. We begin to know the scoop on things. We see that a litter-strewn roadside is a sign of our arrogant relationship with nature. We see that our struggle with time is a real invitation to see that things that seem in the way may *be* the way to our own conversion. We see that our tendency to dismiss others reveals our own insecurities about the true nature of our different neighbors. We see that a beautiful municipal flower garden and cement sound barrier hide what lies behind them—a community of homeless persons living in cardboard shacks. We see that an ordinary loaf of broken bread and a cup of wine represent the power of death and resurrection and speak of brokenness and healing.

Contemplation enables us to see reality with hearts that pound with the presence of God. In this sense, "the great mystery of the contemplative life is not that we see God in the world, but that God in us recognizes God in the world."[8] It is this seeing things as they really are that makes contemplation a way of living. It is an everyday way to begin to see that God has pitched a tent in our hearts, and consequently in our world. By careful attentiveness to God who dwells in the center of our being, we allow God to awaken every aspect of our lives. As we begin to see, we begin to live with less blindness and fog. An incomprehensible certainty commands a place within us where reason is not discarded "but its wider pretensions with regard to mystery and meaning are displaced."[9] Thus contemplation becomes a lifestyle. Such *seeing* and *inclining of the ear* become integral parts of the journey of faith. This journey requires peculiar concentration and the development of habitual practices; traveling along life's road becomes more delightful, yet at the same time unfamiliar.

Seeing from the Inside

Sometimes a contemplative lifestyle is consciously or unconsciously rejected out of fear of our own capacity for evil, as well as the evil that lies beyond us. As George Eliot once said, we must "hear the grass grow, the beat of the squirrel's heart, the roar on the other side of silence."[10] As we begin to see with the clarity of vision inspired by God's dwelling within our souls, we soon discover the skeletons making creaking noises in our own attics. Reality becomes increasingly less hidden and more visible. We can feel terrified by our own solitude and the roaring we hear on the other side of our silence. Skeletons have been known to terrify us. Understandably, we often defend ourselves against seeing things we describe as ugly. Many of our pent-up fears, feelings of guilt, and frustrations are unpleasant to look at. We are reluctant to admit to the times of bitterness, emptiness, sinfulness, and even those periods when demons seem to have made their homes in us. This kind of experience was reported by the desert mothers and fathers and is described well by Nelson Thayer:

> . . . the intense encounter with the wild beasts of the desert was a metaphor for the frightening encounter with the beasts within. Although the spirituality of the desert Fathers and Mothers was marked ultimately by a profound sense of abiding in God, and the peace and stability of that wordless and imageless assurance, the way there is the way of brutal self-encounter.[11]

As much as we might be tempted to avoid this experience, we need it. Not to be involved in such a process of coming to greater self-understanding and self-knowledge is what leads to destructive behaviors toward self and others. It is part of soul-development to become more aware of the reality of sin and evil at work in us, around us, in systems, and in others. Sometimes the mystery of evil around and within us takes hold through over-attachment to particular things or persons, a will for power, or through an unconscious or deliberate disregard of other people's rights to be agents of their own lives. Such seeing and hearing take practice and involve pain. We know that the pain is there precisely because we find it hard to bear too much reality. Like Jeremiah, we can cry out with regret over what we discover: "Cursed be the day on which I was born! The day when my mother bore me, let it not be blessed!" (Jeremiah 20:14). Any opening to reality, whether intentionally chosen or spontaneously granted, inevitably exposes us to the reality of evil forces within us and beyond us. Yet it is the discipline of contemplation that increases our capacity for bearing reality, for bearing truth, and for learning to be authentically human, delighting in being created in the image of God. Far from taking away our humanness, contemplation deepens it.

Contemplation contributes to our being transformed daily into whom we were created to be. It is a lifestyle of journeying with love into love that risks everything, including life itself.

This is the burning truth of what it means to live contemplatively. If I am to be fully human and created to be in the image of God, then how I see myself is bound up in how I see my brothers and sisters surrounding me. For me to be human, I must become human with others. I cannot become fully alive in isolation, nor through the vision limited by my parochial eyesight. A contemplative approach helps me to see beyond myself, to survive the inevitable encounter with evil, and to discover the linkages that exist between my experiences and the historical experiences of others like Jeremiah who have been on similar spiritual journeys. We need a community, past and present, to support and hold us as reality begins to seep in. Evil may be present in that ever-deepening consciousness of reality, but it is deprived of its power next to the central symbol of the crucified one. Ultimately, the most fertile soil for evil to take root is a soul that is unwilling to meet the violent, bitter, hateful stranger within us that harms us and others. Yet even the voice of such a stranger is heard by God and is valuable, worthy, loved, and gifted by God. The more we embrace that exiled stranger, within and beyond ourselves, the more intimately we become acquainted with God, whose spirit is fully alive in us for the sake of our human freedom.

Seeing from the Outside

Another reason we often avoid taking a closer look at the contemplative tradition is because we are fearful that it will become an escapist substitute for social concern and action. But the suspicion that contemplation is a sure defense against the world is unfounded. While the purpose of contemplation is to gaze lovingly upon God and to adore and enjoy God, a natural outcome of such loving is that we become more aware of the world that God loves. Our seeing from the underside and our seeing from the inside lead our souls to see what lies outside.

The integration of contemplation into daily life is to participate in the process of global awakening and the shaping of a new reality. At the heart of this awakening is a growing sense of the sacred quality of existence. What is regarded as sacred is more likely to be treated with awe, wonder, care, and respect. The great spiritual guides, both past and present, consistently have asserted that recovering a contemplative approach clears blocks and releases the energy needed for effective involvement in the world. Further, they insist that our involvement is the fruit of a valid spirituality. Speaking of this balance between contemplation and action, John of the Cross wrote that contemplation is "a secret and peaceful living inflow of God, which, if not hampered, fires the soul in the spirit of love."[12] Far from alienating us, contemplation may challenge us to a deeper, more responsible personal, prophetic, and social involvement. Often this balance has been referred to in terms of life's basic rhythms of sabbath and ministry, withdrawal and engagement.[13] A mature spirituality will demonstrate a natural flow between contemplation and compassionate service. When we see reality differently, from both the underside and the inside of our souls, we become moved to participate in God's best desires for shaping a new reality for the world.

understanding contemplation as part of our Biblical Tradition

At this time and place in human history, a contemplative approach to life needs to be emphasized over others as a way to address our rampant spiritual hunger. For many Protestants, this emphasis needs to include a respect for our biblical tradition as a way of keeping our future appropriately grounded in our historical roots. Pastoral caregivers can claim examples within our biblical tradition of what it means to live contemplatively. This means reviewing with others the ways we have represented Jesus, as well as other significant biblical characters, and clarifying our understanding of contemplative living as revealed in scripture. Part of caring for others pastorally includes challenging any false understandings we have carried about contemplative living and prayer.

Most of us carry within us particular images of Jesus' own way of praying. We have imagined Jesus as one who found time daily to be alone, pray, and spend some time with just his friends or disciples. We have captured the clasped hands of Jesus in stained glass, on candles, and in wall plaques. He has been pictured as one who prayed regularly and spoke intimately with God on hillsides, in garden places, desert-like spaces, and even from the lonely place of his dying and death.

These images clearly have been important to ordinary persons seeking to imitate Jesus and emulate his life of prayer. It is equally true that such images can also be unduly burdensome. They can set us up to imitate Jesus in ways that are neither relevant nor truthful to our daily realities.

The Contemplative Jesus

To be sure, the gospel accounts suggest that Jesus stepped out from life's pressing rhythms at key moments of his ministry. But the daily reality of Jesus' living seems strikingly similar to ours, where the demands of others, work, and limited finances restrict our capacity to take time apart. There is no reason to assume that Jesus was able to go apart from the crowds each day, or even on most days. The gospels present Jesus as one whose own life was so public and filled with pressure, tension, and activity that he only found time to retreat in rare moments of peace and quiet. Perhaps the gospel writers mention his occasional withdrawals because they were so noticeable, even atypical.

More typical were his prayers voiced in the midst of an event—prayers that took spontaneous form, both as lament and as grateful praise. They emerged from the depths of his being, encompassing extremes of both pain and joy. In his daily actions, as well as in his spontaneous and honest utterances from the cross, we hear the contemplative cries that touched upon critical moments of life and death: "If you, even you, had recognized on this day the things that make for peace! But now they are hidden from your eyes" (Luke 19:41); and "My God, my God, why have you forsaken me?" (Mark 15:34). Jesus uttered grateful praise in response to the work of the disciples: "I thank you, Father, Lord of heaven and earth, because you have hidden these things from the wise and the intelligent and have revealed them to infants; yes, Father, for such was your gracious will" (Luke 10:21). Another occasion when prayer emerged was an expression of thanks for a broken loaf of bread (Luke 22:19).

That Jesus ministered in contexts similar to ours, where most of his day was one of inner and outer noise, helps us to reconstruct our image of him as a contemplative person. Did he pray regularly, daily? We really do not know. Certainly it is probable, given his Jewish heritage and its disciplines. We are told that when he prayed he often did so for hours at a time, sometimes all night long. Writer Marcus Borg suggests that Jesus was a "spirit person" (a "mediator of the sacred," one of those persons in human history whose experiential relationship to the Spirit of God was the source of everything else that he was) who likely practiced a wordless form of contemplation or meditation that was central to the Jewish-Christian tradition.[14] We also know that Jesus addressed God in more intimate fashion and with familiar vernacular endearments (on one occasion even using the Aramaic word *Abba* that, roughly translated, means "Papa" or "Daddy" [Mark 14:36] rather than using the more typical and formal terms of address for God).

Rather than scrutinizing whether Jesus prayed daily, however, it is more significant to note that his prayerful cries emerged from the depth of his soul in response to what he saw and experienced each day. Prayer was motivated by a relationship with God, and he understood God to be present with him in daily situations. Prayer did not operate on a slot-machine principle of putting in words to get out answers. Rather, it emerged in honest expression for a relationship with God and it involved listening and waiting. Prayer is evident if we understand that Jesus' way of being and acting was contemplative in nature. Jesus practiced contemplative living. Jesus focused on the presence of God in the midst of his work, particularly by contemplating the people and their circumstances of life as he encountered them. Ecumenist and spiritual director Thomas Ryan notes that Jesus:

> . . . saw people with insight beyond analysis, with a love that cut through considerations of social status and role. He "tuned in" to their present condition and needs and grasped the essential questions they were living. Taking "a long, loving look at the real" was a way of life for him, and may well have been the dynamic that nourished him, the basic way he prayed day by day.[15]

It is evident from the gospels that Jesus had a way of seeing into people's reality and bringing to light what lingered in the shadowy places of their souls. He seems to have used all his senses, including his heart of compassion and empathy, to contemplate life. This included both individuals and groups that he met. He was aware of the daily conditions in which people lived and moved and had their being, and of the things that spoke to their souls' own struggles. That is why stories of soil, salt, leaven, light, children, vines, sons, lost sheep, and coins were so easily and so frequently brought into the conversations.

Other Models of Contemplative Living

Other New Testament characters also suggest the significance of living contemplatively in the midst of busy and daily routines. We recall Elizabeth, who kept Mary within her vision and whose own baby leaped for joy in the womb at Mary's greeting and response to being a mother. "Blessed are you among women, and blessed is the fruit of your womb" (Luke 1:42). Elizabeth saw divine reality in a teenage pregnancy. The aging Simeon and Anna saw beneath and beyond the surface of things that day in the temple. In the child Jesus, they recognized one who was becoming all that he was meant to be in God, and they witnessed the unfolding of God's saving activity. "Master, now you are dismissing your servant in peace, according to your word; for my eyes have seen your salvation" (Luke 2:29-30). When John the Baptist cast his gaze toward the shoreline and saw Jesus ankle-deep in the flowing water of the river Jordan, he knew he was not about to baptize just anyone from the crowd. "Here is the Lamb of God who takes away the sin of the world!"(John 1:29).

These and other stories suggest that a primary way of praying is our daily contemplative experience, which holds the potential to become graced with God's own vision focused through our eyes. We practice seeing from the underside and inside so we may see beyond the surface to the depths of reality, where it becomes possible to participate in the shaping of a new reality contained in the hope and heart of God.

understanding contemplation as Lifestyle

All of this is to assert that we can develop a sense of God abiding within us and enfolding all of our lives, including the noises of our daily routines and events. Pastoral caregivers can cultivate an understanding that contemplation is a lifestyle. It is not so much a special activity reserved for special persons as an ordinary one that happens for all of us as we go about our daily lives. Everyone can live a spirited life, enjoy intimate companionship with God, and live each day contemplatively.

Noisy Contemplation

In the midst of each day, we can practice what Ryan has appropriately called "noisy" contemplation.[16] God can be as present to us in the inner and outer noises of our scattered and hurried lives as God is in time set apart in retreat from such frenzy or preoccupation. The actions we repeat every day are excellent places to begin to cultivate our capacity for living contemplatively. As pastoral caregivers, we have the opportunity to encourage men and women to see their partners, children, colleagues, students, and significant friends as locations for practicing contemplative habits. Looking lovingly and unhurriedly upon those with whom we work, sleep, eat, and play are contemplative opportunities to linger in the silent language of the soul's own care. We can focus on the other, seeing them as if through the eyes of God.

As we grow stronger in this daily momentary or lengthy contemplative practice, we are given opportunity to discover that truth speaks in our own souls and reveals what is needed for restoration. If we find ourselves turning away, withdrawing, or putting emotional distance between ourselves and others, then our souls are giving us a clue that something needs to be addressed. Or we may be hearing noise between ourselves and others that merits inquiry. Others may be making demands that seem unfair, impossible, or unethical. It may be that the practice of gazing contemplatively upon others leads to the real you finding enough strength in your own voice to say no. Or you may discover that your own soul is feeling heavy because you have not surrendered enough of your ego to let others share the load and participate in addressing your needs.

Noisy contemplation is a way of living and being in our daily routines, and it can begin to be practiced in our most common and frequently accessed relationships. These relationships are our gateways to a greater awareness of how God is with all of us on the road to abundant life. In essence, we weave moments of prayerful empathy into each day. Everyday life becomes our primary location to practice being contemplative. What births life at home inevitably will make all the difference in the world.

Refocusing the Eye to See More Clearly

This may sound easier than it is. What is required is a certain refocusing of the eye and a means for being accountable to the intentionality required to see reality more clearly. It is too easy for us to treat lovers as strangers and strangers as annoyances that do not deserve a second look. It is easier to feel impatient with the slow pace of the checkout line at the store than it is to ponder the patience required in the character of the clerk who is probably receiving only a few cents more than a minimum wage.

Some days we will be at home as contemplatives. Other days it will seem unnatural to us, and our looking will take on the patterns of avoidance for which we are notorious. This variation in our faithfulness is as natural as our shifting energy levels. Sometimes, as the expression goes, we wish our eyes hadn't been opened. But when we share with others our common struggles to keep our eyes focused on reality, we find mutual encouragement and become naturally accountable to the gracious gift of God's companionship with us. It is in constant return to contemplative living that our souls find peace and rest in God, who is revealed in the mystery of human relationships.

A pastoral encounter:
cultivating contemplative living

Natural opportunities may arise in our everyday acts of pastoral care to be cultivators of contemplative living. In the noisy places and ordinary circumstances of parishioners, we can extend invitations to take a long, loving look at reality. What follows is an example of a pastoral situation that prompted a caregiver to respond contemplatively. It happened in the local grocery store parking lot as Phyllis was heading to her car and Mason toward the store.

Phyllis: Oh, Mason, I'm so glad I bumped into you. I was going to call you and find a time to come and see you', 'cause I need to talk about something that happened.

Mason: Sure. I'd be glad to find a time that works for us to get together. But I'm also willing to listen right now if you need to talk, for whatever time you've got.

Phyllis: (*without hesitating*) Last night I came home from work and Joe and I went toe to toe—you could say we had a major confrontation. You know it was only my second week in this new job and I'm just beginning to get my feet on the ground with it and all. It's not easy leaving so early on a Monday morning and not getting home until late Friday night. Living a weekend life with my family is sure not what I'd choose, but unemployment was worse, that's for sure. At least this way maybe we'll gradually get on top of all the debt we incurred over the last several months.

Mason: Things sound incredibly stressful for you, and I'm sure the commuting adds strain.

Phyllis: Well, the whole thing is that Joe feels abandoned. Can you believe it? He says he's already feeling the pressure of being the sole parent, mid-week, for our two kids. Does he think it's a piece of cake for me? Being out of the loop and alone during the week has its own pain. I know he's trying to juggle a lot of things . . . the kids' needs, his consulting business—he does that part-time—and he is taking a couple of night school courses to upgrade his computer programming skills. And he's never been the primary cook or lunch-maker until now. That's why I'm here . . . shopping for lunch fixings.

Mason: Wow, that's a lot of stuff, and all at once. You're both going through a lot of changes with a lot of adjustments to make in your roles, routines, and expectations.

Phyllis: No kidding. The shoe's on the other foot now. But even now it's way different from before.

Mason: You mentioned that Joe feels abandoned. I'm wondering how you feel . . . ?

Phyllis: Worried. The job is a fact of life, for now, so I'm worried about how I can support him and hear what it's like for him, 'cause I can't change the way it is or alleviate the pressure. Well, there may be some things I can do . . . like call the kids mid-week on the phone or e-mail every morning from the office. But, basically, I don't know what else to do. I asked him if he wanted me to quit the job and he said "yes!" But I know he didn't mean it. He was just frustrated. That comment came out in the heat of the argument.

Mason: If it's a given for both of you that things aren't likely to shift with each of your work commitments, then I'm wondering what you need from him and what he feels he needs from you.

Phyllis: Yeah, that's a good question. I'm not sure. I probably need to ponder it for myself and ask him that. Maybe he just needs me to listen and to be sensitive to his fatigue when I get home at the end of the week, although I'm pretty whacked myself.

Mason: What's most important for you in this?

Phyllis: Finding a way to accept that the rhythms are going to make us different . . . to make peace with what I can't change and, I guess, to find enough courage in myself to change what I can for my sake, Joe's, and our kids.

Mason: I hear the refrain of a prayer there. . . . Maybe it's one worth repeating from time to time during the day. Sometimes, Phyllis, I have found it helpful to put myself in the spirit-space of the other person. What I mean by that is trying to imagine what Joe's soul is feeling and how it is for him. Of course you can't know exactly, but it may give you a different way of seeing and hearing the one you love. You can imagine him being held by God and reflect for a moment on how God sees him and your circumstances. Phyllis, you can do this when you're sitting beside Joe on the couch, or watching him as he works on his night school homework, or as you're commuting home on Fridays. If some thoughts come to mind, pray for him. It may bring to mind why you cherish him; what drives you nuts and why? You can contemplate your own rhythms, too. May help you to sort out what, if anything, needs to be challenged or changed in him, in you.

Phyllis: Yeah, I can do that. But don't you stop praying for us, Mason, 'cause we need your prayers. I guess time will help, too. It's only been two weeks, after all.

Mason: Of course I'll keep you both, and your children too, in my prayers. It's probably all quite raw right now and like most new realities they have a way of shocking us until we've lived with them for a while.

Phyllis: Uh huh. That's it all right. I was in shock Friday night, but it's starting to wear off. Oh my goodness . . . I just noticed the time. I'm going to be late. I'm supposed to pick Katie up at the skating arena in five minutes. . . . I'll call you sometime next week . . . catch you up on how it's going and let you know if I want to talk some more.

Mason: Be glad to hear from you. Say hi to Joe and the girls for me.

Phyllis: Sure thing. See you later.

In this pastoral encounter, Mason encouraged Phyllis to lodge the situation and her beloved in her own heart where God dwells. By practicing the contemplative habit of gazing lovingly upon Joe, Phyllis may find herself more aware of how God sees not only Joe but also herself. In essence, she is cultivating her awareness of the presence of God by engaging in some *noisy contemplation*. This is a different kind of approach to pastoral care.

Normally, a pastoral care practitioner might focus on Phyllis herself, uncovering her feelings (possibly anger—"I looked after the children for years, yet he can't seem to do it for even two weeks without complaining"; guilt—"I shouldn't have taken this job"; and sorrow—"I'm not dealing very well with letting go of being the 'stay-at-home mom' who hears all the stories firsthand"). This time of transition and its accompanying emotions unquestionably present a timely invitation to Phyllis to look further into herself and to grow. Such a pastoral approach would be concerned first to help Phyllis process the meaning of her feelings about the transition, both for her own sake and for the sake of her relationship with Joe and the family.

Another familiar pastoral approach might be to invite Phyllis to examine the resources of her faith tradition, faith community, and friends during this time of transition. What supports do they have in place to help them bear one another's burdens? Perhaps less familiar is to inquire what this transition might be saying in Phyllis's own soul. Who is God calling her to be and become? In her saying *yes* to the job, what did she have to say *no* to? Can she view her choice as faithful? What vision of "loving partnership" might be a work-in-progress here for her and Joe? Is she struggling with their understanding of what it means to be stewards of the mystery of their relationship?

These are all valid and significant ways of entering a common pastoral encounter in the grocery store parking lot. Most of these pastoral strategies, however, require more time than presented by the situation and a fuller involvement on the part of the pastoral care practitioner. In contrast, Mason's encouragement to Phyllis to try practicing a contemplative response is a helpful approach for a time-limited pastoral event. It models a less frenzied response to a harried encounter. Further, it may encourage Phyllis to adopt a contemplative posture that can empower her in similar situations. Practicing a contemplative approach in a particular situation such as this may lead to the development of a lifelong habit for the soul. To encourage contemplation is to foster Phyllis's personal empowerment for all of life's journey.

Whether we cultivate contemplative living in parishioners, who can learn to view their relationships and circumstances as God-revelations, or whether we design intentional opportunities for individuals to come together in groups to explore a contemplative lifestyle, both strategies encompass a pastoral care that focuses on preventative and restorative learning. We learn how to be contemplative through regular practice and mutual sharing. We form the habit of seeing what is normally invisible to the eye but is visible to the heart in which God dwells.

cultivating contemplative prayer

Inasmuch as contemplation is a lifestyle, it is also strengthened by the actual discipline of what is known as contemplative prayer. Contemplative prayer is something that can be practiced within a contemplative lifestyle. It is not meant to contradict the practice of noisy contemplation, but to supplement it. It is to contrast the ordinary and continual noise of our world with experiences of quietness and moderation. When much of life is spent on the run, we find ourselves running out of breath. Contemplative prayer allows us to catch our breath and pause as we simply rest for a while in God.

Contemplative Prayer as Resting in God

Contemplative prayer is most characterized by its simplicity. By simplicity, I mean that prayer is wrapped in quietness, patience, and a spirit of waiting and restfulness. To pray contemplatively is to be lovingly aware of God and to be fully present to such moments of being in communion with God. Unconscious of time, contemplative prayer means resting, delighting, and lingering in God in such a way that we are drawn into the eternal realm that transcends time. In contemplation, we tend to merge with the subject/object that we are contemplating. Remember the father who rocked his daughter to sleep? To be so absorbed in what we see that we do not know where the time goes is an example of what it is like to be present only in the moment, waiting for whatever will be, simply unconscious of the passage of time yet experiencing a sense of awe and wonder.

In this sense, contemplative prayer is characterized by the simplicity of slowness and quiet. It is about the dimension of our relationship with God that goes beyond words and inner reasoning. Usually we think of prayer as our way of speaking with God. Contemplation is more an attitude of open awareness, free from any restricted focus or projection of thought. It is a time when words and inner speeches fall away, when we let go of any effort to speak. Instead, we simply become quiet before God and rest for a while in the presence of the lover of our soul.

Thomas Merton once referred to this as resting in a place beyond thought and concept—a place of direct awareness.[17] When we are quiet and receptive in this way before God, the Spirit of God is free to restore our souls and to love us into wholeness. Our overstimulated minds and overextended bodies can find peace and rest. Marjorie Thompson suggests that "in a world driven by the need to accomplish and acquire, in a world where we judge one another on the basis of performance, God calls us to the radical trust of rest."[18] When we join God in divine rest, we engage in an inner sabbath that allows us a time to be quiet, receptive, adoring, tender, even joyous. We are contemplative so that we love God for whom God is, not only for what God does for us. In contemplation, we become totally fascinated by God, who is already fascinated by us.

Contemplative Prayer as an Intuitive Way of Knowing God

It is this suspension of speech and rational thought that further describes what is meant by the simplicity of contemplative prayer. A contemplative approach is more concerned with the much-neglected intuitive form of knowing. By this I am not referring to the popular notion of the sixth sense, a gut reaction, or a hunch. By intuition I mean a way of knowing or a state of apprehending or appreciating that occurs before we try to figure something out. Contemplation becomes a subtle awareness of the truth that seems to be present before or after the mediating influence of our intellects. It is an unmediated awareness characterized by openness, a sense of relatedness, and awe and wonder. The presence of God becomes known to us in descent from the mind into the heart where it can be sensed in our innermost self. In other words, the source of contemplation is not the mind, although the mind certainly can and does affirm and challenge the contemplative insights that emerge. The source of contemplation is less linear and rational and more reliant upon the intuitive faculty in us that makes it possible to be in communion with God.

St. Bonaventure once described the contemplative experience as knowing through the "third eye." The first eye is of the flesh, where we perceive the external world of space, time, and objects. The second eye is reason, where we know through philosophy, logic, and reflection. The third eye is contemplation, where we gain knowledge of transcendent realities. At this level, the distinction between subject and object disappears. It is this third illumination, "lumen superius, the light of transcendent Being which illumines the eye of contemplation and reveals salutary truth, truth which is unto liberation."[19]

Some have referred to this means of coming to truth as the apophatic path—the way of knowing that is imageless. This intuitive way of knowing does not eliminate the role of the imagination or experience, but it does aim to suspend, for a time, any ideas or efforts to define, construct or interpret meaning. In such "suspended time," new meaning can be discovered or revealed. In essence, we might compare it to beginning with a blank screen rather than one that can be called up or that already is filled with images or words. It does not deny the particularity of persons and their contexts, but it tries to begin from a place of silence.

In contrast to the apophatic path of intuitive awareness, the more analytical way of knowing moves through the *kataphatic*, the reasoned or imaged way.[20] The kataphatic path begins with an idea or an image (from the past or present) that becomes the source for contemplation. Each of these paths has its strengths and weaknesses, but the more intuitive way of becoming aware presents a particular set of fresh possibilities in our time which seems so obsessed with rational ways of knowing. It assumes special significance for feminists who have repeatedly and painfully found that images constructed by patriarchy can dominate their ways of knowing and exclude their reality. While no path in itself is necessarily better than another, an emphasis on the apophatic way is extremely helpful for Protestant faith communities. It serves as a corrective to a much-neglected way of knowing and becoming more aware of God's presence and action in life. It serves to complement our rational and patriarchally imaged ways of understanding God.

The goal of contemplative prayer is to reach beyond the discursive, thinking phase of meditation, the restrictive nature of concepts, and our constant confrontation with external stimuli, to a state of openness and awareness in which our comprehending gives way to our apprehending. "Apprehension," write Earle and Elspeth Williams, "is openness to being embraced by, rather than embracing, reality. This is the 'knowing through unknowing' of the contemplative tradition."[21]

Contemplative Prayer as Praying God into Speech

The discipline of contemplative prayer is characterized by simplicity, but also by our obedience. Here, again, I am using *obedience* in the sense of what it means to listen to the other in ways that give the other voice. What otherwise might remain unheard becomes heard. To be obedient in contemplative prayer is to listen deeply for God's breath, voice, compassion, and revelation to us. We give ample opportunity for God to reveal God's self to us and are willing to wait in stillness until our hearts are moved, our wills stirred, or our minds enlightened. We listen to hear God's own voice speaking to us whenever, however, and wherever God's voice sounds.

Macrina Wiederkehr refers to this form of prayer as "the beautiful darkness of trusting God to pray within me."[22] To quote T. S. Eliot, when "words strain, crack and sometimes break, under the burden, under the tension, slip, slide, perish, decay with imprecision, will not stay in place, will not stay still,"[23] then we discover that words themselves can obstruct the gift of God's companionship with us. Rather than listen to our own minds racing forward in thought and struggling to find words to speak, we wait in the seeming emptiness for God to form speech within us. It is in this seemingly chaotic realm of wordlessness that the creative presence of God is brooding and bringing things to birth. At such times we resonate with the assurance of the apostle Paul that the Spirit "helps us in our weakness" and "intercedes with sighs too deep for words" (Romans 8:26). God is praying within us and is being heard into speech through us.

Challenges to Contemplative Prayer

As is true with contemplative living, there are many people who also find contemplative prayer to be problematical. One of the difficulties contemplative prayer presents is that it requires us to forfeit our preferences for the outcome and to be prepared to hear that which we may not want to hear. It is not easy for us to leave things in the hands and hearts of others, let alone God's. But the aim of contemplative prayer is not that our own will be shattered into nothingness, but that a healthy will be formed so that choices we make are in keeping with our growth into spiritual wholeness. Sometimes it is difficult to surrender a will for power. But such surrender is required only when God's own dream for the world stands in contrast to the schemes arising from our willfulness. The invitation of contemplative prayer is to stop deceiving ourselves that we can go it alone and to begin to cooperate with God and all of God's partners at work in the world. The propensity for self-deception is so great that the role of contemplative prayer in helping us discover and sift through our own motives is essential.

Another problem associated with contemplative prayer is that, all too often, it is used to disguise some subtle ego desires. These can emerge in either misdirected assumptions about direct contact with God or in a superior sense of pietistic pride. For example, a lack of self-confidence, a faltering sense of purpose in life, or a shaky understanding of a healthy use of personal power can surface in ways that abuse others and the aim of contemplative prayer. Perhaps we have heard someone say: "I prayed about it and God has told me that you should do this." Such claims may be inappropriately motivated. It is possible that such an individual is more concerned with exerting ego strength and maintaining a proper appearance of spiritual piety than listening for how the other may be genuinely experiencing the presence and movement of God. Many of us have experiences where we encounter those who profess to practice contemplative prayer, yet their behaviors are incongruent with a contemplative spiritual practice. At its best, contemplative prayer allows us to see reality, which includes taking a "long, loving look" at our own motives and unuttered spiritual assumptions.

Also, as already mentioned, extroverted personalities in particular can be uncomfortable with contemplative prayer. Usually they need to put words to their thoughts in order to know what it is they are hearing. Contemplative prayer, however, invites us to enter the realm of wordlessness and discover the gifts that await us there. Still others resist contemplative prayer because it feels too much like another spiritual exercise that needs to be mastered or achieved, and they fear failure in the experience of prayer. Persons concerned with their own performance and self-esteem see contemplative prayer as but another means of earning identity and approval. For such persons, contemplative prayer may serve the important and effective function of restoring a personal imbalance between *achieving* and *receiving*.

Yet another problem we have with contemplative prayer is that many times we feel nothing is happening, or at least that we are not aware of anything happening. We can feel frustrated by a silence that seems meaningless or vacant. But if we later become aware of the fruits of the Spirit growing within us, then we can be assured that God has spoken to us and we have heard. Then again, we can become too quickly frustrated by a lack of silence and by the inevitable distractions that surface in contemplative prayer. Even our best efforts to minimize distractions can be destroyed by the unexpected sounds of a beeping car alarm, a chain saw, or a gaggle of geese flying overhead. It is best to be prepared for distractions, and in such cases, simply to accept the sounds, be patient with them, note that a wandering from the focus has occurred, and then to return gently to the intentions of prayer. Persistent inner distractions, however, may represent something we need to pay attention to and welcome for closer examination. Perhaps there is something we need to reconcile or confess. In Jewish tradition, such inner distractions in prayer are seen as "blemished deeds in our lives that crowd their way into the time of prayer in expectation of a blessing."[24]

The ultimate challenge presented to us by the contemplative tradition is well captured by Dag Hammorskjold: "The more faithfully you listen to the voice within you, the better you will hear what is sounding outside."[25] If we bypass or neglect the path of contemplative prayer, we can end up hiding from truth, or at least freezing its dynamic quality. One of the many marvels of our creation is that human nature is endowed with the capability of perceiving and functioning at the numinous, inner level of the soul, not just at the level of physical reality. It is important to bring into some sort of balance all the ways we experience the reality of our soul and its dialogue with the divine. If it is our soul's longing to know God, then we need to open ourselves to new dimensions of relationship, including the quiet and more intuitive ways of knowing.

Otherwise, we are in danger of becoming absurd. The word *absurd* is rooted in the Latin term *surdus*, which refers to a kind of deafness, incongruity, or not being capable of perceiving sound and meaning. Whereas obedient contemplative prayer has an open quality of questions and process, engagement and connectedness, absurdity has a closed quality of answers and indifference, distraction and denial. The absurd life is the opposite of the obedient life. Without this obedience, this listening to the God of our heart, we remain blindfolded, hearing-impaired, closed, and our life grows absurd. Contemplative prayer that is simple and obedient fosters a style of life where we see more clearly, love more dearly, and follow more nearly, day by day.

Incorporating contemplative prayer in pastoral care

There are many ways to practice contemplative prayer that aim to have us linger in the presence of God. Because God holds us tenderly and desires the well-being of all men, women, and children in the world, our commitment to try contemplative prayer matters. Some people find it easy to embrace contemplative prayer as a habit. Others find it difficult to do with any regularity. Sometimes this is because we are too self-absorbed and do not find it easy to look beyond ourselves and to notice God. Whether we are naturally inclined toward contemplative prayer or extremely uncomfortable with the notion, it remains obvious that contemplative prayer is both a method for pastoral care and a resource within it.

What follows are some simple ways to pray contemplatively. I begin by sharing some approaches that may be less threatening for those who are unfamiliar with contemplative prayer. Other forms require a little more practice and commitment to making them rhythmic on a daily, weekly, or monthly basis. Some forms are shared as ways congregations can engage in contemplative prayer as a common action. Most of these contemplative forms of prayer can be used to deepen the life of the pastoral caregiver as well as serve as spiritual resources for the pastoral care that is provided. They also can be taught to congregants as methods for prayer that will enhance the formation of a contemplative lifestyle. They can be taught in small groups, as part of Christian education experiences, as part of confirmation, baptism, and membership sessions, within council or board meetings, at church retreats, or within the worship service itself.

Cherishing Activities That Are Naturally Contemplative

For those who find the notion of contemplative prayer foreign or difficult, I recommend beginning with a natural activity in which individuals can find themselves readily absorbed and which already brings them much enjoyment. The activity should be one that has a contemplative aspect to it, such as listening appreciatively to Bach or Mozart, noticing the thrill of a harvest moon, admiring the architecture of a city while walking, or touring a rose garden at the peak of the blooming season. In essence, there are a variety of activities that are naturally contemplative and that normally are understood to nurture our *right-brain*. The beauty of nature and appreciation for the fine arts are among these right-brain opportunities that can become primary and vital resources for enhancing the ability to pray contemplatively. Music, art, drama, dance, gardening, humor, and stories are but some of the artistic forms that help free the more intuitive responses of our souls.

Just as one might share such an experience with a close friend or lover, such an experience could be a wordless one of inner appreciation shared with God. If the act of looking, noticing, listening, and paying attention to what gets stirred within oneself is truly valued, then this can be a way of connecting our spirits with the living Spirit of God. It is especially meaningful to encourage contemplation through a cherished right-brain activity when someone is feeling overwhelmed by stress, the dynamics of change, overwork, illness, or loss.

Taking a Contemplative Walk

Extroverted people may find it helpful actually to *do* something that encourages a contemplative response. Walking slowly in a beautiful place, for example, may be one way to foster an appreciation for the practice of contemplative prayer. In this case, we walk not to arrive somewhere but just to enjoy the walking. Each step can embrace a sense of peace and joy.

Sometimes I like to recommend counting each walking step so that it correlates with our pattern of breathing. As I walk, I count "one, two, three, four" for each step and breathe in over the course of those four steps. The process is then repeated in sequence while breathing out. Counting is but one way of centering oneself while walking. A simple, repetitive phrase also can be substituted for numbers. "Breathing in God's love, breathing out my fear." Or as we breathe in—"God take away . . . " and while breathing out— " . . . the sin of the world."

Yet another phrase, based on a chant by Ira Groff, can be used also. As we breathe in—"Turn to God in all things . . . " and while breathing out— " . . . in all things to see God."[26] Becoming conscious of the simplicity of walking and breathing brings us into a clearer sense of ourselves and our bodies. It also can enlighten us about the dark side of life, giving us time to notice the fear, the greed, the poverty, the suffering that surrounds our walking. We become present in our walking to the experience of God being with us, for us, and in the world.

Habitual Mindfulness

Another way to begin experiencing contemplative prayer is to carry out an exercise in *mindfulness*. By this I mean becoming mindful of our posture, breathing, body, smells, sounds, and breezes. Most of us go through the day with a busy, constant pace and rarely pay conscious attention to our posture, breathing pattern, or the immediate environment around us. Howard Clinebell once compared this form of quieting and centering one's consciousness to turning off the ignition on a car: "Letting one's mental motor idle for even ten minutes each day can quiet one's consciousness, increase awareness of one's body, and put one in touch with one's spiritual center."[27]

When first practicing mindfulness, I find it helpful to select an object that can serve as a reminder to devote a few minutes (at least five to fifteen minutes is recommended within a period of hours, or each day, or once per week) to pausing and becoming mindful. The object could be something that sits on a desk, hangs on a wall, or is worn on the body. Whatever it is, it is selected to serve the purpose of stopping our minds for a moment and bringing our hearts home to where God is. When I have suggested this previously, people have chosen a flower, a candle, a leaf, a rock, a sculpture, a piece of jewelry. Some might say it is like having an icon present. The point of the icon is not for it to become an idol, but that it serves to point us beyond ourselves toward God.

Since I am prone to sitting at a computer for endless hours at a time, I have a small Inuit sculpture that sits on my desk as my reminder to be mindful. When I am on work-related travel, I often pack it and place it in a prominent place in the room where I am staying. Whenever my eyes notice this playful, wide-eyed penguin (usually at least once or twice every few hours), I let him remind me that it is time to pause, recollect, and become aware of the presence of God. I spend a few minutes correcting my posture and moving through some simple exercises to relax my body. Next, I pay attention to my inhaling and exhaling rhythms and take deeper and longer breaths. Since the penguin is a playful character, usually I try to think of something that carries me, even momentarily, away from my work and into a spirit of play. I rest there for a while. Then, when I am ready, I give thanks for God who meets me there and loves me in my *being* as well as my *doing*. This gratitude is usually a felt silence, and by dwelling in this experience of appreciation, I welcome the Spirit who lets me go into her playful rhythm of life.

Practicing such mindfulness is a good way to introduce contemplative prayer into the workplaces, marketplaces, schools, homes, and overall daily routines of people's lives. It is also a helpful gift to bring to a person who may be hospitalized for a time. The gift may be the suggestion to practice mindfulness through attending to patterns of breathing, or it may be an actual gift of an object that can serve as a focal point for centering in a contemplative way.

Casting a Loving Look

When we are just beginning to learn how to pray contemplatively, some people are drawn to try visualization as a way to remember the love that God has for us and others. Again, we practice this as a wordless form of praying. This is not yet a move to imageless praying, but it is a way to pray that stands in contrast to a more verbal or analytical approach.

We simply picture someone—a child, our life-partner, a student, a church member, an abused woman, a cantankerous neighbor, a prisoner, a homeless teenager sleeping on a grate, and yes, even ourselves—and imagine God's love streaming over that person. We gaze upon that face and imagine God's own eyes looking through ours. We see the value and beauty that God sees there. We lift that person into the light and glory of God.

Visualization, sometimes referred to as *mental imaging*, has been proven to spark healing and growth in cases of illness or brokenness of spirit. Although the reasons why this is so are not yet fully understood, the transforming contribution visualization makes to situations of intense suffering is not in dispute.

A friend recently shared with me what it is like to go through life with the knowledge that he has an inoperable tumor. This tumor is the size of a small orange and it is wrapped around the base of his brain stem. The tumor is so entwined with the nervous system that surgical removal is out of the question. The diagnosis was given several years ago, and his doctors were convinced that he had little time left before it would grow to massive proportions, gradually overtaking his body's ability to function. Among his various responses to the news was a decision to pray regularly and contemplatively using the technique of visualization. He prayed daily, picturing the tumor as a friendly organism that simply needed a host body in order to survive. Just as he wanted to live, so too did it. In his prayer, he regularly visualized the tumor and himself coexisting, becoming good friends with one another. In this way, the body that they both needed for life would not be destroyed.

Obviously there are many pastoral situations where we might well encourage someone to visualize a cancerous tumor as a beastly demon that needs to be cast out before wreaking irreparable damage. It is my experience, however, that people usually carry sufficient internal wisdom to direct the course of their own contemplative prayer. And as we discern the pastoral situation before us, we can pray contemplatively for the other. By imagining the healing light and goodness of God surrounding the one for whom we pray, we pray for the presence of God to be known and experienced.

Prayer of the Heart

This form of contemplative prayer, although it does use words, has a long history in Christian prayer of moving us from the head to the heart. Prayers of the heart are characterized by simplicity. They involve repeating succinct phrases until they take on a life of their own deep within us. When such prayers become ingrained within us, they truly become prayers of the heart.

The origin of this prayer is in what is known as the "Jesus Prayer," combining an early confession of the Christian church ("Jesus is Lord") with the prayer of the tax collector found in Luke 18:13 ("God, be merciful to me, a sinner"). In short form, this becomes, "Lord, have mercy." Consistent use of this phrase has been a contemplative prayer for many over the years. After several repetitions, the words usually fall away into a state of awareness of God as the bestower of mercy upon us.

Another way of understanding prayer of the heart is what has been referred to as *centering prayer*. In this way of praying, a single word or simple phrase is selected that reflects the nature, being, or action of God. The phrase is then repeated as a single focus and in silent concentration. Obviously, it bears resemblance to the Eastern meditative forms that employ *mantras*, but it has its own strand of development within the Western mystical movements of Christianity. The use of a repetitious phrase becomes a means for centering oneself in God.

Over time, rather than becoming redundant, phrases that are repeated tend to deepen and expand in meaning, often as their meanings are influenced by different circumstances in life. As the phrase is repeated, it usually drops away from consciousness, and we find ourselves giving way to the presence of God, which the words point to. Even though a prayer of the heart begins with words or images, the aim is to have it draw us past these to the place where we meet our beloved God in gracious union within our soul.

Scripture phrases can be used in this way, such as "Lord, if you had been here" (John 11:21) or "Lord, I believe; help my unbelief!" (Mark 9:24). So, too, lines from hymns can become memorable prayers that induce a spirit of contemplation, such as "Take all the dimness of my soul away" or "Wake now, my senses, and hear the earth call."

Here are some other examples of prayers of the heart:

+   Gracious, persistent God.
+   God whose tears flow.
+   Holy One of blessing.
+   Fear not, for I have redeemed you.
+   Help me be present in the simplicity of my heart.
+   Here I am. Speak, for I am listening.
+   Into your hands I commend my spirit.
+   Whimsical God.
+   Heaven and earth are full of your glory.
+   Jesus, lover of my soul.
+   Old, aching God.
+   You are the vine. I am the branch.
+   God in the burning bush.
+   Bread of Life.
+   Suffering God.
+   God, do not be silent any longer.
+   Connect us, you and me.

The prayer of the heart can be practiced while jogging, driving a car, swimming, doing dishes, chopping onions, soaking in a tub, munching on a sandwich, repairing a leak in the plumbing, waiting for a meeting to start or the kettle to boil, or walking the dog. It is a prayer that can go with us throughout the day and be recollected in an instant, at a later time in the day, as a quick recentering act. It fits well with the many ordinary tasks we find ourselves engaged in during the day

This form of prayer also may be very helpful to the bereaved, those facing surgery, or those dealing with a major loss or change in life. A prayer of the heart may also comfort persons who are trying to come to terms with a life-altering medical diagnosis. I recall the story of a woman who had just heard that she had to have her fourteenth surgical procedure to deal with the healing of severe burns that resulted from being trapped in a burning car. Disillusioned with God and unable to pray, she finally found sustenance and a strange sense of inner peace by repeating, over and over again, the psalmist's own prayerful lament: "Will the Lord spurn me forever? Has God forgotten to be gracious?" (Psalm 77:7, 9). Sometimes it is helpful to suggest gently to people that they do not need to pray only sweet things. The bitter prayers are also prayers of the heart that can ensure authentic contemplation.

A Poustinia Day

Another contemplative habit which can be cultivated as a form of prayer is what Thomas Ryan has termed a *poustinia day*. The poustinia day is in honor of Catherine de Hueck Doherty, who described what it meant to find "a place of sustenance in the center of her own heart where . . . all is silent and where I am immersed in the silence of God." She called this place her poustinia, a secret room where she would be gifted with God's own self if she went there in faith.[28]

A poustinia is a place of quiet and solitude which people choose to enter with a spirit of anticipation for meeting the God who dwells within them. The Russian term literally means "desert," but it means much more than arid, geographical isolation. It is less desert and more oasis. It can refer to a room, a sanctuary, or a chair that one identifies as the place reserved for entering the quiet room of one's heart. In essence, it is a place within one-self where one remembers to incline one's ears toward God and contemplate the contact of love between God and oneself. One might dare to say that the poustinia is the place where we make love. This loving contact can be made anywhere, even in the midst of a city, so long as the place is safe for us. A poustinia might be a conservation area or a public park full of benches and walking paths. It might be a cabin in the woods that we rent from time to time. It might be a retreat center that has nourished us in the past and to which we treasure returning on a regular basis.

Wherever it is, a poustinia day then becomes an intentional time for withdrawing into a space where we live simply and in a spirit of rest. Ryan recommends that we claim a poustinia day—a day without a particular agenda—at least once a month. A poustinia day is a time for detachment from things, routines, and demands. We take with us a bible, perhaps one other book, and some simple refreshment of bread and water. What do we do? We spend the day *being*. We sleep, walk, relax, read, appreciate, notice, and listen. It is a day without a productive agenda. It is a time simply to be on holy ground and to "take off our shoes." It need not always be done alone, but if accompanied, it is best to reach agreement in advance about respecting one another's needs and rhythms, including the need to keep silence.

Admittedly, whether a person is single or is living with a partner or family, such a form of contemplative prayer that lasts for a full day, perhaps even overnight, requires some accommodation of schedules. Yet with mutual support and advance arrangements, it is possible to go off for a full day of personal restoration and soul-attention. Churches might encourage poustinia days by making comfortable rooms or chapels available for such purposes. Walks around the church neighborhood, sitting in a sanctuary pew, or a nap

on the couch in the church lounge might be some of the ways the simplicity of halting for a day could be embodied in the church context.

contemplating as a congregation

Prayer Vigils

On Remembrance Day, during Advent, Holy Week, or Pentecost, days for
prayer vigil can be identified on the church calendar. The high seasons of
the church year are ideal occasions for fostering congregational forms of
contemplative prayer. Extraordinary events such as a natural disaster, a com-
munity-wide protest against homelessness before winter sets in, or a tragic act
of a random shooter in a local school may also evoke a congregation's desire
to watch and pray.

A prayer vigil is the church's commitment to pray without ceasing for a
certain period of time, even through the night. Church members are
encouraged to drop into the church and contemplate the presence, actions,
and hopes of God in and for the season. A lighted candle can serve as a focal
point in the sanctuary or chapel for contemplative prayer. A sheet with simple instructions for silent prayer can be left in the pews or can be available
upon entry. The instructions may reflect the season or occasion, or may simply list church members so that the entire congregation can be remembered
in contemplative prayer. Prior to the vigil, the church can post a schedule
for signatures. Individuals, groups, or families can make a commitment to be
present in prayer for an identified period of time, usually a half hour in duration. The noon hour and twilight hours as people head home from work can
be left as open slots for those who find such hours more convenient.
Frequently the contemplative periods of prayer are supplemented by a few
scheduled times where public prayers are offered. A prayer vigil needs to be
well organized and planned, and issues of safety during the night hours need
to be considered.

A modified version of the prayer vigil is to schedule a monthly time when
the whole congregation is called to prayer. For example, at noon on the first
Monday of every month, congregational members, as much as they are able,
may stop whatever they are doing and devote five minutes to contemplative
prayer. Again, a brief instruction can be given in advance to assist this prayerful act of solidarity. It is a way of inviting the congregation as a whole to
become more mindful of God's presence in the midst of their daily activities
and workplaces. The congregation thus remains together even though they
are separated physically. Their contemplation may even include the awareness that God is everywhere they are and is not restricted to place.

Quiet Days

In addition to prayer vigils, a congregation can identify *quiet days*. These differ from prayer vigils in that congregational members are invited to spend such a day in quiet. It is similar to a poustinia day except that as many of the laity as possible are taking the very same day to "incline their ears" toward God. Quiet days are days where men and women retreat on an individual basis, but it is the congregation's commitment to have as many persons as possible contemplating at the same time. Quiet days become the faith community's way of being contemplative in solidarity. Such days serve to remind us that prayer is not limited to the church or to certain times.

Alternatively, the church can schedule quiet days to be held in common as members of a congregation retreat together. Such a quiet day can be held anywhere that engenders solitude. The purpose is to spend time in relative silence in the presence of God with other Christians. Minimal instructions are needed. The day can begin with a scripture reading and prayer, and can end with prayer and communion.

Contemplative Prayer in Worship

A simple yet meaningful way of praying contemplatively as an act of community is to include contemplative moments in the service of worship. Before the prayers of the people or prayers of thanksgiving and intercession are offered, the church may give a simple instruction followed by several minutes of silence. Or the congregation may be invited to view the offertory itself as a contemplative prayer, or to pray contemplatively during the offertory. A prayer of the heart may be printed in the order of service as a way to become centered and focused on God, as people gather and before the first words of the service are uttered.

contemplative Living: Recovering the core of pastoral care

Because spiritual growth is the ultimate aim of pastoral care, pastoral care-givers need to embrace methods of fostering contemplative living and teaching contemplative practices. Contemplation is highly relevant today, and it is basic to recovering the core of pastoral care. The contemplative tradition has significant preventative and restorative possibilities for congregations as a whole and for individual members within them. Contemplation may help to satisfy spiritual as well as physical and emotional needs, and may heighten an appreciation of God as both immanent and transcendent. And it may help to restore a much-needed balance between traditionally lived opposites such as private and public, sacred and secular, being and doing. Contemplative living and contemplative prayer may lead to wholeness and a deeper intimacy with God, who dwells inside the soul.

Although contemplative practice may vary in style and meaning for people, it can arouse a deeper relationship with God that leads to an outside vision and a more justice-centered and compassionate gaze upon the world. That is probably why Secundo Galilea was moved to say that "authentic Christian contemplation transforms contemplatives into prophets and militants into mystics."[29] When we begin to see more clearly, then we will love God, others, and ourselves more dearly and will follow God more nearly into the places where wounded spirits abound. Contemplative living prevents our souls from burning out, leads us to rest beside still waters, and restores us for the work of restorative justice. As we become increasingly conscious of the presence of God in us and taking a long look at the world through us, then our experience of the divine may well lead to significant personal and societal healing and transformation.

--==◉⊂==--

Reflection Questions

1. What do you see as the goal of contemplation?

2. What other benefits and forms of resistance can you imagine as you encourage the development of a contemplative lifestyle among Protestant laity and clergy?

3. In this chapter, some ways to practice contemplative prayer as part of our pastoral care were identified. These included encouraging contemplative prayer before surgery, prayer vigils within the sanctuary (during Advent, for example), and scheduled times for the congregational community to practice contemplative prayer. What other ways can you envision for incorporating contemplative prayer?

4. How might we include in theological education and pastoral care training an emphasis on contemplative prayer as an essential approach for a spiritually aware pastoral care?

5. How are you a pastoral caregiver who prays?

◦→══◉═══◦

spiritual exercise

Read and recite the following several times until you are familiar with every word. Repeat it slowly and refrain from analysis. Then put it down and center yourself by whatever means suits you best. Recall the refrain and listen to whatever emerges in the silence that follows. When you are done, give thanks for the time you have spent with God.

> I call to you from deep within.
> Do not let me turn from you.
> Hold me in your eternal truth
> Until I reach my end.[30]

◦→══◉═══◦

A contemplation for pastoral care: Blessed Hands for Blessing

The following meditation is suited for use by pastoral caregivers prior to a pastoral encounter or visit. Allow yourself at least fifteen minutes for the contemplative experience.

Make sure you are comfortable, sitting upright, with both feet on the floor. Close your eyes. Take a few deep breaths. Tighten and let go of your muscles. Work your way up your body from your toes to your head. Be aware of your breathing. Free your mind and focus on your breathing and relaxation.

Now, open your eyes and read 1 Corinthians 12:12-27. Read the passage a second time. Set the passage aside and put your hands in your lap. Take a few more deep breaths. With each breath you take, draw your hands up toward your lungs as if you are moving the air into your lungs. With each breath you exhale, sweep your hands in a down and out motion away from your lungs and away from your body. Now you are ready to notice your hands.

Look at your hands placed in your lap.
Notice them.
What is your immediate reaction?
Look at them front and back.
Put them in different positions.
Hold them up.
Hold them down.

Hold them away from you.

Close them.

Open them.

Bring them together.

Take them apart.

Cup them.

Stretch them until they are taut.

Be aware of your hands.

Tickle your palms.

Feel the tingling.

If you are wearing any jewelry on your hands, look at it. Remember its origin and story.

Contemplate what your hands do and have done for you.

Contemplate how you have used them in your ministry of pastoral care.

Take a moment to give thanks for what faithful servants they are.

Lift up your preferred working hand and form a cup in your hand.

Contemplate your work as a container for God's truth and grace.

Lift up your other hand and form a cup in your hand

Contemplate this hand as thirsty, yet ready to catch the drops of God's truth and grace.

Contemplate your day and the people you will meet as it unfolds.

Bring someone to mind for whom you have a special pastoral concern.

Reach out to them with your hands.

Contemplate how your hands are blessed.

Contemplate how your hands will bless.

Contemplate how your hands and the hands of the other will be open to receive and offer God's truth and grace.

Hold out your hands to the other. Bless with one hand. Receive a blessing with the other.

Now, give thanks for the hands of God joining with your hands to bless the world.

Ask God to use your hands for receiving as well as doing.

When you are ready, reread the scripture passage from 1 Corinthians 12:12-26.

Go . . . to live simply through the day.

This contemplative exercise is an adaptation and expansion of "Meditation on Hands" by Earle and Elspeth Williams.[31]

3
The soul's Rhythm:
Death and Resurrection

⊸═◉═⊷

For you have delivered my soul from death,
  my eyes from tears,
  my feet from stumbling.
I walk before the LORD in the land of the living.
I kept my faith, even when I said,
  "I am greatly afflicted."

  Psalm 116:8-10

We do not live to ourselves, and we do not die to ourselves. If we live, we live to the Lord, and if we die, we die to the Lord; so then, whether we live or whether we die, we are the Lord's.

  Romans 14:7-8

The Rhythm of Life and Death

AS KAZANTZAKIS'S MAIN CHARACTER ZORBA, THE GREEK, SAYS: "Life is what you do while you are waiting for death."[1] Yet even as we dance life with Zorba while we wait for death, our lives, like his, are full of many deaths. We continually feel the sting of death and the challenge to let go of someone or something and take hold of a different reality of life. Because we are a part of all that we have met, parts of us die when loved ones die. This is also true when strangers die or when an entire village is destroyed by the brutality of ethnic cleansing or the gale force of torrential rains and mud slides. We can feel strangely connected and sorrowful in such times. Personal assumptions, such as "the world ought to be a safe place," can die when personal safety is threatened. A professional identity can be hailed in one country, yet be classified as dead in a new homeland. Dignity, self-esteem, blood cells, beloved pets, routines, dreams, family relationships, jobs, and a host of other realities can die. While we wait for death, "life is difficult"[2] precisely because it carries the sting of death.

73

Sometimes we resist death for good, necessary, or prophetic reasons. When an unwelcome cancer invades the body, access to clean water is denied, or we witness the mud-caked graveyards of mass executions, then we understandably call for a moratorium on death and dare to hope that our resistance to death will generate new hope and breathe new life into dry bones.

Most of the time, however, fearful that life will be extinguished, we avert our eyes from death. When we face death, we confront a thing over which we have no control. Our very helplessness prompts an even stronger desire to deny what we cannot tame. The multimillion-dollar anti-wrinkle cosmetic industry, age-defying plastic nip and tuck surgeries, a heightened fascination with the afterlife, angels and near-death experiences, and the rapid market increase of pharmaceutical drugs and herbal life-enhancing products all reflect a culture that cannot bear the sting of death and, while it waits, averts its eyes.

Yet every day the rhythm of death and resurrection pulsates. We are participants in life's natural rhythm of dying and rising. Every morning the sun rises in the east. Late in the day, it dies in the west. A seed falls to the ground and dies, only to push through the soil in the spring as a shoot yearning for sunlight. A snake sheds its skin so that a new form of life can slither once more through sand and grass. A placenta is expelled and dies as a baby writhes its way into the light of day. We can easily acknowledge that nature is alive with this rhythm of dying and rising. What remains difficult for us to accept is that this rhythm is also part of our everyday human existence, and death is something that does not have to put us off nor be put off.

To consider this natural rhythm of death and resurrection as a lifelong spiritual rhythm—one in which the whole people of God participate—is a timely challenge for a pastoral care committed to listening for the soul. Pastoral caregivers generally have been inclined to focus on helping people cope constructively with their losses and deal with their grief primarily as it pertains to a physical death. Our way of approaching and describing pastoral care has often reflected our own denial of death's constant and rhythmic presence. We have not adequately integrated the rhythm of death and resurrection into our pastoral care, nor have we claimed the rhythm as a way to provide sustainable and soulful pastoral care.

Not only do we live and die; we also die and live. What would happen to our pastoral care if we did not save our dying until the end of our lives? That is the underlying question that this chapter explores, first by considering how death and resurrection is a spiritual rhythm for life, second by clarifying the role of pastoral care in matters of life and death, and third by examining four methods for providing a pastoral care that is both sustainable and soulful. These methods are (1) being intentional about using the language of death in pastoral word and deed; (2) listening for the soul during liminal time and reinforcing the soul-awakening capacity of liminality (the time in between death and life); (3) fostering communal occasions for fully lamenting death; and (4) providing opportunities to discern resurrection. Combined, these pastoral methods can help individuals and congregations to embrace the soul's rhythm of death and resurrection.

Death and Resurrection: A spiritual Rhythm for Life

Death and resurrection have received varied theological, liturgical, pastoral, and spiritual treatment through the years. Catholic and Protestant spiritualities have generally diverged in their approaches to the rhythm of dying and rising. A brief analysis of these differing approaches advances our understanding of what needs to be addressed in order to enhance soulful pastoral care in the Protestant congregational context.

The Catholic Tendency: Participating in the Paschal Mystery

Over the years, and with varying degrees of success, Roman Catholic spirituality has intentionally endeavored to make death and resurrection an integral rhythmic dimension of the Christian's spiritual life. Sharing in the deeper mysteries of Jesus' passion—the *Paschal Mystery*—is the spiritual invitation offered to the soul by Catholic streams of spiritual direction. By sharing the Paschal Mystery, death and resurrection become a spiritual journey for the soul.

In Ignatian spirituality, for example, the focus is upon the mysteries of the death-life of Jesus, from his prayers in the Garden of Gethsemane to his prayer from the cross, from his burial in the tomb to his appearances as the Risen Lord. To be united with God in Christ means that we share not only his glory, but also his passion and suffering. We are invited not only to live with him but also to die with him (Mark 8:34-38). In Ignatian spirituality, praying upon the Paschal Mystery serves as a reminder that God in Christ suffers for the redemption of God's creation, and we too can share in that suffering. We too can shed tears and bear the cost of living and telling truth for the sake of the broken world and its healing.

To share in the Paschal Mystery also involves personal transformation. Participation in the resurrection of Jesus requires approaching life differently. In most streams of Catholic spirituality, this is referred to as *discernment*. Only the grace to discern the heart and mind of God will do. Choosing to be in union with God in Christ will release a flood of new possibilities. There is a constant renewing of life with unlimited potential and consequence as we realize and act upon the grace we are given to find the Risen Christ already present in the events of our lives.

Participating in the Paschal Mystery becomes a way to integrate death and resurrection into daily spiritual life. It involves our personal participation, and it is taken, not just once, but several times in life.

The Protestant Tendency: Resisting the Soul's Rhythm

In contrast to this personal, intense, and rhythmic spiritual focus on the Paschal Mystery found within streams of Roman Catholic spirituality, Protestants generally have tended to distance the power of the Paschal Mystery by treating the matter thematically rather than rhythmically. The theme of death and resurrection has been treated in the context of worship (in the Eucharist, and seasonally during Lent, Holy Week, and Easter), in topical study groups, and during baptismal and funeral rites. As such, death and resurrection have become more of a religious matter for confessed faith than a spiritual matter for lived faith. As a spiritual rhythm for life, death and resurrection are noticeably absent from the daily spirituality of most Protestants.

Protestants' reluctance to embrace death and resurrection as a rhythm for the spiritual life may betray our neglect of a central part of our own Christian tradition. The wilderness or desert experience—which Catholic spiritual directors often refer to as the "dark night of the soul" and intentionally incorporate in such devotional practices as silent retreats and pilgrimages—has not been fully integrated into the spiritual lives of Protestant Christians. Generally, the wilderness experience has become liturgically restricted to the season of Lent and confined to its annual forty-day time period. Within the Lenten cycle, even fewer days of intentional focus are given to reflecting and praying about the voices that speak temptation and truth to our souls in desert-like and barren times. Because wilderness has too often been misunderstood as life-destroying, our greatest urge, even as we enter the Lenten wilderness, is too often to find a way out of it so we don't have to think of it again for another year.

It seems oddly difficult for Protestants to enter the way of death when the cross has been so central to our Christian identity. There are several possible reasons for this apparent contradiction between what we confess and what we live. First, certain periods in Protestant history, reputed for fire and brimstone preaching and an overemphasis on the deathly side of things, may well remain too fixed in our minds. Second, our highly consumptive and religiously pluralistic culture has made the concepts of crucifixion, suffering, and death troublesome. We have felt shame for the ways that our central symbol has become a tool of alliance supporting agendas of power, imperialism, and alienation. Third, the gloomy and gruesome aspects of a cruciform love of God seem incompatible with our frenetic pursuit of happiness and the cheerfulness we like to project on the Christian spiritual life.

Recent and necessary feminist reformulations of Christology have also contributed to an increased reluctance on the part of many Protestants to embrace our central symbol uncritically. As Rita Nakashima Brock suggests, the ghost of the punitive Father-God lurks in the corners and never completely disappears.[3] To a large extent, it is in response to the feminist invitation to reimagine the meaning of the cross, in the light of patriarchal bias, that our discomfort with biblical and contemporary cultures of violence rightly has increased. But just as feminists have repudiated threads of patriarchal domination in the Jesus story of the cross, so too have many feminists revealed a Jesus whose life, death, and resurrection exemplifies a redemptive paradigm of feminist liberation. Just as the cross failed to silence the story of a man who opposed religious and social systems of domination that marginalized the poor and despised, most notably women, so too "all the appropriations of [Jesus] into constructions of ecclesial domination through the centuries also have failed to silence the subversive power of his name."[4] A Jesus whose life and death on a cross represents redemption from patriarchy challenges Christian patriarchy and grounds Christianity in the story of a cross that is truly liberating. Thus the way of suffering tied to the cross becomes a factor in the liberation process, not as a necessity of redemption but as the risk one takes when one is engaged in the struggle to oppose the radical evil of unjust structures, systems, and people who resist change.

As we struggle to relate to our central symbol in the light of a reformulated theology of the cross, we can affirm that a tenacious reality of our heritage in the cross is its dismantling, exposing, defalsifying, and subversive power.

The Protestant Invitation: Reclaiming the Soul's Rhythm

This apparent contradiction in Protestant life—between our central symbol and the lived spiritual journey of the people of God who profess discipleship as dying and living in Christ—stands over and against our own powerful heritage. Dietrich Bonhoeffer, faced with the Nazi reign of terror and persecution, reminded us that it is impossible to shun death. As part of the cost of our discipleship, Christ calls each of us to "come and die" and embrace change, with all its subsequent personal and systemic upheaval, as an essential part of the Christian spiritual life.[5] Acknowledging the need for change and the process of change are often difficult and treacherous. Yet Bonhoeffer understood that change is intrinsic to living an authentic spiritual life. Stasis is neither healthy nor desirable. Spiritual growth cannot happen without death. Because of our human nature, we must expect to change, and change requires that we let old patterns and beliefs die in order to move beyond them and experience release from captivity to former ways of understanding and being. Change, upheaval, wilderness experience, and death are all part of the risk of becoming increasingly open to God who "makes all things new."

As for death and resurrection in daily work and life, Protestants have generally avoided the language of spiritual discernment and have preferred to speak of "knowing the will of God." While Catholic spirituality tends to emphasize the process of continual discernment in the Christian life, Protestants have tended to stress the goal. The often anxious search for God's will has frequently resulted in considerable confusion for people, even hindering their capacity to make decisions about life along the way. The impossibility of ever fully and finally knowing God's will for a changing self and world makes the search a monumental task and contributes to the feeling that God is remote and inaccessible. Calls to surrender to the will of God have often blurred the principles of human freedom and agency, resulting in a more passive approach that seeks to leave matters in the hands of God. Moreover, for many Protestants, finding God's will seems to be more a matter of intellectual pursuit and vocational assent, and less a lived, rhythmic, and decision-making process that recognizes the need for both the head (our thoughts) and the heart (our affections) to be involved.[6] Rediscovering discernment as a lifelong process of active, human decision making for the whole people of God in the midst of life's many possible choices will mean that some choices cannot be made. Facing death and then making the choices that are life-giving will be central to discovering what it means to live the spiritual rhythm of death and resurrection.

It is impossible to reclaim death and resurrection as a lived spiritual rhythm for the soul without a willingness to become a full participant in the rhythm. This means listening for the sounds of death in the soul and entering, not avoiding, the stark and discomforting realities of death.

soulful pastoral care: a matter of life and death

Soulful pastoral care deals consistently with life and death matters. It attends to physical death, but beyond this, it listens for death in various life events. Most events in life are God-given opportunities to attend to the rhythmic necessity of dealing with death. Pastoral caregivers need to listen for the rhythm as it pulses through all sorts of events and circumstances of life, including ordinary and unusual ones.

The gradual decline in membership of an aging congregation may not be readily acknowledged or interpreted as an event of spiritual death, but it warrants soulful attention and care. The relocation of a church's pastor can be a time for probing feelings of death and loss. Even seemingly joyous occasions may contain themes of death. We can expect people to cry at weddings and graduations. This is not just sentimentality or nostalgia, but a form of grieving passages of life that, as some poet once said, are lined with tears. Such occasions present opportunities to explore the death of previous forms of relationships and phases of life.

Recently, a woman and her infant daughter were returning to their car in the parking lot of a shopping mall. Just as she was fastening the seat belt on the child-carrier seat, a masked man pointed a gun at her side and demanded the keys to her car. Several hours later, local police found the stolen car. It had been abandoned on a country side road and, to everyone's relief, the child was still fastened into her seat and was physically unharmed. Although no one actually died and a suspect was captured and scheduled for trial, the young mother had genuine experiences of death that affected her self-image, parenting, and faith. Her belief that she could create a safe and protected world for her daughter died in an instant. Her image of herself as a non-violent woman died as she easily pictured herself shooting anyone who threatened her daughter. Her belief in a God that would not allow such harm to befall innocent ones was shattered. No one had actually died, yet she was immersed in death.

If all the dimensions of our dying can be regarded as a natural part of the human journey, then death will no longer need to be restricted to the physical and private realms. All matters of death—physical, emotional, and spiritual—can become a public and communal reality. Death's meaning for the soul can then be heard and discerned by the whole people of God. Inviting people to participate in the rhythm of death and resurrection throughout their lives will not be easy, yet this is the basic pastoral challenge. It means inviting people to discover *death in life* and *life in death* as well as *life beyond death*. It involves drawing people into the deeper realization that death is not to be denied, but needs to be included as a part of life and the healing of self and world.

Denial of Life and Death Matters: Crisis Addiction

Most people display a widespread reluctance to discuss death openly and accept that it is a recurring reality in our lives. Our discomfort with visiting the elderly residents of long-term health care facilities, our inclination to cover up the true causes of some types of death (AIDS or suicide, for example), and the increasing number of private funerals are just some of the ways we demonstrate our denial of death. Studies show that "many psychophysiological (psychosomatic) illnesses are related to unhealed grief."[7] Our inability to talk openly about death and to normalize its reality in our lives can lead to a protracted grieving process and diminished capacity to live creatively and with purpose.

A major consequence of this widespread reluctance is that we have become culturally addicted to crisis. The language of crisis has become the preferred means to describe, tame, and even deny the reality of events that are about death and resurrection.

An Addicted Culture. Almost everything in life has been labeled a crisis, and we have turned crisis into a typical and even trivial occurrence. We scramble from crisis to crisis. If we have a bad day at work or a bad hair day, our life is in crisis. When someone takes our parking spot, or we forget to pick up that missing recipe ingredient at the grocery store, we claim to be having a crisis. We daily observe the havoc of natural disasters, drawn-out jury trials, and "reality TV" in abundance. We snack on crisis from our armchairs and become home viewers of the crises of others. Rather than enter subjectively into the heart of our own crises, we remain at arm's distance from them by living vicariously and voyeuristically through the critical situations of others.

This objectification of crisis contributes significantly to our inability to understand life's various crises as real death-events. Most theorists, counselors and citizens do not refer to life's crises as death-events, nor do most interpret them as opportunities to enter death as a way to find spiritual meaning for life. Rather, *developmental* or *circumstantial* crises have become the normal terms for labeling life's events that include significant losses. Clearly absent from all of this is the bold, truthful, spiritual language of death.

An Addicted Church. The church has mirrored society's addiction to crisis. The church's addiction to crisis is most evident in our approach to pastoral care. Crisis has become a standard means for measuring pastoral effectiveness in ministry. It is now far too common to hear pastoral caregivers, both clergy and lay, making reference to "dealing with a number of pastoral crises." Whether it is fact or fiction, the truly caring clergy or lay caregiver seems to be one who never misses a crisis and is on the run from one pastoral crisis to the next. Pastoral caregivers keep statistics on the number of pastoral crises they have addressed as a means of accounting for their time and reporting to their congregations on their ministry.

The church's addiction to crisis can also be seen in the way crisis has become the normative means for describing and responding to pastoral situations. For example, most textbooks on pastoral care and counseling employ the language of crisis to describe events in life that are dying episodes. Specific chapters may address pastoral care in times of physical death, but other death-events in life are usually captured under chapter headings that reflect the church's accommodation to the more clinical language of crisis. Intervention is the predominant method for responding pastorally to crisis, and pastoral caregivers continue to be trained to provide short-term methods of crisis intervention.

It is clear that a crisis-oriented approach continues to be both descriptive and instrumental in the work of pastoral counselors and therapists, bereavement and hospice workers, and clergy and lay caregivers. There are recognizable benefits to a crisis-oriented approach. Crisis intervention theory asserts that people in a crisis are in a state of heightened psychological and spiritual sensitivity that makes them less defensive and more open to change. Often they have neither the will nor the energy to protest or protect themselves from intervention. This gives pastoral caregivers a way to understand their role as distinctly advantaged by their trusted, timely, and privileged access to those appearing to be in crisis.

Crisis intervention methods have also sharpened pastoral assessment processes by encouraging greater reliance upon interdisciplinary resources and networks. Increased insight and skill in dealing with crises (especially in the areas of bereavement and palliative care) have enabled pastoral caregivers to identify more readily when it is appropriate to acknowledge their own real limitations and refer persons whose lives are too deeply shattered by change and loss.

Despite these ostensible benefits, the church's addiction to a crisis-oriented pastoral care is causing harm. It has led to an unsustainable pastoral care. When crisis intervention is used as the basic means for pastoral response, pastoral caregivers often forfeit their legitimate and unique spiritual role. The framework of crisis has also led pastoral caregivers to develop addictive behaviors. These addictive behaviors work against the provision of soulful pastoral care.

Unsustainable Pastoral Care

Role Confusion. By trying to sustain a crisis-oriented approach to pastoral care, pastoral caregivers lose a clear sense of the distinctiveness of their role. A crisis-oriented approach requires a caregiver to be interventionist. The problem is that most pastoral caregivers are reluctant or unsure of how to intervene in ways that attend to crisis not merely as a problem to be solved, but as something to be respected as a deep matter of the soul.

The goal of crisis intervention is usually to help people find constructive ways to get out of crisis and to facilitate new ways to cope with or adapt to life's difficulties. Pastoral caregivers can feel confident in tending a wound, analyzing a problem, assisting in the circumvention or elimination of a hazard, or determining some new resources for coping. Usually, such pastoral interventions are welcomed precisely because they serve the purpose of reestablishing a sense of order and security in the midst of chaos and confusion. The role for the pastoral caregiver in this kind of pastoral intervention is *managerial*—the immediate management and resolution of specific problems.

Pastoral caregivers who seek to manage crises are usually more concerned to help people *exit* rather than *enter* the depth of crisis. This kind of intervention deflects people from the shades of death and longings for life that speak within their souls. By moving people too quickly toward resolution, crisis becomes something *aberrant* to be fixed (the *what* of the problem) instead of a *natural* dying moment that pulls us deeper into the heart of God, who is life for us (the *why* of the event). Rather than interpreting a lived experience of death as an opportunity for the soul to find deeper meaning in God, crisis intervention strategies can effectively divert people from the agony and ecstasy of discovering that, in the sting of death, there is an invitation to new life.

This is not to say that pastoral caregivers ought never to be interventionist. Rather, it is to assert that pastoral caregivers intervene differently and in a unique way. Their role is to be an *interpretive* interventionist—a gracious intruder who invites people to enter the heart of a crisis more fully and helps to interpret it as a spiritual event of death and resurrection. As long as pastoral caregivers maintain a problem-solving approach, they deny their vital and legitimate pastoral role, which is to help people take the time that is necessary to seek out the spiritual meaning in crisis.

A crisis-centered approach too easily masks the face of God. It tends to deny the reality of death as part of life, and therefore effectively colludes with society's reluctance to enter the reality of death more fully. It is almost as if the church's caregivers have been co-opted by a worldly grief that denies the very death it produces, rather than encouraging "godly grief . . . that leads to salvation" (2 Corinthians 7:10). As long as crisis intervention methods dominate our approaches to pastoral care, we disguise the reality that we are spiritual beings on a human journey that includes entering death and rising to new life on a regular and rhythmic basis. Our pastoral role is to intervene so as to enable persons to interpret and take—not avoid—the spiritual journey into the heart of death and life in God.

Addictive Behavior in Pastoral Caregivers. Sustaining a crisis-oriented pastoral strategy has also led to some addictive behaviors on the part of pastoral caregivers. Pastoral caregivers who have their emotional radar antennae on constant alert for the sounds of crisis are likely to end up in crisis themselves. As caregivers find themselves running from one pastoral crisis to the next, they may grow increasingly out of touch with their own limitations, inner tensions, and personal responses to stress. To try to keep up with the pace of crisis is to live an addicted life. If pastoral caregivers deny their own humanity, fallibility, and limitations, they are addicts, and they promote addiction in parishioners by their example.

Our cultural addition to crisis means that pastoral needs and demands are now exceeding the church's capacity to respond as it has in the past. Since *crisis* evokes the expectation of "911" immediacy in pastoral response, the numbers of people perceived by others to be in immediate crisis and deserving prompt pastoral attention usually exceed pastoral caregivers' capacities to respond at the expected pace. As long as the church tries to sustain a primarily reactive and individualistic delivery mode for pastoral care, the cost will be revealed in our frantic attempts to make ourselves available or to secure the required human and spiritual resources. Our frenetic and desperate addiction to servicing individuals in crisis is one of the main reasons we are experiencing a substantial increase in the rate of burnout among pastoral caregivers.

As long as we sustain this addiction to crisis we will have an unsustainable pastoral care. What is now needed is a sustainable pastoral care. A sustainable pastoral care will redefine crisis as an opportunity to discover life *in* death and not just *after* death. A sustainable pastoral care will employ intentional, communal methods that have the potential to reinterpret crisis as a spiritual matter that deals with the rhythm of death and resurrection. Pastoral methods that invite the faith community to listen in daily life for dying sounds in the soul hold potential for bringing new life, sustainability, and soulfulness to our pastoral care.

pastoral Methodologies for communal participation in the soul's Rhythm

Discovering death *in* life, not just *after* life, will mean taking a countercultural approach in our pastoral care. Instead of succumbing to the culture's addiction to crisis (that life is a series of problems that we must manage and solve), we will practice pastoral methods that understand life as mystery, and death as integral to that mystery. Our methods will include (1) intentionality

in pastoral word and deed; (2) listening for the rhythm of death and resurrection in liminal time—the time between death and life; (3) individual and
communal forms of lament; and (4) opportunities and means to discern newness of life in the soul. Listening for the soul in the midst of moments of death
can guide us away from addictive responses to life toward more constructive,
truthful, hopeful, and faithful responses.

Intentionality in Pastoral Word and Deed

To promote participation in the soul's rhythm requires intentionality in our
pastoral words and deeds. The choice of words we use and the approaches we
take will reflect the strength of our commitment to advocate for a different
way of listening for the soul. Including the language of death and resurrection in our pastoral care, within congregations and beyond, is an important
step in this regard. It is both more faithful and more spiritually truthful to
describe life's crises as opportunities to locate God in our universal experiences of dying. Even these deeply disturbing and uncomfortable experiences
of human tragedy, confusion, failure, and weakness do not fall outside the
presence and activity of God. Can we view these miserable crises as opportunities to discover what is dying in our relationship with God and how our
faith is being born anew? We need to rename life's circumstances and
reframe life's developmental crises so that they are understood to be times
when we find God through our participation in death and resurrection.

A fundamental place to begin is to speak openly about death. It is only
when we stop colluding with our culture's denial of death and become
intentional about opening its private and hidden tombs that life's natural
rhythms will be restored and our souls set free for abundant living. There is
no area of life today where our nostrils are free from death's stench, yet we
have allowed our souls to be spiritually numbed so that we no longer smell
or name what surrounds us. Neither can we admit that death is more than
we can cope with on our own.

Our denial and our hiding of the truth that our numbness is itself a form
of dying must no longer be indulged. More than ever before we have an
opportunity to awaken souls to the inner pursuit for life that emerges precisely at the point of death. The gift of courage will need to be ours to be
truthful and name death for what it really is. Talk of death is hard talk, but
as theologian Douglas Hall reminds us:

> [I]f Christians cannot endure taking into their consciousness the terrors
> that our secular neighbors spend so much time and energy repressing; if we
> with our living symbol of life emerging at the point of death, of healing
> breaking through where only disease had been before, of shalom as the

unwarranted but real outcome of human violence, if with the cross and resurrection of our Lord at the core of our faith we Christians cannot waken
our minds to the darkness at noon, then how can we expect people who
possess no such cornerstone, no such foundation for reflection and meaning in life, to open themselves to such realities. The whole point of the
cross at the center is to give us the courage to be truthful about what is
wrong with the world; for there is no evil, sin, or death to which our God
is stranger. God is there in the midst of it. We may open our eyes to whatever scourge threatens us. We must open our eyes! Because only the truth
can save us. Let us not deceive ourselves.[8]

Naming Death in Pastoral Conversations. The language of death and resurrection can be employed in our pastoral care in several ways. Coffee and cor-
ridor conversations in church may yield significant opportunities for pastoral
caregivers to elicit the spiritual naming of life's crises. Ordinary conversations are not void of experiences of death. When we hear someone say, "Oh,
just put on a smile and you'll feel better; tomorrow's another day," we can be
sure that death-avoidance is happening.

For this reason, it is helpful for pastoral caregivers to come together periodically to practice telling the truth about death in their own lives, their
wider community, and in the world. Public worship is also one of the most
important contexts in which this kind of naming takes place on a regular
basis. In our preaching, prayers, music, and litanies, and in birth, confirmation, marriage, burial, and Eucharistic rites, we can ensure that the truth of
our faith is affirmed and spoken aloud in participatory ways: the God who
saves us for life is with us in death, and we are not alone.[9]

Our public and private conversations need to name on a regular basis
where death is happening and to identify our reactions as responses to death.
We can use judicious phrases such as, "I sense that something is dying here.
What seems like it is dying in you?" Our intentional use of language will also
include bold resistance to such commonly heard phrases as, "She passed
on," "He is resting in the Lord," "They are no longer with us," or "The coal
mine has been shut down." Instead, we practice and model truthfulness by
saying, "She died last night," or "The coal mine is dead." Our souls yearn for
candor and authenticity, and it is more candid and authentic to name the
heart of crisis as death.

Because the language of crisis surrounds us, we do not always recognize immediately when something or someone is dying. We can dismiss the
reality of death or trivialize our own reaction of grief over the loss. Pastoral
caregivers can listen for people's tendencies to disregard the depth of an
experience and the death that is buried there. Naming monumental deaths

(such as the death of a beloved life-partner) is, at least, somewhat more natural for us than naming a seemingly inconsequential death. For example,
an eighty-year-old woman's loss of a driver's license may appear to be a routine outcome of the aging process, yet it represents the painful death of a
certain measure of independence. This is a moment dying to be named.

In a death-avoiding, death-denying, and crisis-addicted culture, caregivers have the opportunity to model truthfulness in speech about the journey of the soul. Recognizing death as a part of the daily rhythm of life helps
us to live as authentic spiritual beings. Pastoral caregivers also can assume
responsibility for ensuring that people hear the language of death and resurrection enacted within the church's various ministries. These days, this is
especially pertinent for the church's bereavement ministries.

Naming Death in Bereavement Ministries. Even at times of bereavement,
people can be reluctant to name death boldly. Pastoral caregivers have an
extremely significant role to fulfill in this regard during the initial hours and
days of death. Death needs to be intentionally named. Next, it is important
to provide immediate and varied outlets for expressions of grief (individual,
familial, public, and small groups) that can help people put the many names
of death on the disorienting event. If we use the language of death and resurrection on a regular basis within all of our congregational ministries, then
individuals may be increasingly equipped to do this naming themselves.

In cases of physical death, funeral services obviously make a critical contribution. Ritualizing death in a public context is another form of naming
that helps reinforce death's reality. If someone chooses to kill him or herself,
let us not avoid naming suicide in the public funeral service. If it is a death
that affects an entire group or community, then special services that ritual-
ize the death become vitally important. A public announcement of the clo-
sure of a local industry can be ritualized. Local churches might plan and
hold a service in which the entire community has the opportunity to express
its grief, confusion, worry, and anger. This is an opportunity to remember
that even the most severe tragedy is an opportunity to experience the presence of God impaled on the cross of human pain and suffering.

A sensitive yet bold use of the language of death and resurrection is also
important for those within and beyond the church. Many whose familiarity
with the church has decreased (if indeed it ever existed) still turn to the
church for assistance with some sort of service for the dead. As society has
become increasingly secularized, we see new trends emerging around grief
and burial rituals that reinforce cultural patterns of death-denial. For-profit
businesses are springing up in response to recent consumer demands for

low-cost services, quick cremations, and interments. Pastoral caregivers need to listen carefully for signs of death-denial and to counter these with a more forthright and public approach to death.

Church members are not immune to current trends and the increasingly profitable and conglomerate-controlled funeral industry. Congregants can pre-plan funerals without consulting their local church resources or those who will be the grieving survivors. In the past, we could assume that surviving family would make the first call to the church rather than the funeral home. Today, the reverse is usually true. This places families, at their most vulnerable time, in the guiding hands of funeral directors who may not see it as their role to challenge decisions that support an avoidance of death's reality. The nature of their investment in the planning process is different from a church's. It is becoming increasingly common to omit a ceremony of any kind that allows time for a final goodbye. We have all heard people say, "I just couldn't bear to sit in church ever again if we held a funeral here. I will always see his open coffin in front of the pulpit and break down crying." This reluctance to acknowledge death directly, and to bring one's grief to a faith community that ought to be the most able to receive it, can contribute to severe emotional, physical, and spiritual blockages.

Another recent trend in funeral services, one that avoids dealing with grief openly and that denies the wider community a forum for their grief, is to have a private family ceremony without visitation. In rare instances there may be appropriate reasons for this kind of decision, but generally, to collude with this kind of counsel is to deny that death and grief are universal, timeless, and communal experiences. Every death is experienced on an individual plane but also on a collective or systemic plane. No death is a completely private affair. Even though it may seem as if we are desperately alone when death confronts us, in fact we are joined in one great empathetic and interrelated human family. Another contemporary pattern is for cremation to occur first, followed by a memorial service. Less and less common is the tradition of seeing the body in an open casket, followed by a funeral service and graveside burial, at which throwing earth upon the descending casket makes death dramatically real.

Pastoral caregivers can take a proactive role by recommending that the public dimensions and realities of death be acknowledged and by helping people discuss funeral preparations in advance. It is important to prepare people to die well and to consider the psychological and spiritual benefits of making death real at a time when we are most prone to want to deny its reality. Hearing and talking openly about death—both at the time of death and prior to death—helps everyone learn that death is a natural part of the rhythm of life and that it deserves communal acknowledgment, affirmation, and support.

Listening for Sounds of Death in Liminality and Soul-Awakening
Listening for the soul as it enters death and experiences liminal time—the time between life and death—will strengthen the pastoral care of congregations. Death expresses itself in many ways, but if we listen carefully, we will often hear it articulated in the actions and words people use to express what is happening in their lives. The invitation is to listen for the sounds of disintegration and disorientation, for it is there that we are most likely to find the sting of death.

Is a dream falling apart? Is innocence shattering? Is a self-image crumbling? Is the capacity to control something fading? Is it no longer possible to keep it all together? Is energy too dispersed and divided? Is grief, or a series of losses, internalized and hidden? Is an image of God no longer adequate for faith? These less ordered, messier, and unwelcome parts of what happens to people are precisely the places where the soul encounters the rhythm of death and resurrection.

Whether it is a person dying or the local pulp mill shutting down and putting hundreds of people out of work, the grief that accompanies loss invariably results in profound disequilibrium. "This can't be happening to me." "It feels like a terrible dream that I'll wake up from tomorrow." Beyond shock and denial, other responses may reveal the signs of death: physical pain, confusion, disorientation, numbness, anger, guilt, crying, restlessness, and nervous energy.[10] Such responses are instinctual and often lead to the most primitive expression of fight-or-flight. Our bodies try to mobilize an adequate response, but sometimes we are uncertain where to direct our urge to fight. And when there is nowhere to flee, our frustration can bring on tremendous emotional, physical, and spiritual stress.

As with most ordinary life-events, an experience of something or someone dying is an opportunity to discover God with us in steadfast and new ways. When things are going smoothly, we are more content to live with a superficial connection with God. When suffering disrupts our lives, however, upsetting our equilibrium and throwing us for a loop, we become more motivated to do serious soul-searching. Death is a profoundly spiritual issue that disturbs and awakens our souls. It confronts our connection with God and beckons us to deepen that connection by asking who and whose we are and how we choose to live and die. What can be affirmed, discovered, defied, or deepened? When we are in crisis and name the sting of death at its center, the soul is awakened to the pursuit of ultimate meaning.

Questions about meaning and God's presence in the midst of confusion, emptiness, decay, or tragedy explode to the surface. Like the psalmist of old, the questions cannot be contained: "How long, O Lord? Will you forget me forever? How long will you hide your face from me? How long must I bear pain in my soul, and have sorrow in my heart all day long?" (Psalm 13:1-2). There is always the danger that, if we do not provide the opportunity for such thoughts and feelings to explode, they will implode. Questions of spiritual meaning and relevance are most likely to find their natural voice when death is physical. "Why did this happen to me?" "God, where are you?" "God, what am I going to do?" "God, why are you so cruel and unfair?" "Why did you allow this to happen?" "God, how much pain is enough?" "Will there ever be light in this relentless darkness?" Other experiences, such as being forced to sell a family homestead due to bankruptcy or experiencing the emotional withdrawal of a spouses, may not be as readily acknowledged or interpreted as spiritual death-events, but they, too, warrant soul attention and care.

Pastoral caregivers are ideally situated to listen for both the obvious and hidden sounds of death. They can help persons and communities give expression to the soul-disturbing sounds that are pounding in the depths and affirm the seemingly unanswerable questions that are stirring in the soul. Critical dimensions of our pastoral care are how we are present with people and how we hear them into speech during a dying episode. The experience of death is a crucial moment for exploring the ultimate meaningfulness of life lived in relationship with God. Before we can affirm that death is a turning point inviting us to discern how we will live, the fullness of the death must be experienced.

Affirming the Liminal Phase. Experiencing the fullness of death includes affirming and accepting liminality as an essential phase in moving from death to life. Liminality is the phase we experience between the certainty of death and the certainty of life.[11] Liminality is what most people, including pastoral caregivers, are least equipped to handle and most prone to resist.

As our listening for the soul intensifies in this phase, pastoral caregivers can tune their ears to listen for the usual sounds of resistance and fear. We quip about skipping over the darkness of Good Friday in order to get to the Easter Sunday alleluias as if our lighthearted confession is a preventive strategy for avoiding the reality of death in our own lives. Entering the Saturday places of death and facing the depths of our loss and pain is hard work. Looking into the heart of whatever is dying in us can be exhausting and can feel more debilitating than healing. Remembering can seem more like dismembering, especially if we feel alone, lack resources to help us negotiate the way, and have no previous experience of death to draw upon as a memory that even the tomb is within the scope of God's transforming gaze and action. I think it was philosopher Matthew Arnold who once described this time as akin to living between two worlds, one dead and the other powerless to be born. People can feel terribly afraid and unsafe during this liminal tomb-like phase in which we experience our souls straddling death and life. A major component of listening is to hear and normalize these feelings of fear.

What has inhibited us most as pastoral caregivers has been our general reluctance to claim the middle liminal phase as a central focus for our caregiving ministry. We have rarely given adequate attention to the soul-awakening potential of this zone. Rather than encouraging people to enter the time of chaos, contradiction, and liminality even more deeply, and naming and lamenting what is dying or whatever needs to die, our discomfort with the internal chaos that is part of the dying process has motivated us instead to practice means of getting people out of crisis and on with their lives as quickly as possible. We have frequently missed the full potential of a pastoral response that takes the liminal phase seriously. We have neglected to affirm the full rhythm of life of spiritual beings, which includes listening for the soul's need to taste death in the wilderness even as it longs for liberation and life.

Earlier in this chapter, I commented on the reluctance of Protestants to integrate the wilderness image into a lived spirituality. Resituating the spiritual image of the wilderness from a sidelined Lenten position to one more central to the faith is one way to affirm and give words to the soul's experience of liminality. We have always understood the spiritual image of wilderness to be characteristic of the terrain over which life's journey in the spirit takes us. What has been missing is offering this image as a way to normalize our fear and resistance to death. The image is helpful because it recognizes that danger, threat, and risk are part of the spiritual journey and cannot be avoided. It is also helpful because it affirms the primal thoughts, feelings, and words that need expression before a new identity and way of being can emerge. Consistent with the image, one must be willing to engage "the beasts" as well as be served by "the angels" (Mark 1:13). Pastoral caregivers can assume the responsibility of listening for the soul until it is heard into speech. The troublesome questions and feelings (the presence of beasts) that emerge in the wilderness can be vocalized and at the same time the individual can be assured that they are not abandoned (angels are present) even as they project primal rage and sorrow onto pastoral caregivers, others, and God.

Affirming Expression of Liminality. For the soul to awaken to new life, it needs to express its most primitive voice during the liminal phase. The role for pastoral caregivers here is to encourage this expression, listen intently and passionately to it, and persevere with its expression until it is spent. By listening and encouraging primitive expressions, pastoral caregivers provide a corrective to those who assert that such soul-expression is aberrant. Maria Harris reminds us that "if we grieve the loss in the world, if we are in bodily distress due to its poisons, and if we feel we are out of place and no longer fit, we may be acting the sanest ones of all."[12]

For this reason, a vital dimension of pastoral care that listens for the soul is helping the whole people of God understand that the expression of primitive emotions can feel endless (and usually includes rage). In the heart of the wilderness, people are seized by many so-called negative feelings (distrust, breakdown, failure, and anger) and experience their self-control slipping away. It is as if the pain will never end, that nothing makes sense anymore. Feelings of isolation, powerlessness, emptiness, restlessness, and deadness emerge. Rage can be pent-up and people can suffer "an inwardness with a jammed lock," to use Soren Kierkegaard's familiar metaphor. During these moments, as poet Dylan Thomas phrased it, we "do not go gentle into that good night" but we "rage, rage against the dying of the light." It is in this critical liminal phase that pastoral caregivers can enable persons to locate and put into words before God the precise destination of their grief and rage. Anger is a signal to the soul that all is not well with the world, and to affirm anger as an ally in our spirituality is to begin to see the power of it in the work of soul-awakening.

The challenge for congregations and pastoral caregivers is to dignify the soul-awakening process by keeping focused attention on this phase. It is too tempting to shut it down prematurely or to bypass it altogether. Allowing the most painful questions and negative emotions to flow, no matter how uncomfortable we may be with them and no matter how destructive they may seem to be, is vital to awakening the soul. If there is anger at the deceased for dying, that anger needs expression. If there is rage at God for a creation scheme that makes death necessary, then that rage needs expression. If there is invective toward an employer or company for a costly reduction in work hours and salary, then that invective needs expression. And this is still not the core of death. There is more that needs to be heard into speech.

These intense, sometimes surprising, and conflicting feelings can lead to despair. The soul can feel as if it is losing touch with God and its foundation of being. Communication with God can break down and people can lose any sense of how to relate to God. Former images of God may seem useless and shattered into irreparable pieces. Scapegoating behaviors surface, and the individual may engage in self-blame and suspicion. The individual may fear or encounter the truth that personal failure and mistakes may have created the very experience of wilderness. It is at the core of death that people tend to abandon God and prayer, a marriage, a friend, a minister, a church, colleagues, or a community. They can forfeit any genuine hope or the maturity of love and mutuality that lies on the other side of their hopelessness. Dorothy Soelle describes this experience of forsakenness as relentless suffering. It feels as if it will never end and that the soul will never see light in or out of the darkness again.[13]

What is happening in the soul at this moment—when we are in the very core of the crisis—is that we are living the central paradox of Christian faith: the Paschal Mystery that life comes through death, that one gains oneself by losing oneself (Mark 8:34-36). When we come up against our own helplessness and human limitations and realize that we have come up against that over which we have no control, then we are in the heart of death. In the heart of death, narcissistic egoism dies so that the soul can be awakened and set free for authentic love of self, God, and others. When one is in the midst of such an experience, one cannot be primarily in the business of defining oneself. As Gerald May puts it: "One's ego, sense of identity, self-image seems to evaporate almost magically. And one is left, just simply being."[14] Death provides the opportunity to cease human flailing, to accept our full humanity and fallibility and to rest in the mystery of God. It is "not to do anything," and instead to be supported by the life-breath of God.

It is important for pastoral caregivers to remember that during the liminal phase, sometimes people need to leave the faith community for a time because their personal resources are just too battered to find one more ounce of energy that will allow them to remain. And we need to let them go and trust them to God. This is not the same as fulfilling their experience of abandonment, for we need not be disconnected, simply respectful for a time. The danger of the liminal phase is that individuals can become so self-preoccupied that they are unable to sense, rethink, redescribe, or reimagine a different or larger reality on their own. Self-preoccupation often leads to destructive behavior toward self and others and seldom yields transformative energy, freedom, or hope. This is why communal connection remains necessary in some form as the soul fully enters the rhythm of death and resurrection.

One form may be helping people discover that they can give full and honest expression to death in the faith community, and people will not shrink away in discomfort. Another form may be for the faith community to affirm people's strengths and latent resources when they are not able to spot them themselves. Yet another form may be for the community simply to continue breathing the spirit of new life into others when they feel they no longer have the energy to draw breath themselves. At the height of people's exhaustion is the faith community's incarnation of the caring promise that they still belong to God and are intensely cared for, even as they walk through the valley of the shadow of death.

The faith community's lived promise of non-abandonment is integral to soulful pastoral care during the liminal phase. Non-abandonment is a measure of the faith community's commitment to be hospitable to the soul as it experiences the rhythm of death and resurrection. Pastoral caregivers can periodically assess whether a congregation is practicing non-abandonment and can share their findings with the congregation so that they can initiate changes. Here is a helpful checklist of questions for pastoral caregivers concerned with developing a congregational ethos that is hospitable and fully present to liminality in all of its potentially expressive force:

* What experiences of death are we hearing in the lives of our people and in the wider community and world?
* How are we regularly naming the rhythm of death and resurrection in our worship?
* What images of God do we hear during the time of death?
* Do we lift up comforting images of God on a regular basis?
* What images of God might we present as a means of evoking a breakthrough to new life?
* Do we acknowledge and accept that the soul goes through a messy and theologically unconventional phase?
* Is the soul given opportunity to express itself fully within the congregation and without fear of increased isolation or recrimination?
* Do people in pain disappear from the church and return months or years later, or not at all?
* Do we have a means to follow up with people who have slipped into isolation?
* Are we talking together about experiences of death and resurrection in ways that can undergird the next occasion when the rhythm occurs?
* How are we preparing members of our community to die well?

A faith community's capacity to be in solidarity with persons who are in the tomb-like places is a measure of soulful pastoral care. Such solidarity assures persons experiencing death that there is an empathetic human family that lives and breathes the rhythmic nature of death and the universality of grief.

A Communal Pastoral Methodology: Lament

One pastoral method for encouraging the expression of liminal time is to legitimate lament as a communal act within the congregation. Lament is a specific and cathartic way to channel primitive expressions of liminality and to normalize these expressions in a public context. Lament is an essential part of the soul's awakening process, and it needs to be brought from its private, neglected, suppressed, hidden, buried, and lonely places and into the context of common sorrow and rage for all the deaths we experience. This will counter our culture's pattern of denial, and our pastoral care will bear witness that as long as someone suffers, no one can be completely happy; if anyone is dying, no one can be completely alive.

Just as we include affirmations of our common faith, so, too, can we incorporate words of lament. If we can practice voicing frustration and complaint to God in the hearing of one another, then our personal experiences may seem less overwhelming, isolated, and peculiar and we may be enabled to sing "blest be the ties that bind." Incorporating lament as a structured and regular opportunity within the faith community is a way to be proactive in our pastoral care.

The Pastoral Role of Lament. Walter Brueggemann describes lament as our most "vigorous mode of faith." Calling it "a spirituality of protest," he says that it is our way of recognizing that all is not right in the world. "This is against our easy gentile way of *denial*, pretending in each other's presence and in the presence of God that 'all is well' when it is not."[15] By holding God accountable for what has failed and seems unjust, our lament speaks against a docile relationship with God. Such a form of speech holds cathartic value, surely. But more importantly, lament helps everyone discover that the life of the world is saturated with death and that the ache of much pain is yet unresolved.

Lament is an honorable means of expressing the unfinished ache of a death, what are normally considered to be unacceptable thoughts (about God or others), and the soul's desire and gratitude for life. Lament usually assumes a pattern that includes addressing God, pouring out the soul's complaints against God and others, asking God for something (such as rescue from a situation) and providing reasons for God to act, wishing for something harmful to come to the enemy or cause of death, and finally moving to some statement of gratitude or confidence. Lament begins in the tomb and ends with the soul's awakening to hints of hope and resurrection.

Integrating Lament in Congregational Life. If lament can be included periodically in public worship, prayers, and songs, then our liturgies will take an important step in bringing death from buried private places out into the open of the faith community. Lament clearly has a place in special liturgies offered during the Christmas season for those who mourn, in services that draw awareness to violence, imprisonment, and AIDS, in rituals that recognize a community's grief over the death of a public or heroic figure, or mass injuries or death (an airplane crash, a multicar pile-up, or the drowning of a group of children). The death of children is an especially poignant time to remember the biblical witness of Rachel's inconsolable grief and lament.

Moving beyond these more obvious examples, it is important to include lament on a regular basis within Sunday worship to underscore that death is a natural part of the soul's rhythm. Prayers of confession are rhythmic and regular means for the expression of lament. Lament can also be encouraged in small groups by inviting people to write and share their own lament psalms or by inviting spontaneous expressions of lament. A guide can lead people to offer spontaneous expression by leading people through the various elements that comprise a pattern of lament. Lament can be used by bereavement groups, prayer groups, study groups, or groups formed for the explicit purpose of giving expression to losses or deaths other than those related to physical death. For example, we might include lament in a marriage preparation weekend, a confirmation class, or baptism or church membership study.

In addition to the biblical witness of lament (particularly of the prophets and the psalms), there are many courageous and helpful published resources that enable us to integrate lament sensitively and appropriately within small group and liturgical contexts.[16] Printed forms of lament, including psalms, readings, poems, prayers, songs, and litanies can embrace the various forms of death and what dies within us. These can include lament against violence, lament against physical death, lament against downsizing, lament against restructuring, lament against the loss of innocence, and lament against the loss of faith. In Ann Weems's *Psalms for Lament*, we find words strong in utterance and insistence that give expression to the many forms of death and the griefs we all bear. A meaningful example of a reading that could be used within Sunday worship, a small group gathering, or a funeral service is her "Lament Psalm Two":

God, find me here
where the sun
is afraid to shine!
Don't you recognize your faithful one?
Haven't I known you
since the days of my youth?
Haven't I sung your songs
in the ears of our enemies?
Why then are you silent?
Why have you forsaken me
and left me to wail
in the empty night?
Why do you give me silence
when I ask for
the nightingale's song?

O God, have pity on me
and enter into
the city of my pain.
Hear my cry
and come to me
that all might know your faithfulness.
From the icy coldness
of the pit,
I will praise your name,
for like a shepherd
searching for a lost sheep,
you will not give up
until you find me.

Here in the gloom
I wait for the light
of your coming.
Then I will shout
that my God is the God
who does not rest
until all are
gathered in
from the threat of night.[17]

Lament as Soul-Awakening Activity. In taking up the pastoral work of lament, we learn that its purpose is not resolution but as an expression that sets things in motion. Through utterance, the soul begins to awaken. In this sense, listening for the sounds of death and soul-awakening differs from helping people merely to survive a crisis or cope in a crisis. Timothy Carson puts it this way: "Transformation is expected as a result of the liminal plunge."[18]

Soul-awakening is sparked by truth-telling protests that cry "the world should not be the way it is."[19] These very utterances are daring declarations of intent toward a new reality and way of being in the world. They are defiant expressions of confidence that there must be something more beyond death. As paradoxical as it may seem, when the hurt, despair, demand, and invective are fully voiced, we are *alive in death* and have begun to glimpse the possibility of life beyond death.

Even when God seems terribly absent, it is in voicing despair that the soul is most keenly alive to the reality of God. The power of hope is enacted in the utterance of despair. New life comes through an embrace of death wherever we find it implanted in our lives. When the soul awakens enough to cry for a moratorium on death, then this moment is not outside the presence and activity of God. "A raw, ragged openness is linked to the awesome reality of God's holiness."[20] It is in such fullness of death that it becomes possible to discover that there is a deep incongruity in life that we need neither resolve nor deny.

The pastoral work of lament is this simultaneous resistance and embrace of every pressure toward new life. Even so, we know that some people can become stuck in their grief and rage, bogged down by the sheer immensity of their pain and sense of loss. Some people may continue to defy the promise of new life by turning back toward death-denial, which is a numbness to the fact that death holds life within its grasp. There is an arrogance in human nature that can strongly resist freedom and that would rather remain in self-chosen misery than have to live with the uncertainty and unpredictability of dying and assenting to the new. Yet the spiritual paradox remains that the heaviness will not lift until it is fully embraced as a natural part of the process of moving from death to life. By ourselves, it is difficult to obtain release from the powers of death and the deep fear that accompanies new life. When we are in the heart of darkness, facing death, stranded in the liminal zone, we may be unable to face death or find life on our own. Sometimes we are simply unable to distinguish the difference between a death-event and a life-moment. As Alan Jones put it, "The womb of the new life is often identical with the tomb of the old."[21] To embrace our capacity to live the rhythm of death and resurrection, and in particular, to move from the liminal phase to the soul awakening to new life, we humans need the help of God's spirit manifested in one another.

Listening for Resurrection

Rather than struggling to *get through* the crisis of death, we have entered it in order to *see through* our dying to what lies ahead. The Greek word for discerning is *diakrisis*, which implies seeing through crisis. Discerning suggests, once again, that listening for the soul is a critical skill for pastoral caregivers to develop. Now we are listening for ways that death invites us and others to become more aware of the lifelong call of God revealed within such experiences. In other words, listening for new life involves developing in ourselves and others a posture of discerning and a method for discerning. People want to find the truth for which they can die and live. They continue to ask the question: "What am I to do?" Our pastoral care can include discernment as a helpful avenue for assisting people in working with this spiritual matter of how God is inviting a person to awaken in the soul to new life. Such new life will enable us to embark as fully human persons on a spiritual journey to live in the glorious image of God.

To listen for the sounds of resurrection and help persons discover new life, it is important in our pastoral care to claim insights from the rich reservoir of our tradition. But before doing so, a word of caution is in order. Discernment is not about gimmicks or quick fixes for the grief that resides within us. Rather, discernment emerges from deep engagement with an experience of something or someone dying and from opportunities that present themselves for choosing newness of life. What discernment offers is a way to incorporate new dimensions of ourselves that we have discovered in death and to test choices for life so that they further prepare us for full participation in the lifelong spiritual rhythm of death and resurrection.

Listening for Resurrection: Cultivating the Posture of Discernment
Although discernment is the way that many Christians through the centuries have sought the will of God for their lives, a posture of discerning and methods of discernment have not always been cultivated well or practiced within most Protestant churches.

There are some exceptions. The Quaker tradition, which values the role of the local community in discernment, assists in determining if a spiritual leading or call is consistent with the experience of God as found in scripture, the Quaker tradition, and the local meeting of the faith community. Methodists have also sought discernment by means of the *Wesleyan quadrilateral*, which also relies on community, past as well as present. The four elements of the quadrilateral are scripture, church, reason, and experience, with scripture understood to be the primary source of guidance, and experience understood to mean spiritual experience or "testing" the leading of God. Notwithstanding these and other processes specifically designed for the discernment of "call and gifts for leadership in ministry," Protestants are generally inclined to draw upon secular processes for making everyday life and death decisions or determining new directions in the spiritual journey.

Protestant churches often have put processes in place for potential ministry candidates to discern a call to ministry but rarely offer parallel processes for helping laypersons discern their ministry in the world. Moreover, what ought to be a continuous process of discernment for all ages and at all stages of life is often restricted to a prepubescent vocational discernment and occasional congregational inventories that seek to discern gifts for the church's internal ministry programs. In spite of these limitations, an obvious strength in what Protestant churches have done is that discernment has remained an ecclesiastical matter and a concern for the faith community. Discerning vocation has rarely been viewed as a merely private affair.

We can build on this foundation and reassert the importance of the church's proactive role in assisting people of all ages to discern how God is beckoning them toward life-giving choices and activities. Any focus on discernment will first encourage a lifelong posture of openness that listens for how death-laden experiences consistently summon us to new life. Painful death-events inevitably jolt us with questions that touch our deepest motivations for living and that probe the implications of experiencing resurrection in the soul: "What is most important in my life now?" "Why am I (still) living?" "Given what I now know, how can I be most authentic?" "How can I best live my life so that I am deeply connected to God?" "Who is God inviting me to become?" "How does this experience of dying speak to me now about my leisure, work, relationships with family, friends, and enemies, public and private life?" "How does it challenge or change my motivations and aspirations and strengthen the struggle against death-denial and this world's powers of death?"

Listening for the emergence of these kinds of questions in the soul, as well as helping people to ask themselves such questions, is part of our pastoral care ministry. At the point, but not before, when people experience themselves on the verge of "something different," "something shifting," "something inviting us to a more abundant life," pastoral caregivers can listen for how souls are being awakened to act and live in dialogue with a larger meaning and mystery in life. Caregivers can respond by participating in the intentional act of helping others discern the consequences of the soul-awakening for their ongoing lives and experiences. God's invitation to resurrection life may emerge as a new self-image, identity, worldview, or image of God. Each of these realities will lead to different situations and decisions that will need to be made.

For example, a heterosexual orientation, a judgmental image of God, or an idealistic expectation of the institutional church all may have died. In liminality, the soul may have died and awakened to a gay or lesbian identity, a God of unconditional love, or the realization that the church is a fallible and, at times, oppressive and damaging institution. What it means to live authentically in God with this new awareness, and as a spiritual being on a human journey, is now the matter at hand. The awakened soul is in a process of discerning what is needed in order to flourish as a person made in the image of God.

When and how, to what and to whom we give our *yes* or our *no* are part of the experience of our dying and discerning how we are to live as resurrected beings. As Shawn Copeland puts it: "Tough decisions and persistent effort are required of those who seek lives that are whole and holy. . . . (W)e need to renounce the things that choke off the fullness of life that God intended for us . . . " and say "yes to a way of life that makes space for God."[22]

A critical aspect of this listening does include discerning vocation. By vocation, I am referring to one's vocation in God, which is about more than career choices. Whenever people experience something or someone that is dying, they will find themselves visiting or revisiting their vocation. To use Walter Brueggemann's well-known phrasing, vocation is to "find a purpose for being in the world that is related to the purposes of God."[23] Or to recall Frederick Buechner's phrase: "The place God calls you to is the place where your deep gladness and the world's deep hunger meet."[24]

In this sense, our vocation is not a one-time decision merely related to career. Nor is vocation simply a personal concern. It is the ongoing matter of how our own growing authenticity and personal needs come regularly into conversation with our deepening understanding of God's desires and needs for the world. Our vocation is a way of being in the world that is constantly challenged by the new life in God that we discover through our participation in the rhythm of dying and living. When we understand vocation this way—as the ways we choose to live in deep connection with God's love and desire for the world—then it needs to be discerned continually throughout life, and we need tools and the faith community to assist our discernment.

Criteria for Discerning. Discernment allows people to see their choices more clearly and to make decisions in a way that considers what will be most life-giving for themselves as they live in an interconnected world. Because there is usually more than one possible choice before us, the criteria for choosing become important. As we face potential changes in our lives, we may sometimes need to make a choice among several apparent goods, or it may seem as if a choice must be made between the lesser of two evils. Saying yes to one thing may mean giving up something else. How do we know when we have made a good decision?

Pastoral caregivers can suggest criteria that individuals and groups may use for discerning choices that will be life-enhancing and life-giving. For one thing, discernment seeks to move us toward a life-giving, creative spirit, not a destructive, self-indulgent spirit. For example, if a student identity is dying and a nine-to-five identity is coming to life, the question "How much will I make?" becomes far less important than "What is God calling me to do?"

Yet the most encompassing criterion by which to discern what God may be inviting us to is the extent to which concern for our own well-being is balanced by concern for others. When we are both true to ourselves and deeply aware of others and the world God so loves, then we are experiencing the fullness of God's vocational call to life. Discernment is not finding out what is best for ourselves, but assessing how to live out what is best for ourselves in relation to others. Our own experiences of death and resurrection can arouse our sense of smell for death elsewhere and make it untenable for us to turn away from the world's pain. When we have discerned an authentic vocation in God, we will be involved in a constructive and enlarging engagement with otherness.

As is true in the liminal phase, when we are in this phase of integrating new realities and discovering new life, our spirituality is neither a private nor a spectator activity. Discernment is not something that just happens; rather, it is the intentional exploration of one's living and one's personal relationship with God. This intentional exploration may begin in private prayer and a process of personal discernment, but it is only brought to completion through a testing of decisions with others in the faith community. All discernment is aided by the shared wisdom of the faith community. Our *yes*'s and our *no*'s will be strengthened through sharing with others our hearts' desires and how we are holding these in the light of our deepening connection with God and others. And, when we share, we must be open to hear and respond, even reconsider our *yes* or our *no*.

Integrating Discernment in Congregational Life. Incorporating discernment groups as part of a congregation's ministry is a preventive and spiritually life-enhancing means of providing pastoral care. Some groups may want to meet weekly (perhaps over a meal) or monthly, others at the request of an individual to assist with discerning how an experience of something dying may be a resurrection event.

Someone may need help assessing whether it is time to sell the family home and move into a health care residence. Maybe a woman seeks help in discerning what it means for her to be single and now past the point of being able to have children. Perhaps the outreach committee is having difficulty accepting that it no longer has the human or financial resources for two equally important ministries and must choose between continuing to provide an elementary school breakfast program or being involved with a neighborhood halfway house for mentally challenged persons.

Several discernment methods and guidebooks already exist, and these methods can be shared as means for making faithful choices in life.[25] Some of these processes include designs for an entire faith community to reach consensus on a decision. Ordering a congregation's ministries by discerning the vocation to which the church is called will stand in bold contrast to those models of decision making in most Protestant churches that are founded upon parliamentary rules. Other methods are more suited for individual and small-group responses. The *Ignatian* and *Clearness* processes are two of the most familiar methods for discerning the movement and call of God throughout life's rhythm of death and resurrection.

The Ignatian discernment process[26] is an important one with which to become familiar, although it is meant to continue over several months and to be used in conjunction with daily praying with scripture and regular meetings with a spiritual guide or group for reflection. The thoroughness of the process, integrated with prayer based on the life of Christ, is one of its many strengths. The process is meant to be used for individual discernment, but it can be expanded for the purposes of communal discernment. The main elements of the process include:

1. Gathering information from various sources (scripture, reading, community, interviewing, and so forth)
2. Imagining the possible change (placing the choice before the mind's eye)
3. Weighing the pros and cons (not to count them, but to determine which list is more reasonable and influential)
4. Offering the decision to God in prayer and listening for inner consolation or desolation (consolation leading toward peace with God or desolation leading away from God in distress)
5. Testing the decision against past experience and vocational passions

It is possible to use the Ignatian process as a template for discernment and to condense the process into a shorter time frame, but this is less effective than engaging in Ignatian discernment as originally intended.

The Clearness Committee is another discernment process developed by the Quakers.[27] It was originally developed for discernment about marriage, but is adaptable for a variety of situations where something is dying and someone or something is yearning to find new life. A person seeking "clearness" and wanting to discern the most appropriate course of action prepares a written statement of his or her situation in advance and circulates it to a group of trusted and invited persons. The group begins with centering prayer, perhaps a scripture reading followed by silence, after which the "focus person" gives a fresh statement of the concern. Others then respond with questions for clarification and discernment. Sometimes there is silence, which is an opportunity for further quiet reflection and interior prayer. It is common to hear clearness committee questions begin with phrases such as "Have you considered . . . ?" or "How do you see that affecting . . . ?" After a time of response and questioning, observations are collected from around the circle. "I think I am hearing you say that . . ." It may be that a clear choice emerges or that there is still sufficient fuzziness so that not to decide is the best decision at this time. All of this is done in a prayerful atmosphere, in a spirit of thanksgiving for members of the group, and with a commitment to reconvene either to continue the clearness process or to hear how a clear decision has unfolded.

In addition to these two traditional methods, here are some guiding questions that may be helpful for any discernment initiated by individuals or groups:

+ What is dying and what will new life look like?
+ What am I clinging to? How am I being called to greater freedom?
+ What will this decision say to me about my relationship with myself, others, and God?
+ In what ways are others going to be affected by this decision?
+ What are the benefits and costs of saying *yes* or of saying *no?*
+ What will life look like if I/we say *yes* or *no?*
+ What obstacles will be encountered?
+ How are personal limitations being considered?
+ How will this choice influence future choices?
+ If the choice is *yes/no*, does that limit possibilities for growth (mine or others)?
+ What might be said to others in this same situation?
+ Is there adequate spiritual and emotional support either way?
+ Are all alternatives being fully considered?
+ Which alternative stimulates and which stifles?

* Who do I/we hope to be become through this?
* Will this represent a step in the direction of embracing otherness/ respecting creation?
* How does this choice further prepare me for living the soul's rhythm of death and resurrection?

Whatever circumstance of death arouses the need to discern new life and vocation in God, the church community can be involved in prayerful, attentive, challenging, and supportive ways.

Dying into Life: A New Basis for Pastoral Care

Listening for the soul's rhythm of death and resurrection requires that we state a new purpose for providing pastoral care in relation to crisis. For obvious reasons, we need to continue to respond to individuals experiencing genuine crises. The time has come to go beyond solving the problems of crisis, however, and to regard our primary pastoral task as developing communal participation in the lifelong rhythm of learning to die and live anew. Our goal now is to reinterpret crisis as a death-event, to encourage people to enter the reality of death as fully as possible, and to discern the spiritual meaning that will awaken the soul to new life.

To reframe our purpose in this way necessitates a shift in focal attention and pastoral tasks. Rather than giving primary attention to helping persons survive a crisis, we turn to place our focal attention on the heart of the crisis that is the spiritual matter of death. If our churches can become hospitable places for those raw expressions of death's sting, then our acceptance of liminality and our encouragement of communal lament will help awaken souls to this rhythm in which they will die well and live abundantly. Once souls are turned God-ward, the work of resurrection is under way. Encouraging postures of discernment and the use of discernment methods within the faith community enhances the soul's awakening process. Such God-vocated discernment occurs moment by moment in our lives and begins where all journeys of the soul begin—with listening for God and God's nudge upon our hearts to listen for the rhythm of death and resurrection in this world and the next.

Reflection Questions

1. How have I experienced the culture of death-denial operative within my congregational context?

2. Locate that part of yourself that does not want to grieve or rage and that does not want to be aware of that need, or even to think about it. It may be something in you about which you have kept silent. Can you describe this part of you? What sort of pastoral care would be helpful to this part of you?

3. How can pastoral caregivers best be equipped to offer pastoral care that focuses on liminality and soul-awakening?

4. If a shift in pastoral method is required, moving from crisis intervention to communal participation in the rhythm of death and resurrection, what will help evoke that shift?

5. In what ways is pastoral caregiving a vocational call to live the rhythm of death and resurrection?

Spiritual Exercise

Meditate on the following excerpt from T. S. Eliot's poem "Journey of the Magi":

> This: were we led all that way for
> Birth or Death? There was a Birth, certainly,
> We had evidence and no doubt. I had seen birth and death,
> But had thought they were different; this Birth was
> Hard and bitter agony for us, like Death, our death.
> We returned to our places, these Kingdoms,
> But no longer at ease here, in the old dispensation,
> With an alien people clutching their gods.
> I should be glad of another death.

A Pastoral Tool to Assist Discernment

Read and meditate on John 11:1-6, 17-45.

Take a sheet of paper and record your soul's responses to any or all of the questions below. These responses may be shared within a small group that has gathered for the purpose of discernment.

After completing the sheet, offer a prayer to God and repeat as a mantra throughout the day:

"Both in our living and in our dying,
we belong to God,
we belong to God."[28]

1. What is dying in me is . . .

2. This death is an intrusion in my life because . . .

3. Like Martha, I feel that if only . . .

4. What I most need from Jesus is . . .

5. What I most want to scream is . . .

6. My faith is challenged because . . .

7. Like Jesus, I weep for . . .

8. Like Lazarus, I wonder what my life will be like when . . .

9. What I need to be unbound from is . . .

10. When Jesus yells to me "Come out!," I hear . . .

4
credible caregivers:
sustaining spiritual practices

⋅→═◉═←⋅

Admonish the idlers,
    encourage the faint hearted,
    help the weak,
    be patient with all of them.
See that none of you repays evil for evil,
    but always seek to do good to one another and to all.
Rejoice always.
    pray without ceasing,
    give thanks in all circumstances;
    for this is the will of God in Christ Jesus for you.
Do not quench the Spirit.
Do not despise the words of prophets, but test everything;
    hold fast to what is good;
    abstain from every form of evil.
May the God of peace himself sanctify you entirely;
and may your spirit and soul and body be kept sound
    and blameless at the coming of our Lord Jesus Christ.
The one who calls you is faithful, and he will do this.
Beloved, pray for us.

    1 Thessalonians 5:14b-25

THIS CHAPTER IS NOT WRITTEN TO EVOKE GUILT or to add one more burdensome item to a list of essential tasks for pastoral caregivers. Rather, I hope it will be a gentle reminder of what is already known—that credibility depends upon one's willingness to sustain spiritual practices that enhance personal soul development and enrich pastoral care. Too many caregivers unwittingly reinforce the ideas that the Christian life is about compartmentalizing faith and daily life, working oneself to death, neglecting self, family, and significant relationships, and embracing too many good causes. Such patterns and practices are destructive to body, mind, and soul. When pastoral caregivers neglect their own spiritual well-being, the pastoral care they provide is seriously compromised. Neglect leads to diminished energy and vapid spiritual resourcefulness, and it delivers a detrimental message about the nature of the Christian life. What we embody can be more harmful than helpful to our pastoral care.

credibility as a form of pastoral care

A significant dimension of pastoral care is what is offered by way of example. The observable patterns and practices of the lives of caregivers become substantive means for fostering spiritual well-being. We care for the souls of others whenever and however we demonstrate that we are attending to our own. Our credibility as pastoral caregivers depends upon whether we value and embody spiritual practices that sustain the soul.

If we have lost touch with our own souls or neglected our own spiritual thirst, then it will be difficult, if not impossible, to respond to the spiritual thirst of others. British sage Thomas Carlisle once quipped, "What this congregation needs is a rector who knows God on more than hearsay."[1] When we are grounded in a daily awareness of God's love, and our faith is alive and growing, then parishioners are more likely to seek and know the face of God. Their own yearning to connect with God may increase, and subsequently, their lives may become more integrated, balanced, and healthy. If people experience us as healthy, fully human, and seeking an ever-deepening connection to God, then they may be more drawn to take hold of the abundant life promised by God. Pastoral caregivers are living sponsors for the cultivation of the soul in everyday life. The spiritual lives of pastoral caregivers have the potential to make a substantive contribution toward soulful pastoral care.

Credible Pastoral Caregivers

For several decades now, studies have shown that the laity seek, above all other qualities, *spiritual* leadership in their ministry personnel and church leadership.[2] They want persons who have learned more than facts and who have mastered more than technique. They hope for, even demand, persons whose faith is vital, whose experience of the gospel's freedom is real, and who live out that faith in the midst of a fractured world with a deep sense of their own humanity and vocation.

Laypersons want pastoral caregivers who possess spiritual wisdom and who serve others with compassion. They search for church leaders who have a deeply anchored spirituality and who can offer pastoral care grounded in a lively relationship with God, led by the Spirit, and prompted by a genuine call to serve. They want someone with whom to share their deepest and most personal experiences. They look for people who can talk naturally and openly about their faith and how it connects with the joys and struggles of daily life. Above all, they seek caring persons who are centered in God and open to hearing God's voice in the midst of the people. The laity want authentic, trustworthy, and credible pastoral caregivers.

It is precisely this search for *spiritual* leadership that opens up for us the possibility of viewing credibility as a substantive dimension of our pastoral care. A common yearning motivates the search for soulful leadership. Laypersons and church leadership alike continue to struggle with maintaining spiritual practices that will sustain them in the course of their daily lives. To paraphrase the words of the apostle Paul, "the good we would do we do not." Not only do we know what we should do, but for the most part, we even know why it is that we do not do it. In the morning, we arise with the anxieties and demands of the day already before us, even in our own households. During the day, people, paper, and pressures to produce come and go, and it seems there is no time for prayer. In the evening, the fatigue of the day meets up with the needs of hearth and home and finally we fall into bed, too exhausted to pray. It becomes so easy to convince ourselves that our "busyness of care" is our prayer and that our "prayers on the run" are sufficient for the day. Sometimes they are. But more often than not, such forms of prayer leave us wanting, waiting, and searching.

The credibility of pastoral caregivers should increase to the extent that pastoral caregivers can be open and honest about their own search for relevant and meaningful spiritual practices that can be appropriated in the midst of daily life. When pastoral caregivers are perceived as credible, then the ways they sustain their spiritual lives become living examples and resources for others who seek soul sustenance.

Credible Spiritual Practices

How do pastoral caregivers sustain spiritual practices that nourish their own souls? What spiritual practices foster credibility and increased openness to listen for the stirring of God in others? As I have intimated, most pastoral caregivers already acknowledge many of the things that contribute to credibility in pastoral practice. We need not be persuaded one more time of the importance of care for the caregiver, receiving regular spiritual direction ourselves, and developing prayerful habits for our ministries of pastoral care. Through the literature on pastoral care and various denominational and clergy-based materials, pastoral caregivers consistently have been exhorted to incorporate personal spiritual habits into their lives for the sake of their ministry. Most pastoral caregivers acknowledge that solitude, prayer, self-examination, devotion, meditation, scriptural reflection, and spiritual direction are all significant means for developing the spiritual life that is then embodied in pastoral care. These various personal habits enable caregivers to see themselves and others differently and to place pastoral situations in the hands and heart of God.

Notably absent from this customary emphasis upon the spiritual life of the pastoral caregiver, however, is the notion that credibility is enhanced by more than our personal and private spiritual habits. In fact, much of our credibility as pastoral caregivers is based in our capacity to affirm that all spiritual habits are embodied and therefore public, regardless of whether those habits are primarily directed toward the inner life or outward action. The spiritual habits of pastoral caregivers will exemplify what is valued or disregarded. They bear moral weight and communicate to the public our personal and communal identity, our theological and pastoral convictions, and our orientation to life.

The realization that spiritual disciplines are not a private matter leads us to consider how cultivation of the spiritual life shapes participation in the Christian life and faith communities. The credibility of pastoral caregivers increases when inner and outer spiritual habits are understood to be constitutive of the Christian life. That which is embodied and enacted publicly communicates to others about the spiritual life and what it means to be connected in deepening ways to God. When spiritual habits are understood to be embodied and enacted, they become less a personal discipline and more a public practice.

Credible Terminology: From Spiritual Discipline to Spiritual Practice
The language we use to describe soul-sustaining spiritual habits is exceedingly important. Nowadays, in terms of habitual activities, people generally are more comfortable with the notion of *practice* than of *discipline*. We speak of practicing a musical instrument, quilting, bread-making, marathon running, yoga, or our golf game. Rarely does our speech refer to such practiced activities as disciplines.

In terms of spiritual habits, this shift from the more classical notion of discipline to the more contemporary idea of practice may be grounded in our dismay over the ways spiritual disciplines can so easily become punitive tools for disciplining others. Despite the many positive outcomes of disciplined activity (such as the achievement of regularity, agility, stamina, and skill), the word *discipline* is too readily associated with an achievement motivated by guilt and based upon fears of disobedience and correction. If spiritual disciplines are understood as a way to control, correct, or enforce behavior, then the spiritual life may be expressed with others in similarly controlling and coercive ways. Too often, spiritual disciplines have degenerated into means for measuring the adequacy or inadequacy of another's spiritual life. Moreover, the notion of discipline can feel overly burdensome to many and suggestive of a spiritual destination attainable only through extensive pain and self-inflicted deprivation.

The idea of spiritual practices provides a more helpful way of "addressing the yearning of contemporary people for deeper understanding of and involvement in the redemptive practice of God in the world."[3] Spiritual practices are personal and public activities that enable us to participate in God's practice toward the world. In this sense, spiritual practices become life-giving forms that sustain us and allow us and others to flourish. They address the fundamental human need to live as spiritual beings connected to God and to one another. They may hone skills, but more importantly, they help us develop postures and pathways for transforming life. They strengthen our participation in a way of life that is more whole and touched by the presence of God. When spiritual practices are enacted in daily life, they can change the ways we live each day. Spiritual practices become a means for restoring, liberating, and integrating self and others into community.

When pastoral caregivers undertake spiritual practices that sustain their lives and contribute to a different way of seeing reality and participating in it, then such spiritual practices become both *content* and *method* for pastoral care. The credibility of pastoral care is heightened, as is the credibility of pastoral caregivers themselves.

The Precariousness of Credibility

Before exploring specific spiritual practices that can sustain our lives and enrich our pastoral care, some words of caution are in order. The postures we assume and the beliefs we hold as we engage in spiritual practices can jeopardize our credibility.

If we assume a perfectionist posture, others will surely question our credibility. Morton Kelsey once suggested that the single most important credential for anyone offering spiritual guidance or facilitating spiritual growth is "to have taken the inner way himself or herself and still be on it."[4] When we take the inner way that leads to outward action, we dare not give the impression of having it all together. To do so would damage our credibility.

We have all had the experience of trusting someone who appears too confident in their ability to pray, too saintly, and who seems piously perfect in their spiritual journey. Spiritual practices can become a new form of legalism or a way of "binding the conscience and of producing the smug, self-satisfied attitude that destroyed the framework of Puritan piety."[5] We need to be careful not to make any spiritual practice into a new legalism or burden. One can better trust a pastoral caregiver with the agony and ecstasy of the soul if that person admits honestly to wandering off the spiritual pathway and to having days of wondering about ever making it through the doubt or darkness. We feel more freedom to disclose our own soul's struggles when we believe that people who understand the ways of the soul are hearing our revelation and how it functions.

The precariousness of our credibility also is affected by whether or not we view spiritual practices as lifelong opportunities for spiritual development or as immediately achievable habits. Attending to the soul can seem very complex at first, and it is important to remember how many false starts and stumbles a new practice takes. It is impossible to become an expert at a spiritual practice, because spiritual practices are not static entities that are achievable but rather dynamic processes subject to change. There is always something new to discover, experience, and pursue. For this reason, assuming a supportive, reassuring, forgiving, and challenging posture toward ourselves and others is vital to the maintenance of our credibility.

Recently, my beloved life-partner and I took ballroom dancing lessons. Besides the waltz, the tango, and the fox-trot, we practiced the jive. There is one basic set of steps to which six other patterns are inserted. With each new pattern, our feet tripped over each other. Our guide gently reassured us: "Once you have the mechanics committed to memory and have practiced the steps, the dance will become more natural. Then you can just concentrate on the music, enjoy the spirit of the dance, and advance to other dance forms." Once the basic routines are solidified, the rhythms of trying, waiting, concentrating, and experimenting with additions become the way for fully engaging the practice of dancing.

Allowing others to see that we are open to new spiritual practices and experiences, and that we are able to learn and grow from them, is itself a pastoral action infused with care for the soul. People best learn spiritual practices when they are regularly active in them, are actually doing what those practices involve, and when they are connected in some way with others in the doing of them. People will view us as credible pastoral caregivers when we engage in spiritual practices as lifelong opportunities that are full of pain and promise. We discard what does not work, try out new forms, affirm what helps, and acknowledge what hinders. Ultimately, our credibility is strengthened by our capacity to acknowledge our humanity, try new things, and sustain a willingness to practice. Our credibility is also enhanced by our capacity to view spiritual practices as public activities. When we are connected in some way with others in the doing of them, then the shared experience of discovery and reflection deepens and transforms our spiritual practice in an ongoing way.

spiritual practices for pastoral care

This chapter explores three spiritual practices based in ordinary activities that have both a personal and public dimension to them. These three spiritual practices can help pastoral caregivers be faithful to nurturing their own souls, enhance their credibility as pastoral caregivers, and promote spiritual well-being as a form of pastoral care. Included in the exploration of each practice are some suggested ways to deepen the development of the soul in relation to the pastoral care we offer.

While these three spiritual practices are not meant to be an exhaustive set, they have the greatest potential to animate pastoral care in a contemporary context. They can move us toward soulful pastoral care because they aim to resist fragmentation in society, the breakdown of human relatedness, and relentless competitiveness and drivenness. These three spiritual practices suggest a way for us to cultivate life so that people flourish and have their spiritual longings addressed. Persons who regularly and intentionally embrace these three particular practices can lead people individually and communally to a deeper connectedness with God, each other, and the world.

The three spiritual practices are hospitality, sabbath-keeping, and simplicity. These faithful practices may seem deceptively simple or too down-to-earth. Then again, the ways we include others at our dinner table, what we read and when, or whether we take time to enjoy cycling down a country lane are all actions that reveal to us and others who and whose we are.

The fruits of our pastoral care will be known in and through our spiritual practices. The ways we go about sustaining and developing our souls will serve as guideposts for others seeking to live with integrity and in right relationship with God. It is not just about getting by, but about ways we can flourish in concert with our souls, with others, and in communion with God. Our commitment to these three spiritual practices will strengthen our credentials as pastoral caregivers, thus providing windows through which others may glimpse ways and means for living as authentic spiritual beings.

practicing hospitality

When pastor Andre Trocmé was once asked why he inspired an entire French village to risk giving shelter to Jews during World War II, he replied simply, "I cannot bear to be separated from Jesus."[6]

Hospitality as a Spiritual Practice

Hospitality is a spiritual practice because it links us to God, ourselves, and others. The spiritual practice of hospitality is a way to meet, recognize, and receive the presence of God. It is the act of receiving another with openness, respect, and delight, offering to another the freedom to reveal himself or herself as he or she chooses. Not only do we offer what we have, but we also offer who we are. Hospitality is the virtue that allows us to break through the narrowness of our own fears and open ourselves and our space to the stranger.

By using the term *stranger*, I refer to those parts of ourselves that are foreign to us, as well as to persons who are *other* and who represent the unknown to us. The stranger within and without represents challenges to the familiar constructs of our personal world and spirituality. Strangers have things to tell us that we may not have heard said before, and those things may stimulate our thinking and help us to see more clearly. This may be precisely why we do not often greet the stranger with hospitality or acknowledge the stranger as someone made in God's image. By paying attention to those who are unfamiliar to us, as well as to the mysterious dimension of our very selves, we open ourselves to the possibility of our spiritual development and to the discovery that God is up to far more than we can think or imagine.

We know by experience that those whom we host frequently end up giving us the blessings of their presence. We respond to a hospital referral to visit someone we have never met before, only to find we have received at least as much from the wounded one as we have given. As we practice hospitality, we "learn to value the strangeness of the stranger."[7] This notion that strangers bear "surprising gifts" is part of our biblical heritage. "Do not neglect to show hospitality to strangers, for by doing that some have entertained angels without knowing it" (Hebrews 13:2). The surprising appearance of a baby in Bethlehem becomes the Word made flesh. The three guests who visit Abraham and his aged wife Sarah bring the startling news that she will bear a child. Much later, in Matthew's gospel, we are reminded that the face of the stranger is indeed the face of Christ (Matthew 25:38). When it is most fully realized, hospitality not only welcomes the surprising and unfamiliar, but it also recognizes the presence of holiness within. It sees and meets something of God in the stranger and in that which seems strange.

Hospitality as a Form of Pastoral Care

Practicing hospitality is a way to become more whole and at home in God. The spiritual practice of hospitality reminds us that at the core of every human soul lies the same basic longing—to be included and invited to share the full gift of our common humanity. Being welcomed into shelter—into space where we can feel safe and at home enough to grow, receive, challenge, and give of ourselves freely to others—is a basic step toward offering pastoral care that attends to the soul. When hospitality like this is extended to us or by us, we are experiencing pastoral care. At the same time, we are modeling for others a way to care for the soul. We are helping to ensure that future acts of pastoral care will be graced with a spirit of compassion and openness.

Through faithfulness to the practice of welcoming strangers and difference, we care for others. At the same time, we embrace ourselves as people whose own souls regularly need the assurance of safety and the gift of inclusion. We might wonder if pastoral caregivers can truly care for others if they lack such personal experiences of shelter or homecoming. Probably not. Their own soul's yearnings will supersede their abilities to focus upon or reach out to others. Pastoral caregivers can practice being hospitable toward their own selves and finding hospitable places where the stranger that lies within them can be known and received. We can open ourselves up, as Margaret Guenther suggests, "to be the needy, vulnerable, weary traveler as well as the generous host."[8] Once we acknowledge and welcome the stranger within ourselves, we will be more likely to develop an empathy for others who find themselves marginalized or confronting the reality of being an outsider.

A word of caution about this spiritual practice: Finding safe lodging, whether physical, emotional, or spiritual, is not the same as feeling secure. Although caregivers need to have made a home within themselves and with others where they experience safety, this also should be a space where appropriate challenges can be given and received. A hospitable environment is not one that is immune to threat, risk or change, and there can be as much risk in refusing hospitality as there is in offering it. The one offering hospitality, however, provides the possibility for the other to be treated justly, even if comfort or freedom from oppressive forces is not always possible.

Developing the Spiritual Practice of Hospitality

It is important for all pastoral caregivers to think about how this spiritual practice can be sustained on a regular basis. If we become too settled, we run the risk of being unconscious of those alien parts of ourselves and of remaining indifferent to those who wander without shelter.

Some may find that a personal spiritual director is a good way to remain open to strangers and to claim the joy of the soul's own homecoming to God. Finding someone who can warmly welcome us and regularly and lovingly tell us the truth that keeps us honest is crucial to our credibility. John

Ackerman reminds us that even the old desert fathers and mothers "insisted on complete transparency before a director. This is the only safe way to keep from fooling ourselves."[9] We all need at least one person who can see us and love us as we are, yet point us toward the call and grace of God. Otherwise, that which is *strange* within us will remain unknown. Everyone who practices hospitality needs someone who cares for his or her soul.

Others may find that sheltering refugees, working with new immigrants, getting to know neighbors from differing cultural backgrounds, or serving dinner regularly to the homeless may enable personal soul transformation and turn strangers into friends. Some may wish to practice extending the home's table so that the elderly are no longer isolated from sources of affection and care, or so that children find an after-school welcome, or life-partners find table-time to greet and learn from the stranger in each other. Too often we become estranged or torn asunder from those we love by our neglect of this spiritual practice of hospitality.

In many respects, the spiritual practice of hospitality begins at home. Our significant relationships are one of the first public places in our daily lives that we can practice it. How we embody inclusion, affirmation, and challenge with our children and our adult relationships will be an expression of hospitality that extends beyond home life and into the daily public realms of workplace, neighborhood, church, and world. Practicing hospitality may start with those who sit intimately at the table with us, but it extends outward to circles that welcome differing gifts of persons and cultural communities.

An Enriched Pastoral Care

Fruits of the regular practice of hospitality are increased generosity of spirit, capacity to support others, and readiness to participate in liberating activity. Pastoral care is enriched whenever the soul's anxieties are transformed from suspicion into magnanimity and confident witness. Caregivers are more likely to spot the vulnerability of those who are dislocated in life. In their daily routines, caregivers may notice persons who are experiencing uprootedness in physical, emotional, and spiritual ways. Support and solidarity are more likely to accompany an increased capacity to listen to stories of flight, exclusion, and alienation.

The spiritual practice of hospitality is one way to sustain our own relationship with God and become increasingly open to the diversity of persons and circumstances facing those who require pastoral care. When we practice hospitality, we are listening for the soul's desire to flourish and feel at home. If such a desire remains unfulfilled within the caregiver's own soul, then its fulfillment will be sought at costly expense to those who genuinely seek pastoral care. Experiencing hospitality strengthens our credibility to practice public hospitality. If the stranger within us and at arms' reach becomes both gift and challenge—a way to connect to God—then what is important is to sustain the spiritual practice of hospitality so as not to miss God's own knock at our door.

practicing sabbath-keeping

The Sabbath expresses the heart of the Good News, that God in Christ reveals an infinite love for us that does not depend on our works. It depends simply on our willingness for it, on our desire to turn to that Great Love with our deepest love, through all our little loves. . . . What better way to reveal God's love beyond our works than to stop our usual works and discover that Love is not withdrawn, but strongly visible for us? Not only is this a witness for ourselves, but also for others as they see us intentionally celebrating an identity and love that is not dependent on our worthy productions. In our simple sabbath rest, doing nothing but appreciating the giftedness of life in God, we can reveal the Gospel to our neighbors in a demonstrable, non-aggressive, yet very challenging way.[10]

Sabbath-Keeping as a Spiritual Practice

The practice of sabbath-keeping is another way to connect with God. Pastoral caregivers will be enlivened in spirit and more able to offer care from a strong, healthy foundation if they are regular keepers of the sabbath. Understood as rest and devotion to God, the sabbath can be kept through the regular practice of setting aside one day a week or making some special quality of time available. People may not use the term *sabbath*, but as harried citizens of a frenzied world, they yearn for the reality of the historic practice of the sabbath.

In differing ways, this is true for both clergy and laity. Just as dimensions of work and ministry can spill over into sabbath time, so too the desire to cultivate and appreciate sabbath time can spill over onto days other than "the Lord's Day." Deep down, we know that when we fail to guard sabbath, the world would have us to itself. We do not want to be on the run or having to watch the clock, but we no longer seem to know how to protect leisure for praying and playing. As a new century lies before us, the practice of keeping sabbath may be a soul-sustaining gift just waiting to be unwrapped once more.

The Erosion of Sabbath-Keeping

Until the beginning of the twentieth century, the spiritual practice of setting aside one day in seven was central to Protestant spirituality. Keeping the sabbath is a pattern threaded deeply in the fabric of the scriptures. The pattern is six days of work followed by one day of rest and recreation. But rest from labor is only the beginning of sabbath-keeping. The sabbath pattern is related to the creation and exodus stories. Having created everything, God rests on the seventh day and makes it holy. On this seventh day, God takes delight in what has been made and loves humanity in the form of time shared with them. In the exodus story, as Dorothy Bass points out, the commandment to observe the sabbath is "tied to the experience of a people newly released from bondage. Slaves cannot take a day off; free people can."[11] Sabbath is seen as a social institution, a shared and public act that commemorates liberation. The fundamental truth arising from sabbath about God's relationship with humanity is that human beings are made in the image of God, and no one is to work in a spirit of captivity and without rest. Thus, we flourish as human beings when we honor God's creativity, imitate God's rest, and experience the freedom to be creative and festal.

For numerous reasons, our sense of sabbath has eroded over time. For many, sabbath-keeping assumed a burdensome quality and simply lacked enjoyment. Past interpretations of the sabbath, some of which were overly harsh and legalistic, led to a more popular understanding that sabbath-keepers were killjoys. Howard Rice, reminding us of the severe regimen that became associated with sabbath, cites a list of things from which Christians were to refrain:

> First, from all the works of our calling. . . . Secondly, from carrying burdens, as carriers do; or riding abroad for profit, or for pleasure. . . . Thirdly, from keeping of fairs, or markets. . . . Fourthly, from studying any books of science, but the holy Scriptures and Divinity. . . . Fifthly, from all recreations and sports. . . . Sixthly, from gross feeding, liberal drinking of wine, or strong drink; which may make us either drowsy or unapt to serve God with our hearts and minds. Seventhly, from all talking about worldly things, which hindereth the sanctifying of the Sabbath, more than working.[12]

In addition to finding these sorts of restrictions intolerable, sabbath-keeping suffered because of the diminishing quantity of discretionary time available. The dominant cultural rhythms and global market economies have solidified changes in patterns and hours of work that make it impossible to have a common "pause" day. Contributing to this is the reality of our increasingly pluralist, multifaith, and secularized culture. Legislation that served to protect the Lord's Day was amended, allowing businesses and tourist industries to be open on Sundays. Moreover, commitments to group activities and sports that compete with traditional Sunday worship strained the spiritual practice of sabbath-keeping, especially for the baby-boomer generation and their children. These varied cultural, political, and societal events place the church in the vulnerable and uncomfortable position of trying to find an alternative between over-accommodation to the culture and inappropriate withdrawal from it.

What has happened is that the time we do have, no matter when that is, no longer seems able to refresh us. In spite of our freedom from our ancestors' bondage to sabbath laws, our practice of sabbath-keeping is remarkably inferior. There is no common societal day of rest. The pause button is never pressed, and all of creation groans seven days a week. Too many people find Monday morning the most exhausting time of the entire week. Too many experience Sunday morning as the only day of the week they do not have to set an alarm clock. It is almost as if we have flat-lined time so that each day is like every other. There is little balance between work and leisure, and even less time for devotion to God or to compassionate deeds.

Despite our best intentions to allow for a different quality of time in our lives, we have been guilty of turning too much of our time into work time. Social forces that prompt us to consume things material and immaterial have also reinforced this reality. Tilden Edwards argues that it is this individualized way of life, even during leisure time, that sets off a rhythm of life that "emerges as one that oscillates between driven achievement (both on and off the job) and some form of mind-numbing private escape. This crazed rhythm based on a distorted view of human reality increasingly poisons our institutions, relationships, and quality of life."[13] The notion of sabbath as a protected, shared, and public time has gradually disintegrated into viewing days off in private terms.

Sabbath-Keeping as a Form of Pastoral Care

The Importance of Rhythmic Rest. Whether one day in seven or in some other pattern, sabbath-keeping is a distinct practice that claims the importance of rest. By encouraging people to have a rhythm of rest in God, we care for their bodies, minds, and souls. Rest clears the way for other activities that are otherwise difficult to make time for in our hectic lives. Sabbath-keeping enables us to pay attention to the presence of God in our week, helps us affirm the centrality and indispensability of public worship, and makes us mindful of others who need rest and relief from oppression. Sabbath is a structured opportunity to be intentional about realizing how much our sense of time is different from the fullness of God's time, which is presenting itself ever anew through us.

Sabbath-keeping helps us sustain a more sane and holy rhythm of life. With it, we are gifted with an alternative to our culture's deadly rhythm of drivenness to make and spend money and to escape in an increasingly numbing sort of time. Sabbath-keeping saves us from a dialectical way of living and being. The church may be one of the few institutions in society that can foster and be accountable for an authentic rhythm of resting with God and caring effectively for the world. Sabbath can free us from that deadening sense that every day is the same. Our sabbath-keeping will bear witness to and promote a more life-giving rhythm that balances rest and work.

Reframing our Theology. The spiritual practice of sabbath-keeping is also a pastoral care strategy for reframing the theological thinking and actions of the laity. How we understand *time* is a profoundly theological matter. Pressing the pause button on our work tests our thinking about the very nature of God. It tests our behavioral capacity to trust in the sufficiency and goodness of God. Whenever we encourage persons to practice sabbath-keeping, we are caring about their relationship with God and their understanding of who God is and how God acts.

Will the world, or I, fall apart if I stop working or stop making things happen? What gives God pleasure, and what can I do that contributes helpfully to God's realm? Is life really blessed by God and God's Spirit moving in it? Can I truly rest and taste this spirited caring?

Keeping the sabbath means relinquishing a theological paradigm based on dominance and submission and moving to one based on partnership. A consequence of this shift means that we then support even the environment's need to rest. We become partners with creation as we rest in freedom from work, commerce, and worry by allowing ourselves to "be in that fresh space in such a way that we realize appreciatively and joyfully our holy connectedness"[14] with the earth and all who dwell therein.

Another consequence of this paradigm shift is discovering that we cannot develop or sustain the spiritual practice of sabbath-keeping in isolation. The spiritual practice of sabbath-keeping invites us to claim a theology of *community.* The public dimensions of sabbath-keeping become increasingly clear to us, as does our need to remain accountable to one another for the ways we keep sabbath. The spiritual practice of sabbath-keeping draws us from isolation into a community of blessing and accountability.

I have a good colleague who periodically sends me e-mail. She specifically asks me what I am doing to keep sabbath and then tells me what she is doing. "Right now, I'm reading a book by Kathleen Norris, about half an hour each morning." Or "this weekend for playtime, I'm going to browse the nearly new shops, try on crazy hats, and laugh at myself in the mirror." This kind of mutual accountability helps us learn to rest and rejoice. It reinforces a different understanding of time and keeps us mindful that the spiritual life is less something to achieve and more something to experience. Mutual accountability also helps us determine together what is good and holy and what is not.

Developing the Spiritual Practice of Sabbath-Keeping

The spiritual practice of sabbath-keeping and the development of a partner-ship paradigm are strengthened by the ways we choose to regard time, our physical bodies, and corporate worship.

Qualitative Time. "The Sabbath is the poetry in the prose of the week."[15] To keep sabbath, it is vital to let go of our normal routines, demands, and work and allow a different quality of space and time to be created on a regular basis. The intent of this sabbath time is neither to escape from the world nor to overindulge in the things of the world through extreme sensual gratifica-tion. Some people who have extremely high-stress jobs may need, however, to restore some balance by catching up on some sleep before being able to move into a deeper sabbath time.

The sabbath is an opportunity to be creative, celebrate life, make joy manifest in our experiences of the day, and spend time with those we love. Honoring sabbath means living in the presence of God and in some way being useless all day long. Rather than killing time or making the most of the time, we can waste holy time on the sheer pleasure of noticing God-given life and being together. Taking a walk or a drive, napping, talking with loved ones, reading, listening to music, appreciating art or candlelight, or cuddling with a beloved partner are all good ways to connect with holiness on the sab-bath. We might even consider the restoration of fading traditions such as inviting the isolated or lonely to join our table, writing a letter to a faraway friend, or visiting a person confined to home.

Bodily Rest. Another important dimension of sabbath-keeping is to recog-nize that full rest includes paying attention to our physical bodies. The more we rest in God, the more attuned we become to the flesh God embraced and in which God dwells. We delight in our body's flexibility and learn how to bear its tensions and limits gracefully. By so doing, we glorify our Creator, the one who chose to call human flesh home. Sometimes, Christians have had difficulty comprehending that time allocated to the physical body is nei-ther self-indulgent nor decadent. In truth, a rested, healthy, energized body is as indispensable for the Christian life (and our pastoral caregiving) as the practices of prayer or meditation.

One of the greatest hungers today, next in line to the search for spirituality, is the search for a fit body. The number of people looking for a meaningful spirituality is exceeded only by the jump in memberships at health facilities and fitness clubs. People seem to have difficulty, however, making the connection between body and soul. For whatever reasons, they do not seem able to see that swimming, skiing, running, dancing, laughter, or play have important places in their relationship with God. We arrive at wholeness by using the full stuff of human experience, including our bodies. It is vital that we neither deny them nor view them as somehow outside the realm of the spiritual. Physical activities that put our bodies in motion are important. They help us deal with rattled nerves and stressed living. They teach us to respect and cooperate with others, and to discover the limits of our own bodies and the qualities of perseverance and judgment that underlie all spiritual practices.

Generally, the church has given insufficient attention to this connection between body and soul. The linkage between rest for the body and rest for the soul can become much more overt in our pastoral care. Do we encourage persons to view physical activity as a way to greet God and become more aware of God who dwells within us? Many people resist physical activity simply because it is not enjoyable for them. They associate exercise with inconvenience, unpleasantness, and yes, even suffering. Yet as Thomas Ryan reminds us, "there is a fine line between giving of ourselves and giving up on ourselves."[16] If our physical energy deteriorates, we will be of little good to those we seek to care for and care about. It is difficult to offer genuine pastoral care, love others, and invite them to love themselves if we consistently exempt ourselves from this same caring. Such simple measures as getting enough sleep and exercising regularly leave one less prone to fatigue, better able to handle stress, less subject to depression or substance abuse, and generally more alert and relaxed.

It is a significant pastoral act to invite people to care for their bodies as much as their souls. We can encourage persons to begin with experiences of play, movement, and physical exercise that they already take to with spontaneity. If there are some activities that we already enjoy and that engage us fully, these are good places to start.

If physical movement frees us and others from the demons of workaholism, then we will be blessed with liberation. If it moves us toward carefree play, it will be holy. We must, however, resist the pervasive temptation in our culture to turn physical exercise into workouts that result in working at our play. Rather, our physical movement offers us the gift of being free from burdensome preoccupation with unfinished work or worry. In a culture that is so goal-oriented and serious, physical activities provide us with the genuine replenishment of the inner spirit that is the heart of true sabbath-keeping.

Worship as a Festival of Solidarity. At its best, the sabbath is a corporate witness to the way Christians understand life, its rhythms, giftedness, and meaning. Sabbath as a time of rest includes taking time to be in solidarity with others who provide positive encouragement for practicing and living a different quality of time. When we assemble with others, we remember that sabbath-keeping is not just about taking a day off, but that it is about recalling and giving thanks for God's activity in creating and liberating the world. In the best sense, public worship is a festival of solidarity with all creatures that yearn for rest and freedom.

Too frequently, however, corporate worship can feel like drudgery. Worshipping communities forget that hymns or songs need not drag, clothes need not pinch, gossip need not flow, and complaints need not always be voiced. We forget that our public gathering is a sign of the feast that is to come and that our shared worship is a festival, a spring of souls, a sharing in the activity of God that shapes a new creation.

The church's temptation is to violate the freedom of sabbath-keeping by scheduling committee meetings immediately following worship, rather than encouraging congregational members or groups to take delight in eating, conversing, caring for one another, or exploring nature's beauty together as a continuation of keeping the sabbath. Actively resisting the pressures to turn the time of corporate worship into time to fulfill more obligations is an act of pastoral care for members as well as those who are pastoral caregivers.

For those whose available time falls on a day other than Sunday, there can be strategies for saving that day from privatism by treating it as if it were a Sunday. How are the gifts of bread and wine carried by extension to those shut out from Sunday service? If it is not possible for a congregation to provide alternative worship service times, informal gatherings can be organized by bringing together those who are available on another common day. If this is not feasible, we can at least read the same scriptures and offer the same corporate prayers as may have been printed in Sunday's bulletin or order of worship. We can pray in solidarity, and be drawn, even in our solitude, into the church's common life.

New forms of sabbath-keeping will expand the concept of sabbath time so that we no longer restrict sabbath-keeping to a specific weekday. We can add the practice of sabbath-keeping to other days and moments that take into account the complexities of our lives. Such days and moments may be viewed as *mini-sabbaths*. Mini-sabbaths need just as much intentionality. We can set aside a certain time (20–30 minutes) each week to cease our work and rest in God in whatever ways are determined to be good for us as individuals, small groups, and households. Mini-sabbaths may take the form of spiritual reading, gardening, belonging to a wood-carving association, or meeting for breakfast once a week with some chosen companions in the faith.

Whenever such mini-sabbaths are set aside, the time can still be viewed as sabbath rest. Our regular commonly held sabbath day can be combined with this kind of regular rhythm of spiritual renewal during the week.

An Enriched Pastoral Care

The practice of sabbath-keeping bears much wisdom for pastoral caregivers who seek to care for souls maneuvering their way through the stresses of contemporary life. The focus on appreciating rather than manipulating time offers a spiritual value that is a vital corrective to our current social context. It serves as a beacon for a society that needs to be reminded that our ultimate yearnings will not be addressed through the acquisition of material gods. Moreover, our natural environment needs a rest from all the burning, buying, and bargaining that takes place. Keeping sabbath will go a long way toward balancing the claims of work and festivity, rest and ministry. One day a week may make a difference each day of our lives for the rest of our lives.

practicing simplicity

When we are truly in this interior simplicity our whole appearance is franker, more natural. This true simplicity . . . makes us conscious of a certain openness, gentleness, innocence, gaiety, and serenity, which is charming when we see it near to and continually with pure eyes. O how amiable this simplicity is! Who will give it to me? I leave all for this. It is the pearl of the Gospel.[17]

Simplicity as a Spiritual Practice

Pastoral caregivers strengthen their credibility by practicing simplicity. Simplicity means living in such a way as to foster a sense of right proportion and right relation within the various circles of our lives. The spiritual practice of simplicity is not itself simplistic. It is fraught with ambiguities and dilemmas, but it can, over time, set material goods and the tools of life in a just, faithful, and global perspective.

Simplicity is a spiritual practice because it deepens our connections with others, and thus with God. A commitment to simplicity reflects a desire not to be harmful, ostentatious, or competitive, but instead to elevate the human spirit through choices that honor the interdependence of all life. Simplicity is the only thing that can sufficiently reorient our lives so that the things of this earth can be genuinely enjoyed without destroying ourselves, others, or the earth. The spiritual practice of simplicity helps us participate in God's restorative practice for the world.

Simplicity as a Form of Pastoral Care

Simplicity helps us begin to take the inner and outer path toward eliminating the toxicity created by economic anxiety. By promoting simplicity, we are caring about the bodies, minds, and souls of persons who are battered by society's competitive orientation to life. The spiritual practice of simplicity is a way to live differently in the face of such relentless pressures. It has the potential to draw persons into community from places of fragmentation. Practicing simplicity can diminish vapid frenzy and create meaningful life-orientation.

The spiritual practice of simplicity is a way for ordinary persons to reclaim their rightful role in conversations and actions normally presumed to be something understood only by the so-called experts. Bankers, stock brokers, accountants, lawyers, politicians, and other financial advisors have staked out the territory of economics and grounded it in a set of meanings that frequently leave the ordinary citizen feeling that it is all too complex to grasp. Ironically, the root of the word *economics* is found in the Greek word *oikos*, meaning household. This smashes through the manufactured complexity of contemporary market-driven economics and restores it to its original realm of meaning and significance—*taking care of the household* and handling goods and services in such a way as to sustain and enliven the global household.

As shifting economies fuel our anxieties, and the array of products available to us is less *necessary* and more *glamorous*, we are beginning to squirm under the weight of the energy it requires to secure, maintain, and discard goods and resources. Our unsustainable living patterns are beginning to evoke awareness that God may be inviting us, as households of faith, to reexamine our care of our personal homes and our global home. We know that our personal, workplace, and congregational budgets communicate our beliefs and values to the public. Yet we naively continue to think that the domain of money remains privately hidden. This gap that we have preserved between our souls and our material needs and wants is the result of an unexamined, inadequate, and unhealthy spirituality. Our own fear of economic discomfort has blocked us from grasping that the gulf is about how we see and experience God with us, among us, and in us, and in the very matter of creation itself.

The practice of simplicity brings a necessary perspective and needful corrective both to givers and receivers of pastoral care. It nurtures a liberated inner and outer spirit that changes the way we approach and offer pastoral care. As soon as we turn our attention to the spiritual practice of simplicity, our pastoral care will be imbued with outward expressions of care that are less exploitative, and in fact, are more appreciative and restorative. Simplicity sets us free to receive the provisions of God as gifts that are not ours to keep and that can be shared freely with others.

Developing the Spiritual Practice of Simplicity

The spiritual practice of simplicity has an inward reality that is expressed in an outward lifestyle. In order for simplicity to develop, it is important first for pastoral caregivers to listen for internal anxieties, both their own and others, that manifest in external actions.

Listening for Soul-Anxiety. Most North American Protestants live fractured and fragmented lives. Our souls agonize over how to secure our future and we worry continually that we will not have enough. We respond to cultural forces that seduce us into believing that status and position are desirable, that more is better than less, that what others think about us is more important than what we think of ourselves. We crave things we neither need nor enjoy. We are trapped in a maze of competing attachments and are convinced that to be out of step with fashion is to be out of step with reality. Our lust for affluence is virtually a psychosis of the soul inasmuch as we have lost touch with reality and the ultimate source of soul security.

The spiritual practice of simplicity necessitates listening for the debilitating effects of economic anxiety and then expelling the toxicity and behavioral patterns engendered by such internal economic anxiety. These continuous acts of *listening* and *expulsion* can be modeled through the ordinary experiences of pastoral caregivers. Pastoral caregivers can model for others their own ongoing efforts to develop the spiritual practice of living simply in and for God.

Locking everything up bordered on obsession in the house where I grew up. There were double locks on the doors of my childhood home. Not only was I locked out, but I was also locked in. The doors were locked from the inside using a key that was in the possession of the adults, who presumably believed such precautions would protect us and our familial goods! I still double-check the locks on household and car doors before walking away. Old habits die hard. At least now, I realize that abundant living is not the same as securing an abundance of possessions. To paraphrase Martin Luther, if my goods are not available to the community, they are in essence already stolen goods.[18] This anxious practice of securing possessions for the sake of securing the future is futile. I lament the ways it gets in the way of fostering community and generosity of spirit, and so my instinctive reactions require intentional examination, and in many cases, expulsion. My inner anxiety is a God-given challenge to practice living my God-given future in my present days.

When pastoral caregivers first listen for their own debilitating anxieties, then they will be better positioned to listen to the soul-anxieties building to toxic levels in others.

Caring about Money Matters. Listening for economic anxiety necessarily includes listening for the ways people deal with money. Caring about money and the ways people treat, spend, save, privatize, or publicize money is a matter that is vital to the well-being of our souls. The spiritual practice of simplicity is, in fact, an economic practice. Money is a spiritual matter, and our spiritual lives will be characterized by the ways we regard money.

Our biblical tradition is unambiguous in the ways it can ground and guide us in our treatment of money. No serious reading of scripture can substantiate a view that Jesus did not address practical economic questions. Biblical injunctions against the poor and the accumulation of wealth are clear and challenging. There is no absolute right to property, wealth is periodically redistributed, and *mammon* is a dangerous rival to God.

At the same time that Jesus graphically depicts the difficulty of the wealthy entering the realm of God, it is also clear that God intends that we have adequate material provision. We must abandon any thought that we are called to practice a single style of life or a life that denies pleasure, beauty, or material things. The spiritual practice of simplicity is not about denial of the goodness of creation. Clearly, the Bible does not champion a dreary asceticism. Consistently, scripture reveals that creation is blessed and is to be enjoyed. Asceticism and simplicity are not indistinguishable. The former renounces possessions, while the latter sets them in the context of an interdependent world. Simplicity truly can rejoice in the gracious provision of a "land flowing with milk and honey."

Thus, to practice simplicity is neither to fall into the trap of legalistic asceticism nor to capitulate to the monster of mammon. Both are spiritually lethal and lead to corruption, abuse, and idolatry. Moreover, being without material possessions is no guarantee that one is living simply. Neither is having an abundance of things necessarily evidence of a greedy life. It is important to recognize that neither poverty nor wealth can provide absolute assurance of a simple life that is free from internal or external anxiety. But we can listen for patterns that negate or support a spiritual practice of simplicity.

Two Pastoral Care Actions

The spiritual practice of simplicity is difficult, and there are no definitive actions that guarantee its development. Simplicity is a lifelong and evolving spiritual practice. As pastoral caregivers seek to practice simplicity and to cultivate it in others, two fundamental pastoral care actions will further the practice. First, an important pastoral care action is to acknowledge simplicity's complexity. Second, the spiritual practice of simplicity is enhanced by the provision of opportunities for public reflection, communal support, and accountability.

Acknowledging Simplicity's Complexity. Engaging in the practice of simplicity is complex. Making decisions with the goal of simplifying life is usually not simple. For example, some decisions to simplify patterns in the workplace, at home, or in the church can be counterproductive, uncompassionate, and even ridiculous. If someone leaves a high-stress job in order to spend more time with family, it may not simplify life at all, especially if it means losing the benefits of good medical and dental insurance and a high-return pension plan. Likewise, returning to earlier or less cumbersome patterns in the name of simplicity may not be the best solution. For example, a family home may be listed at twice the value of another, but the more expensive home may be closer to the location where both family members work.

To choose to practice simplicity means leaning into questions that do not necessarily present ready-made solutions. It is to take one step at a time and to practice a quality of discernment that includes putting more than our indulgences into the equation. How we take others into account and care for our households, including the restoration of our world home, is an important part of the spiritual practice of simplicity.

In our pastoral care, we can offer people some guiding questions to assist the discernment of what restores right proportions and right relations. Questions that invite us and others to examine the choices we make are helpful in discerning what it means to practice simplicity. The kinds of questions that are helpful are those that hold in tension individual needs and the needs of the wider community and that invite us to consider the difference between indulgences and needs. Obviously, in the pastoral conversations we have, some questions will be more relevant to particular situations than others. Our use of them depends to a large extent upon the particular circumstances presented. Pastoral caregivers, spirituality or study groups, or public workshop leaders can use questions as a means to guide others toward acts of listening, expulsion, and decisions that care for and restore households.

Here are some possible questions to guide decision-making so that the interdependent nature of life is honored:

* Is what I am doing going to contribute to the well-being of my soul, and by association, the well-being of family members and others?
* Is what I am doing going to foster dependence or interdependence?
* Is what I am doing contributing to a system that will enrich or diminish community?
* Is what I am doing going to affect negatively or positively my use of time?
* What will this new material item or investment mean to me, my family, and my community? Is it a need or an addiction? Is it ostentatious?
* What is *abundance* and what is *enough*?
* How can I make this available to others—to the community?
* What will be the outcome of an increase in profit? Who benefits? Who loses?
* Is my job connected to the community's life and needs, or will it deflect my attention from the community?
* What is an appropriate proportional basis of my livelihood to share with the community?
* How am I (or how are we) being stewards of our material goods and environment?
* Are there things I can dispose of?
* Can I enjoy something/this thing without *owning* it?

Opportunities for Public Reflection. The second fundamental act of pastoral care that we can offer is to provide opportunities to talk about economic matters publicly. The spiritual practice of simplicity is cultivated by bringing people together for open discussion both within and beyond the household of the church. By presenting money as a spiritual matter, we affirm that its place must no longer be relegated to the private realm but must be central to the public domain.

It is important to acknowledge in our public reflections that there is considerable discussion taking place about the nature of poverty itself, the feminization of poverty, and the growing number of children living in conditions of poverty. In our public reflections, we can include alternatives to a market-driven economy and can consider the range of personal and communal responses that are possible. For some, the spiritual practice of simplicity will lead to a decision to be entirely countercultural and in opposition to consumptive trends. For others, it may mean choosing to live out a commitment to see and relate to the poor in one's midst. To be "poor in spirit" is to be receptive to the God we meet in our spiritual practice of simplicity.

Once money matters to the extent that it moves from the secret folds of our wallets to the places where it is given, exchanged, sold, and forgiven, then any decisions we make about money are enhanced by shared wisdom. The community has a vital role in helping us remember that our commitment to the simple life is not about one-sided benevolence, romanticizing poverty, or being sentimentally silly in response to the seriously depraved conditions in which many find themselves. The regular support of others who seek to practice simplicity in forms that express solidarity with the poor is essential to sustaining our own commitments. The community keeps us accountable and strong in our attempts to resist consumerism. There is no question that the practice of simplicity directly challenges personal values, vested interests in affluent living and the choices that are made on a daily basis.

An Enriched Pastoral Care

Pastoral caregivers who engage in the spiritual practice of simplicity will find themselves doing pastoral care differently. Their pastoral care will be enhanced by a diminished personal frenzy, an increased compassion for the stress-laden and impoverished conditions in which many find themselves, and an openness to the complexities of personal decision making that confront most parishioners.

A significant contribution of this spiritual practice to pastoral care is that our soul-listening moves to a different depth of concern. We begin to listen with specificity. No longer failing to hear or avoiding subjects normally considered too private, pastoral caregivers can listen for human anxieties related to lifestyle choices and economic matters. Decisions that promote unhealthy independence and neglect soul-sustaining patterns of interdependence can be explored and challenged.

When this kind of listening, expulsion, and discernment for decision making is rooted in the caregiver's own willingness to be self-reflective and publicly accountable, then people experience the pastoral caregiver's credibility. Credibility enables the pastoral caregiver to hear about money matters in people's lives and then to encourage a kind of decision making that furthers God's best hopes for our global home.

Our pastoral care is enriched by the ways we promote a spirit of care for others who still need justice in the world. The spiritual practice of simplicity has as its core the desire to seek God and God's realm of right relations and right proportions first. Sometimes we will need to invest considerable energy in the households immediately within our reach. But our pastoral care will be incomplete if we do not include opportunities for personal and public reflection on how the spiritual practice of simplicity calls us to care for the whole world. We can enhance our pastoral care for others by promoting truthful discovery of what belongs to whom and what needs to be returned to others. Then, and only then, will we cultivate together a household where all live abundantly and where God makes us truly alive.

Enhanced Credibility: Public Spiritual Practices

By focusing on these three spiritual practices that serve to deepen our relationship with God and strengthen community, I am neither eliminating other valid spiritual practices nor arguing that these three are necessarily the ones that should be indiscriminately adopted. What I am suggesting is that pastoral care is neither credible nor complete without placing public practices alongside the more traditional personal spiritual practices of scriptural study, devotion, prayer, spiritual direction, and meditation. While our pastoral care ministry may be strengthened by our private spiritual habits, our credibility is experienced only when our spiritual practices are embodied and experienced by others.

The spiritual practices of hospitality, sabbath-keeping, and simplicity have unlimited potential to enhance our understanding and practice of pastoral care. In this millennial era, they may be the three most relevant spiritual practices for laity and clergy. As soul-sustaining measures, they may go a long way toward helping the world to renew its trust in those who offer pastoral care.

It was the ancient writer of Proverbs who said that "where there is no vision the people perish" (Proverbs 29:18). A congregation does not become a credible, pastorally caring community by chance. It is the result of the faithful, consistent spiritual practices of its pastors, staff, leadership, pastoral caregivers, and members. If it does not happen by chance, then intentional methods are needed. Addressing how laypersons can empower themselves to practice soulful pastoral care is the subject of the next chapter.

⊶⊷

Reflection Questions

1. What practices do you consider to be most central for maintaining credibility as a pastoral care provider?

2. How do you experience God's hospitality? Do you find it hard to receive and give gifts? Why?

3. Does your church/organization convey a spirit of hospitality toward its own members, leaders, strangers, marginalized members of the wider community (the homeless, families of prisoners, refugees, people who suffer from mental, emotional, or terminal illness, divorced people, gays and lesbians)?

4. What, in your experience, makes it difficult to practice sabbath-keeping?

5. How might we encourage the spiritual practice of sabbath-keeping during times of transition from one life passage to another (for example, adolescence to adulthood, singleness to partnership, sickness to death), or during special seasons of the church year (for example, Lent or Advent)?

6. What connection do you make between the practice of simplicity and pastoral care? What difference might it make to your pastoral care if you were freed from the violence of superiority, greed, privilege, and control?

7. Bring to mind a recent pastoral situation. How did you resist or cooperate with God's grace in that event?

⊶⊷

Spiritual Exercise

Here are three daily prayers for a pastoral caregiver. Try praying one or all three of them each day for a week.

Morning Prayer
O God who has brought me safely to the beginning of this day, protect me in your grace. Keep me, this day, from falling into sin or running into danger. Grant that all my thinking, feeling, and acting may be righteous in your sight. Help me live this day to your honor and praise. Amen.

Afternoon Prayer

O God, have I been humble enough to receive your grace from others?

O God, have I heard and kept the seal of confession and granted the assurance of your forgiveness?

O God, have I been an advocate of soul-sustaining spiritual practices?

O God, have I sufficiently declared and magnified in my being the wideness of your grace?

O God, have I been candid with you and mirrored that same candor with others?

In your love, answer and help me to love as you would love. Amen.

Evening Prayer

Thank you, O God, for bringing this day to its close. Thank you for giving rest to my body and soul. Thank you for guarding and preserving me one more day in your love. Forgive me for the wrong I have done this day and help me to forgive those who this day have wronged me. Grant that I may sleep in peace and fall once more into the grip of your love that will not let me go. I commend my loved ones and my own body and soul into your hands. I place the broken world in your hands for tending and mending. Praise be to you, O God. Amen.

⋆⊶⊙⊷⋆

A pastoral situation for Reality-practice within a Group

Select three persons for practicing a pastoral response to the situation described below. One person will assume the role of the pastoral caregiver (in this case, a minister of the congregation), another the woman in crisis, and the third person can assume the role of an active listener-observer. The listener-observer will reflect back to others what was heard and observed.

Following a role debriefing and the listener-observer's response, the whole group can discuss the pastoral situation. Ask yourselves: How do the spiritual practices referred to in this chapter connect to this pastoral situation? In what way?

Background

A retired woman phoned the church to set up an appointment to see the minister. She declared herself to be in crisis because her second marriage of just over a year was in serious trouble. The trouble was that her husband apparently had insisted that, upon his death, his estate go directly to his children from his first marriage. The woman is in her early sixties, well-educated, and with a career background in real estate. Her husband, also retired, appears to adore her and seems attentive to their marriage. Both are members of the church and attend worship regularly.

The Situation

Soon into the conversation with her minister, she declared that "this financial flaw" in her husband had "opened up a floodgate from my past financial anxiety and released a torrent of powerful emotions." She revealed that her first marriage was the result of a pregnancy at the age of sixteen and included physical abuse from her husband, the death of a second child, and finally divorce. Following the divorce, she struggled to make ends meet, worried constantly about money, and struggled to educate herself and support her son, who later developed a drug addiction. She stated that the main reason she married again is that her current husband is kind, and the marriage provided her with present and future economic stability.

5
soul companions:
Listening for the soul
in Daily Life and work

⤙══◉═══⤛

Now on that same day two of them were going to a village called Emmaus, about seven miles from Jerusalem, and talking with each other about all these things that had happened. While they were talking and discussing, Jesus himself came near and went with them, but their eyes were kept from recognizing him. And he said to them, "What are you discussing with each other while you walk along?"

. . . As they came near the village to which they were going, he walked ahead as if he were going on. But they urged him strongly, saying, "Stay with us, because it is almost evening and the day is now nearly over." So he went in to stay with them. When he was at table with them, he took bread, blessed and broke it, and gave it to them. Then their eyes were opened, and they recognized him; and he vanished from their sight. They said to each other, "Were not our hearts burning with us while he was talking to us on the road, while he was opening the scriptures to us?"

Luke 24:13-17, 28-32

F OR OBVIOUS REASONS, WE NOW UNDERSTAND that pastoral care is a function of the entire congregation, and "the aim of the church's pastoral care program should be to develop a dynamic climate of mutual, loving, enlightened concern, which gradually leavens the whole congregation."[1] In word and deed, every church member has pastoral care opportunities to be a neighbor to others in the home, the workplace, the faith community, and the wider world.

This chapter focuses on the laity and their involvement in pastoral care. Usually, when the role of the laity in pastoral care ministries is considered, the subject is examined through the lens of establishing training programs for lay caring ministries. Several books on pastoral care already emphasize the need for equipping the laity and provide clear suggestions for developing and structuring lay caring ministries within congregations.[2] Laypersons already have been helped to provide ministry to persons in need in the congregation and community. This has included ministry to the community's lonely, sick, aging, bereaved, homebound, institutionalized, exploited, violated, and economically oppressed.

Most training programs cover various forms of visitation, as well as the facilitation of self-help groups that deal with concerns such as grief, addiction, caring for elderly persons, and support for family and friends of terminally ill persons. Program components usually include examining the role of lay pastoral care, establishing a care relationship, effective listening and responding skills, caring in various situations (grief, homebound, and so forth), and accountability and referral issues. Since numerous lay training programs already exist, as does evidence that suggests that quality and the supervision of laity in such programs increases their effectiveness, this information need neither be argued nor repeated here. Surely we no longer need to be persuaded that it is beneficial and appropriate to include training programs for lay caring ministries in the life of congregations.

What has been missing, however, from the literature and our pastoral care practice, is an emphasis on how laypersons can reclaim their rightful ministry of caring for the soul and providing spiritual guidance for one another. Some attention, albeit limited, has been given within lay training programs to the faith issues that arise in crisis and other times of need. What these programs have failed to address is the daily care of the soul that is both sought and needed by the laity. In many respects, it is in the experiences of daily life and work that laypersons want and need to find God. They want to have spiritual resources that will help them be faithful to God in the immediacy of their daily lives.

This chapter deals with this commonly neglected aspect. It suggests that by enabling laypersons to give and receive soul companionship, many of their immediate pastoral needs can be expressed and addressed. The immediate daily issues most people struggle with "involve in some way jobs, money, and vocation."[3] Touching on these concerns and providing means for laypersons to do the soul-work necessary for integrating faith and work are the pastoral care agenda for a congregational ministry of soul companionship. To state it more boldly and succinctly, soul companionship is a way for the laity to reclaim their rightful ministry of providing spiritual guidance and soul-care to one another.

whatever happened to lay spiritual guidance?

Deacons likewise must be serious, not double-tongued, not indulging in much wine, not greedy for money; they must hold fast to the mystery of the faith with a clear conscience. (1 Timothy 3:8-9)

At one time within our Protestant heritage, laypersons did exercise care for the soul. In Reformed churches in particular, the roles of the elder and deacon included fostering development in the spiritual life and helping people make connections between their faith and daily living. Until the twentieth century, elders and deacons were vested with particular spiritual care responsibilities that included sponsoring newer Christians, praying for the spiritual concerns of the membership, and visiting church members in their homes.

These were not mere social visits or teacup occasions. Elders and deacons were commissioned to inquire about how persons were maturing spiritually and to assume responsibility for how others grew in grace. The spiritual lives of congregants were elders' and deacons' primary congregational business. As Howard Rice reminds us, elders "were responsible to examine communicants privately before each Communion service and to intervene so as to bring about reconciliation between neighbors found to be at odds with each other." Elders and deacons were chosen because they were perceived as bearers of spiritual wisdom, rooted in the Christian tradition, faithful to their own spiritual development, and trusted to be persons who could pray with others in times of personal need.

The strength of this earlier understanding of the elder and deacon has severely eroded. There are many reasons why this is so. As the role of the pastor in providing pastoral care and counseling was professionalized, the laity gradually relinquished their role in offering soul-care to one another. Also, the understanding that elders and deacons were lay spiritual guides or soul companions altered. In some instances, the concept and language remained, yet the functional expectation that they would provide spiritual guidance vanished. Recently, a ministry colleague shared with me that an elder had refused a request to pray at an annual congregational meeting. The request was to offer a memorial prayer, on behalf of the congregation, for church members who had died in the previous year. The request was met by this response: "I never would have agreed to be an elder if I knew I had to pray." Clearly, there was a disconnection between the office of elder and the spiritual responsibility to hold church members in prayer.

In some congregations, the terms *elder* and *deacon* are simply no longer used; instead, terms such as *councilor, session member,* or *church leader* are substituted. Where the elder or deacon title still exists, persons can be chosen to fill the office more on the basis of their leadership abilities, administrative skills, and general level of enthusiasm than for notable spiritual maturity or wisdom. Sometimes they are chosen simply because they respond to the powers of persuasion and are available and willing to serve.

It also can be argued that, in addition to the guiding influence of elders and deacons, Protestant churches sought to care for the soul largely by involving laypersons in study and prayer groups and by awakening the soul through preaching and worship. While these remain significant methods, it should be noted that they reflect resistance on the part of Protestants to a one-to-one method of spiritual direction and fear of an authoritarian approach to care for the soul. Protestants have consistently maintained that it is God's grace and not the action of any one human being that is the primary factor in spiritual development. Often such prayer and study groups met midweek to share in prayer and exhortation of one another or following a church service in order to discuss the sermon of the morning and its implications for faith and daily life.

The role of lay spiritual guides and group forms of spiritual guidance have played a significant role in particular periods of the history of Protestant churches. The potential of these methods today to provide for the needs of many, without draining the energy of a few pastoral caregivers, is great. In most congregations, church leaders can identify at least a few individuals who are spiritually open and eager to mature in the faith. They may have the willingness and potential to become soul companions for one another and to prepare themselves to enable others to be soul companions. More than ever before, the role of the laity as spiritual guides can be recognized for holding great potential to increase the effectiveness of a congregation's pastoral care ministries.

soul companionship as pastoral care

In many respects, the paradigmatic story in Luke's gospel of two disciples on the road to Emmaus illustrates the pastoral value of soul companionship for the spiritual journey. Luke knows that soul companionship is a source of personal strength, divine revelation, and vocational discernment. These things are felt and found as we journey along the Way with our brothers and sisters in the faith community. Our ordinary world and the world of God come together in the rites of soul companionship.

The rites of soul companionship include sharing our human experiences, dilemmas, and trials, reflecting on scripture, breaking bread together, and discerning the revelation of God. It is in these simple rites that God is revealed in Jesus. Jesus himself draws near, makes himself known, and is recognized. The Emmaus road event tells us that soul companions help us to deal with all the ambiguities of living in a culture that is hostile to faith. Because soul companions care about what really matters to God, they help us to listen for God, discern God's presence and activity, and live our lives accordingly. Soul companions connect us more deeply to God and the grace of God's caring presence in our workday actions. Our hearts "burn within us" when we share together the grace and grit of our daily life and work and find God revealed to us there.

Our capacity to be faithful in the world depends greatly on the soul companionship we experience and offer. Martin Luther King, Jr., once told the story of a woman who came up to him on a particularly trying day when he was feeling drained of energy:

> 'Something is wrong with you,' she said. 'You didn't talk strong tonight.' Seeking further to disguise my fears, I retorted, 'Oh no, Mother Pollard, nothing is wrong. I am feeling as fine as ever.' But her insight was discerning. 'Now you can't fool me,' she said. 'I knows something is wrong. Is it that we ain't doing things to please you? Or is it that the white folks is bothering you?' Before I could respond, she looked directly into my eyes and said, 'I done told you we is with you all the way . . . but even if we ain't with you, God's gonna take care of you.'[4]

This kind of direct, almost confrontational wisdom came by instinct and through a peer. It was offered by a companion in the faith who knew his soul well and who had nothing to gain or lose from telling the truth as she saw it. Such spiritual counsel comes from the heart and is offered naturally as a gesture of care for the soul. It is a good example of the pastoral value of soul companionship when life's labors and circumstances are trying. Pastoral care was given by a companion in the faith who cared enough for the soul to offer unrelenting support, truthful words, and a vocational prod from the rear.

Soul companionship is a valuable means to set daily life in the context of listening for God. It is a dimension of soulful pastoral care because it deepens a way of life in God and keeps us honest before God and in our daily actions.

The Nature of soul companionship

The Importance of Terminology

I deliberately choose the term *soul companion* over *soul friend* or *spiritual guide*. Even though there has been, at various points within the Protestant traditions, a stress on the role of the elder and deacon as a spiritual guide for individual congregational members, there remains a healthy suspicion that authoritarianism and sacerdotalism may creep into any relationship in which spiritual counsel is received. Within Protestant traditions, it is important to retain an emphasis on the priesthood of all believers and to affirm the mutuality involved in giving and receiving soul-care. Whatever term is chosen, it needs to be one that embodies mutuality and can move us beyond the restriction of a personal spiritual guide to what it means to care for souls that live in a communal web.

Given Protestants' understandable reluctance to use the term *spiritual guide, soul friend* may seem to be a reasonable alternative. Kenneth Leech, in his study on the history of Christian spirituality, proposes this term.[5] In part, it is a way of capturing the Johannine notion of friendship. Since God calls us friends, friendship with one another becomes a way to bring the love and knowledge of God to completion within us.

While Leech's work advances our understanding of what a soul-caring relationship can mean, the term *friend* may be too laden with contemporary and individualistic meanings to be adequately constructive. Today, when we say to another, "Meet my friend," we are usually referring to a friendship found in our neighborhood, workplace, or daily activities. Sometimes we even call casual acquaintances our friends. A friend is most commonly understood to be a person with whom one is on terms of mutual affection, independent of sexual or family love. Friends fulfill multiple purposes, including providing avenues for socializing, participating in projects of mutual interest, making common cause, looking after our property when we go away, and being loyal.

In an increasingly secularized culture, it is reasonable to assume that most people neither conceive of friendship as a community-building activity nor as something that embodies a spiritual dimension. Although there are exceptions to this, the purpose of friendship is rarely understood to be a mutual exploration of questions and concerns that are pressing upon the soul. If we could retain the clarity of Aelred of Rievaulx's statement that "to live without friends is to live like a beast," then the term *friend* could become advantageous. In our current culture, however, we have observed the opposite. Friends also have encouraged "the emergence of the beast," leading to despicable acts of violence against family members, friends, schoolmates, and even strangers.

For obvious reasons, it is very important to uphold the mutuality, affection, and tenderness normally experienced in friendships as defining characteristics of soul-caring relationships. Yet soul-care needs to go beyond these qualities in order to make room for the pastoral care values found in the paradigmatic Lukan Emmaus story. Soul-care includes unconditional support, truth-telling, accountability, and vocational discernment. Soul-care sees beyond the secular and individualistic dimensions of life to the sacredness and interdependence of all of life.

In contrast to *friendship*, the term *companionship* suggests people who engage in accompanying activity. A companion goes with another on a journey and is present to that person no matter what happens. Thus, *soul companions* are those whose primary reason for being in relationship with each other is to accompany each other on the spiritual journey. They are in relationship in order to listen for God's presence in their lives. They are guided by questions such as "Where is God in this?" "Who is God in this?" "Who is God inviting me to become?" "What is God nudging me toward?" In contrast to friendship, genuine affection may develop in a soul companionship, but it is not a condition of soul companionship. Soul companions come together in order to help each other hear the voice of God at work in their daily lives and to create a context of accountability in community for what is discerned.

The Importance of Individual and Group Companionship

Soul companionship can happen between two individuals and within a group. Persons can draw alongside each other with the intention of being mutual sources of spiritual support, strength, encouragement, truth-telling, and discernment. Soul companions need not have any formal theological education. Since the point of conversation is to discern God's presence in the midst of daily life, anyone who is willing to listen and talk openly about God and the life of prayer can make a good soul companion. Family members and beloved life partners may well reflect the essential qualities of individual soul companions, but it is important also to include soul companions from the wider context of a faith community and the diverse perspectives it brings. This lessens the potential for bias and narrowness of vision. It is important that soul companions be able to challenge us as well as comfort us.

Soul companionship can be initiated by making an intentional request of another to be a soul companion and by participation in a group whose purpose is soul companionship. Whether drawn from the ecumenical community or a particular congregation, individuals can gather regularly in groups in order to facilitate collegial ways to attend to the soul. Such groups are best limited to eight to ten persons. It is most enriching to have both an individual soul companion and a group that provides soul companionship and is committed to offering it to others. Soul companionship in the context of a small group becomes a helpful reminder to us that we are not alone on the spiritual journey. It is a way for us to participate in the living communal web that keeps us connected to one another, to God at work, and to God revealed through our humanity.

The Importance of Continuity

Whether soul companionship is a mutual relationship between two persons, a group experience, or both, regular gatherings are important. Those involved can negotiate the regularity. A weekly time is most helpful. It is advisable to meet together no less than monthly. The group can negotiate the duration of its meetings. It may be helpful to establish a time limit at the outset with the option to extend it. Experience suggests that for a group to become effective at soul companionship, it needs to meet at least eight to ten times over the course of a year. Some groups will choose to meet monthly, others biweekly or weekly.

There may always be compelling reasons to reschedule or miss a gathering. If this becomes a pattern, however, then regular prayerful support for the absent person needs to extend to follow-up action. It is important to demonstrate care by asking about what may be going on in his or her life that leads him or her at this time to withdraw from the experience. Continuity is a key factor in nurturing meaningful soul companionship. Without it, a commitment to listen for the soul in daily circumstances may wane.

The pastoral inclusion of soul companionship

There are many reasons for deliberately including a lay ministry of soul companionship in a paradigm of soulful pastoral care. Soul companionship is not a therapeutic or problem-solving tool. Rather, *the goal of soul companionship is to help people listen for the soul and for the presence of God in their daily work and lives.* Soul companionship aims to attend to the ways our souls hear the call of God in our lives. Since this is the goal, it is important to state the pastoral care objectives of a lay ministry of soul companionship.

First, *attending to soul companionship increases the ability of laypersons to care for themselves.* Soul companionship offers laypersons a way to accept responsibility for their own soul-care and spiritual development. It can lessen passive and unhealthy dependencies on others perceived to be the contagious carriers of a lively faith and spiritual wisdom. Corinne Ware supports this when she says that "so long as laypeople expect pastors and priests to seek God in their stead and make no effort of their own, they will be disappointed and stunted."[6] By refusing to focus solely on the person of the pastor, soul companionship provides a viable mechanism for increasing the spiritual health and human agency of individuals and faith communities. Soul companionship challenges laypersons to become competent in their own spiritual development and to stop handing over their spiritual lives to the so-called experts. It is no longer someone else's job or the job of specialists.

Second, *soul companionship ensures that in a soul-denying culture, there is still a safe place where the soul can be invited into free and open expression and be fully supported as it finds its voice.* Hearing from others the myriad ways the spirit of God is perceived to be at work in us can increase spiritual openness, provide affirmation, and offer reassurance. Soul companionship reminds us of the commonality of human experience. None of us likes to be alone, especially when it comes to matters of the spiritual life. Being purposeful in the church about attending to soul companionship may address tendencies to privatize and compartmentalize the spiritual life.

Martin Marty was bold enough to declare that "we have friends, or we are friends, in order that we do not get killed."[7] Our survival as spiritual beings in an individualistically centered and competitively based world requires that we relate to one another in ways that are more collegial, less independent, less privatized, more inclusive, and more communal. Soul companionship helps us remember that what happens Monday to Saturday is as important to God as what happens on Sunday. It can get very lonely out there in the world. Many laypersons know firsthand the panic and paralysis that come from losing a job, retirement, or a work layoff. Soul companionship strengthens our inner faith resources. It gives us cause to realize that human life without spiritual meaning and spiritual companions is too hard to manage. It is one way to fulfill Martin Marty's insistence that "friendship is an act of freedom."[8] Soul companions free us from isolation. We realize that we are not alone in our trials and that we can be supported in our efforts to relate these to our faith.

Third, *soul companionship expands our spiritual vision and helps us cross boundaries.* Soul companionship allows us to affirm the biblical axiomatic that "we cannot love God whom we have not seen if we do not love our brothers and sisters whom we have seen."[9] Ultimately, we can only grow so far on our own. It is by being in the company of others who also seek to understand and know the ups and downs of the spiritual life that our spiritual growth is expanded beyond the boundaries of our narrow personalities and insights. It is important that we discover how our souls can be enlarged through seeing God in the experiences and life events that surround us and cross social boundaries. Through interaction with others we are challenged to be more inclusive. Soul companionship enables us to see things differently and to become aware of the many ways that God is at work within us.

Fourth, *soul companionship grounds the spiritual journey in a realistic context.* Since care for the soul has become so popular and people are becoming bloated by indiscriminately devouring trendy programs and publications on spirituality, it becomes important to create a context in which the spiritual life can be probed critically and carefully. Soul companions can give and receive feedback on assumptions, information, and even opinions. Discovering the spiritual legacy left by centuries of practicing Christians, and finding out together how to make it rightfully our own, is the kind of encouragement and provocation that can be provided through intentional soul companionship.

Fifth, *soul companionship offers a means for church members to become more truthful and accountable to one another.* Some things are too valuable to cast to the winds or the whims of the world. Sharing experiences from one's life and work and discovering where God is in our experiences keeps us mindful of God and the intentions of God for the world. Although we need not necessarily tell everything all the time, a regular commitment to tell the truth of our daily lives in the company of soul companions guards the integrity of the spiritual life. It keeps us truthful in a world where falsehoods and capacities to self-protect and self-deceive are strong. Soul companions enable people to tell painful truths about themselves to God and others and to find ways to live in the light of a truth that society frequently does not honor.

A production company that ignores environmental regulations in order to boost annual profit margins does not want to hear about stewardship of resources. A church member that writes a letter to the local newspaper speaking out against the deployment of smart bombs can cause a stir in the world. Being faithful in daily life includes taking our faith into that life. Soul companions care about helping each other become more loving, more like Jesus, and more open to God's presence and activity in their lives. They keep us accountable to participating fully in the activity of God's Spirit in the world. They help us explore obstacles and aids for living in ways that are good for us and others.

All five of these pastoral objectives support soul companionship as an essential dimension of pastoral care. Left on our own, we are at a loss to know how our souls can find companionship with God. In a world full of betrayals, soul companions dare to "furnish proof . . . [that] there are reasons for trust."[10] By including soul companionship, we become more whole, trusting, and alive in God. Our hopes for individual and communal fullness of life are raised.

Implementing soul companionship in congregations

When considering all the issues involved in implementing a ministry of soul companionship in congregations, it is important to remember at the outset that soul companionship is a lay-centered ministry. It is an expression of pastoral care that is given and received by laypersons. This is not to suggest that clergy are uninvolved. Clergy may give some individual encouragement and guidance for deepening the inner life, but it is not reasonable to expect that individual sessions will be available for all church members.

What is more helpful is for clergy to initiate the development of a lay soul companionship ministry and to serve as a resource by preparing and supporting group facilitators. Although it is best if laypersons are willing and able to facilitate groups from the outset, clergy may find they need to manifest their support by convening and facilitating the first experience of a soul companionship group; this will build confidence and familiarity with the purposes of soul companionship.

Clergy can also contribute resources to enable group biblical reflection, study on Christian spirituality, and the life of prayer. Further, clergy and laypersons can work together to develop guidelines for initiating and developing individual soul companions. Minimally, these can include a description of soul companionship, expectations and responsibilities for soul companions, recommendations regarding frequency, place, and length of meetings, guidelines for listening for the soul, and suggestions for inquiries about the presence of God in daily toil and trials.

There will always be some congregations less suited to the small group form of soul companionship ministry. Congregations can adapt the principles of a soul companionship ministry to other formats that may be more appropriate. For example, congregational activities and the work schedules of congregants may suggest that a series of immersion experiences would be more workable. A larger group of persons who express interest in growing spiritually can be brought together four to six times over the course of a year. During a Friday evening and Saturday retreat-style event, the basic elements that comprise a soul companionship group can be elucidated and experienced. The group can easily put into place a means for participants to companion one another between the immersion weekend experiences. Any adaptation of a soul companionship group ministry will want to retain the foundational principle that the ministry be lay-centered, and to the extent that it is possible, also lay-facilitated.

Selecting and Preparing Group Facilitators

Selecting potential facilitators for soul companionship groups requires careful thought and clear criteria. Effective facilitators are persons with natural aptitudes for relationship-building and faith reflection and who have expressed the desire to grow spiritually. They are willing and able to commit themselves to the preparation required to form a group and the time required for convening regular group gatherings. Hopefully, most congregations have at least a few persons with personal qualities that nurture self-respect and caring for others, who are aware that life is an ongoing experience of learning about life in the Spirit, who have some familiarity with Christian tradition and the Bible, and who are authentic, self-aware, open to others, and able to listen. Often such persons will be recognized as those to whom others turn spontaneously for confidential conversation and spiritual strength.

Because soul companionship groups can attract all sorts of persons interested in spiritual matters, it is beneficial to have group facilitators anticipate possible problems or potential abuses that may arise. For example, a group member may be uncomfortable with silence or the anguish of someone's story and may dismiss or negate the presence of God in quiet, doubt, or anger. Or an individual may take on the role of the incessant talker, comic, or spiritual cynic. Anticipating these kinds of situations in advance prepares facilitators to reflect privately with such persons about the implications of their behavior on the life of the group. The facilitator may be able to propose behavioral modifications that will make positive contributions to the group. In some cases, individuals may not be at a place in their lives that enables them to contribute in constructive ways to a group. In such instances, persons may need to be referred to other sources for assistance or counseling prior to their regular involvement in a soul companionship group.

Making Intentional Covenants

Deliberate efforts to give and receive soul companionship require commitment and fidelity. Throughout history, people who share a common desire for a deeper spiritual life have covenanted with one another to strengthen their faith and have willingly agreed to certain things that foster inner and outer renewal. Usually these have included the Emmaus companionship rites of sharing life experiences, biblical reflection, prayer, the breaking of bread, and service. When any of these ingredients is missing, a faith community's connection with God runs the risk of fading. Together, they form a way to live faithfully in daily toil and times of trial. Soul companionship is based on laypersons' regularly doing the things that attune themselves to God's presence and prepare them to take part in God's reconciling work.

Developing a covenant for soul companionship requires some imagination and persistence. Most covenants include an agreement on the purposes of the group, the sorts of commitments that will be made to honor the group's life and continuity (attendance, prayerful support between meetings, confidentiality, meeting time, schedule and place, attention to group dynamics and processes) and a meeting structure. It is always preferable to summarize in writing what agreements are made. The written document serves as a helpful concrete reminder of the importance of the commitments made to be soul companions to one another. Sometimes a visible sign of the covenant is helpful. A laminated poster with the scripted promises and signatures of the group may be one way to reread and reaffirm the significance of having soul companions for the spiritual journey. Covenants can always be renewed or changed to reflect circumstances that may shift over time. A covenant will remain in place so long as souls experience care. A soul companionship will be in place as long as it serves its purpose and is maintained by intentional openness in responding to God.

Forming a Soul Companionship Group

Too often those who come to church have to search themselves for resources for their spiritual growth. Soul companionship groups are one way that the church, the very place where the spiritual life needs to be fostered, can address the truth of what it means to live daily as spiritual beings. Finding members for a soul companionship group is best accomplished by a combination of periodic public invitations and the word-of-mouth approach. A carefully worded bulletin insert, open letter, descriptions on a church Web site, or an orientation event are all means to describe soul companionship in general terms. Rather than go into too much detail, a few contact names can be provided so that interested persons can pursue their questions further. Individuals who seem to have an interest in spiritual matters, and who are personally invited by a group facilitator, are most likely to respond positively to the invitation to become a soul companion.

One of the dangers of a lay ministry of soul companionship is that groups can be experienced by non-participants as cliques of like-minded people. To help dissipate this potential threat to the unity of the whole congregation, the congregation can be advised at the outset that new groups will be formed on a periodic basis. Also, entering group members can be challenged to discern their own gifts and potential for facilitating a soul companionship group. New groups can be started as old ones continue.

The Structure of a Soul Companionship Group

Most soul companionship groups will find that they need at least two hours each time they gather. Recalling the key ingredients for spiritual renewal mentioned above, a gathering will usually include the following (the times are approximate guidelines):

Centering (3–5 minutes) becoming spiritually centered, focused on God and aware of our soul companions

Sharing Daily Work and Life (40 minutes) sharing experiences from daily work and life that connect or disconnect us from God

Bread-Breaking (10 minutes) a brief time for refreshment and nourishment

Biblical Reflection/Study (40 minutes) hearing biblical texts and reflecting on their meaning in the light of our daily work and life, or study of a topic related to Christian spirituality

Accountability (10 minutes) a brief sharing of how companions have maintained awareness of God during the week and are being faithful (as individuals and as a group) in their vocation to God

Prayer (15 minutes) experiencing different ways to pray and praying together

Benediction (2–3 minutes) creating a sense of inner stillness and blessedness in departure by offering a short, memorable (perhaps favorite), unison prayer of benediction

The Content of a Soul Companionship Gathering

Previous chapters in this book have contained suggestions for centering and prayer, so these need not be repeated here. Sharing Daily Work and Life, Biblical Reflection/Study, and Accountability are components of a soul companionship gathering that call for further explanation.

Sharing Daily Work and Life. Work is not intended necessarily to mean *paid* work. Work is simply those labors and activities that occupy our waking time. They can be routine or unusual, voluntary or paid. Work can be a hobby of the heart, the toil of our hands, or the exercising of our minds.

Generally, we have mistakenly thought of work as something outside of the spiritual realm. Yet even the simplest errands or the most menial chores can be holy work. Whatever we do, it is part of our greater effort to participate in the ways God labors to mend the world. Brother Lawrence said to his companions that "our sanctification did not depend upon changing our works, but in doing that for God's sake which we commonly do for our own."[11] The key is in seeing our daily toil as holy activity and our work as "contributing, not simply as making a living."[12] Whatever our work, it can be the very work of God to bring wholeness to the world.

With this perspective in mind, we share something from our daily life and work that has brought us into a deeper awareness of God or caused us to question where God is in the experience or event. "God was telling me to calm down as I began my new job." "God was refreshing me as I swam lengths in the pool." "I keep feeling uneasy about my future there and I think God is trying to tell me it's time to move on, but to where?" The purpose of the sharing is not to solve or fix problems that we or others may identify. Rather, the focus is upon where and how God is revealed in the event from the perspective of the person who is sharing the experience. Others in the group who have had a similar experience may wish to respond by sharing what they discovered about their relationship with God as a result of that experience.

It is not always necessary for everyone to share equally, and it is important to remember that there are times when someone's silence is a valid contribution to the group. This is a time to share the daily spiritual quest and to listen for the voice of God in the experiences that are shared.

Biblical Reflection/Study. During the time of Biblical Reflection, the Common Lectionary can be used as a guide or scripture texts can be purposefully selected. Many scriptural passages are suitable for exploring themes related to connecting with God, spiritual growth, discipleship, discernment of gifts, call, and prayer. The scripture passage is read at least twice with a period of silence between each reading. Group members are then invited to reflect on the text in terms of how it speaks to them about living faithfully in the context of their daily work and lives. The point here is not to analyze the passage, discuss it at a theoretical level, or study its original meanings. Rather, it is to make connections from the heart between the Word that is heard and the life that is being lived.

If the group prefers a topical study on Christian spirituality, there are many books, readings, videos, and resources available that cover the history of Christian spirituality, Christian mystic writers, classical saints, and contemporary writers on spirituality and spiritual development.[13] The particular tradition of one's faith can be studied, as can other spiritual traditions. A study of church creeds, affirmations of faith, hymns, or the meaning of Christian worship can also open up new understandings and practices that nourish the spiritual life. If a topical study is chosen in lieu of biblical reflection, then one or two group members can be responsible for opening up the topic at each meeting. Members may need to be assured that no one is expected to be an expert. Rather, presenters simply share information and insights from their inquiries and interest in the topic and open up discussion from the rest of the group.

Accountability. The portion of the gathering devoted to Accountability is an important piece. At first, groups may be tempted to avoid this element or may fail to keep enough time allocated for its inclusion. This is an opportunity for group members to hear from one another the means they are using to maintain a daily awareness of God. It is important to share how they have been intentional, faithful, or faltering since they last met as a group. Such honest sharing is simultaneously a supportive and challenging act. Some members may share about devotional practices and prayer rituals, others about reading and study experiences, still others about exercise programs or nourishment gained through a movie, a walk, or time set aside to play and talk with a loved one. Whatever emerges, the key is to learn from one another about what is realistic, appealing, doable, and meaningful for creating a pattern for using time in such a way as to sustain a focus on God in all experiences of life.

This also includes sharing the ways we are being invited by God to grow ever more faithful in our daily work, whatever that may be. If we have questions about our work, how is God speaking to us in the questions themselves? Is what we are doing each day harmful or helpful? Is what we are doing rending or mending creation? Are those we work with strengthened or stressed by our presence and style? How are we being Christ-like within our places of work? Soul companions may be able to suggest where the demands of a job may be at odds with the values of our faith. They may express support and wisdom when our faith compels us to take a dangerous risk. Sharing with one another how we re/view our work and ask God to bless the labors of our hearts, heads, hands, and feet is an important part of how we companion one another's souls.

Significantly, as a soul companionship group progresses, it is within this accountability segment that a group often makes the connection between maintaining individual accountability and sustaining themselves through communal forms of service. As a way of maintaining awareness of God in daily work and as a way to sustain themselves in God, members may choose to work together on some sort of service project. Although such an outcome is not the purpose of the group, a different understanding of accountability for one's life and work in God emerges with authentic vitality. A group may choose to serve meals once a month at a homeless shelter, collect litter washed up on shore, sponsor a refugee family, develop a ministry of praying for children, or assume responsibility for visiting church members and others living in a retirement complex.

soul-care for life

Placing an intentional focus on soul companionship within congregations is an essential dimension of soulful pastoral care. It is a means for laypersons to reclaim their rightful role in providing spiritual care to one another and to make real James Fenhagen's dream "that the day will soon come when spiritual guidance is common practice within the Christian community."[14]

Soul companionship furthers individual spiritual growth and contributes significantly toward the development of a pastorally caring community. When souls are accompanied, souls are cared for. Soul companionship grounds us, and the experiences of our daily lives and work, in a context of support, revelation, and ongoing discernment. By finding and sustaining soul companions, we assume responsibility for our spiritual nurture. We ensure that we will be challenged to remain faithfully focused on the presence of God in all that is holy in life. Rather than drift through life, we can choose to be accompanied through it by those who seek, along with us, to give and receive soul-care.

Sometimes soul companions are closer than we think. Whether we believe it or not, someone may be on the verge even now of extending an invitation to us to become a soul companion. Being soul companions to adults is an experience to be treasured for a lifetime. Even more priceless is the experience of accompanying children and listening for their souls. It is to this congregational dimension of soulful pastoral care that we now turn.

Reflection Questions

1. What has been your experience of the church caring for the questions and concerns of your soul as they relate to your daily life and work?

2. What does the term *soul companion* suggest to you?

3. How do you respond to the idea of a lay-centered ministry of soul companionship?

4. Think about what you generally do within a day (prepare meals, talk with family and friends, accomplish work tasks, read the newspaper,

watch television). How can you envision these as places where God meets you and where you serve God?

5. Carefully consider the service of worship from your church. Ask your-self how each element of the service can make connections between faith and daily life and work.

⊷≡◉⊜⊶

two spiritual exercises

1. *A Meditation on Luke 24:13-35*

Read the passage at least twice.

Enter the story. Imagine yourself as one of the disciples on the road to Emmaus. What in your most recent experience has seemed most empty of God or most difficult to let go of? Sense the mood. Name what you are feel-ing. Who is with you on the road? Imagine his or her companionship. What is your reaction to the stranger? What is the stranger saying or doing? What is being revealed to you? Get in touch with how you feel after the stranger leaves. Where is your companion now?

After returning from your meditation, spend a few moments in quiet and in prayer. Listen peacefully . . . pray gratefully . . . remember graciously . . . live soulfully.

2. *Soul Accompaniment in the Workplace*

Since people often have little grasp of the specific challenges and opportu-nities of one another's daily work, you may wish to take a soul companion with you to work for a day or a portion of the day. Talk about his or her impressions and ask him or her to share with you where he or she saw or experienced God.

⊷≡◉⊜⊶

A biblical reflection for use within a soul companionship group

The biblical reflection is based on the story of Moses' encounter with the burning bush.[15] Group members can come to a session having read the bib-lical passage in advance and reflected in writing upon the following ques-tions. Alternatively, the group may prefer to greet the text together and to respond spontaneously to the guiding reflection questions.

Guiding Text: Exodus 3:1–4:20

Guiding Reflection Questions:

1. Pondering your daily work and adult life, identify an incident where "a bush was burning."

2. How would you describe your routine at the time the bush burned ("keeping the flock of Jethro")?

3. In what sense was the experience "an interruption" of your routine?

4. How would you describe your "turning aside to see"? What made the experience "hot"?

5. What was at stake for you in your response? Some risk, cost, changes?

6. Who did you discover you were ("Moses! Moses!")?

7. In what sense was the place "holy"? Is it still sacred to you?

8. Who did God tell you God was ("I am . . . ")?

9. To what or whom were you called or sent?

10. What are the continuing signs of God's companionship (Exodus 3:12)?

11. Do you smell the smoke of any new bushes burning in your life right now? If so, what do you intend to do?

6
children's spirituality:
Listening for the soul of the child

Then the Lord called, "Samuel! Samuel!"

And he said, "Here I am!" and ran to Eli, and said, "Here I am, for you called me."

But he said, "I did not call; lie down again." So he went and lay down. The Lord called again, "Samuel!"

Samuel got up and went to Eli, and said, "Here I am, for you called me."

But he said, "I did not call, my son; lie down again."

Now Samuel did not yet know the LORD, and the word of the LORD had not yet been revealed to him. The LORD called Samuel again, a third time.

And he got up and went to Eli, and said, "Here I am, for you called me."

Then Eli perceived that the LORD was calling the boy. Therefore Eli said to Samuel, "Go, lie down; and if he calls you, you shall say, 'Speak, LORD, for your servant is listening.'"

1 Samuel 3:4-9a

CAN YOU RECALL who listened for your soul when you were a child? About the time I was learning to read, my grandmother gave me a birthday present. It was an illustrated book of children's prayers. Among them, and quickly committed to lifelong memory, was the classic childhood prayer:

Now I lay me down to sleep,
I pray the Lord my soul to keep.
And, if I die before I wake,
I pray the Lord my soul to take.

Whatever motivated my grandmother to choose this particular gift, it became an absolute means of assurance. The words of that prayer led me to believe that my soul was safe, and whether I lived or died, I belonged to God.[1] I knew this certain assurance went beyond the physical and emotional security provided by my parents. Somehow, somewhere in the depths of my childhood soul, I felt that this assurance was about more than any household or familial experiences of safety. Although I could not have stated it then, I knew that assurance was about divine gift and the mystery of life.

After two or three years of schooling, I remember having a conversation with a woman who seemed to me to be older than anyone I ever knew. For some reason, I trusted her. She seemed wise, perhaps because, even at my youthful age, I sensed her desire to listen for the voice of God in the mouth of a child. Rose had been appointed as a lifelong deacon in my home church. One day, following the worship service, I wandered over to where she was still sitting in a pew. I asked her when and how I would know if God wanted me to do something. Rose's response was simple, yet forever memorable: "If it is of God, you will know. Wait and see."

It is exceedingly important to recognize the soul of the child and to affirm and respond to a child's soul-longings. Feeling safe in God and finding God clearly were two key themes of my soul's early movements and desires. These two childhood experiences stand out for me as examples of the kind of soul-yearnings that reflect a child's spiritual potential. What enabled the development of my soul is the fact that it was reverenced. My grandmother and Rose treated my young soul with dignity and respect. My soul's existence was validated and it was listened to with sensitivity and delight. No matter how deep my early yearnings may have been buried, there were elders around me who waited with me and for me and who bent down to listen for words that hinted at the soul's desire to be set free to flourish.

In this chapter, I want to present the notion that young children have tremendous and often untapped spiritual capacities that deserve greater pastoral attention. There is a noticeable gap in our pastoral care with children, and that gap concerns our care of the child's soul. We are endowed at birth with embryonic capacities for faith. "How these capacities are activated and grow depends to a large extent on how we are welcomed into the world and what kinds of environments we grow in."[2] The cry of alarm is sounding in the environment of the church. We can respond to the alarm and bridge the gap by learning ways and means to listen for and reverence the souls of our children. By listening for the soul of the child, we can do much more than bring instruction, grace, or comfort. Like Jesus, we can position ourselves beside children (Luke 9:47) to welcome them, to hear what God is saying to them, and to intervene on their behalf by providing ways and means for them to meet and respond to God.

Paying attention to the souls of our children is more radical than we may imagine at first glance. It will mean moving beyond our familiar ways of attending to the young ones among us. For most of our churches, this will involve us in tilling new ground.

Ages Three to Eleven:
An opportune Time of Their Lives

The focus for this chapter is upon children between the ages of three and eleven, an opportune time of their lives. Children in this age range are remarkably open and sensitive to the spiritual dimensions of life. This particular age range allows us to consider children who have developed the capacity for outward expression (speech, art, and movement) but are not yet fully at home with abstract conceptualization. It is an advantageous time to reverence the child's soul and to encourage the development of a living relationship with God.

Faith development theorist James Fowler and Christian educator John Westerhoff have both observed that children within this age range crave acceptance and affection, have active imaginations, and are able to make solid links between symbol and reality. As Fowler has also stressed, children hear meaning that is often hidden in stories and symbols, and as children develop, they begin to investigate why things are the way they are.[3] This is not to say that children understand symbolic meanings in the way that adults do. In this age range, thinking is still concrete, and children are not yet ready for the abstract thinking that characterizes adolescence and adulthood.[4] Nevertheless, young children do make meaning from story and symbol. These meanings are genuine reflections of their lives and the divine presence within them. The child's inner deliberations may be rudimentary in form, but they are no less real or spiritual.

The characteristics of three- to eleven-year-olds and their developmental and spiritual needs provide important clues for us as we aim to provide effective pastoral care for young children. Adult listeners (the "Eli's" among us who provide assurance of God's presence), rituals that engage the imagination, comfort and meaning, and activities that foster a sense of wonder and gratitude are essential elements that enable children to hear God's voice calling them by name. Of course children entering their teenage years have deep soul-needs too. But the focus here will be upon young children, for it is during this time of their lives that we can establish constructive patterns for listening and attending to the soul. These patterns can then become foundations for all of life's journey.

our pastoral care Legacy with children

For the most part, Protestant churches have not regarded children pastorally. Our legacy confirms that we have failed to give serious consideration to the pastoral and spiritual needs of children. We have been more concerned with providing instruction in the faith than with listening to children's souls and hearing and valuing what is important to them. Generally, we have allowed our concern for children to be wholly expressed in preventative and instructional ways. In spite of the caring intentions embodied within these means, they are inadequate for addressing the depth and range of spiritual and pastoral issues present in children. Nor can they be classified as forms of pastoral care. The effectiveness of these educational and preventative strategies has varied considerably, and it is obvious that our muddled responses to children leave considerable work to be done. Only rarely have we genuinely remembered to include children in the provision of our pastoral care and in our work of training people in the faith community to become better caregivers. Mostly, we have failed miserably to grasp that children need to receive the care of a church community. Our pastoral neglect of children has included our blindness to their spiritual questions, longings, and needs.

It is not only within Protestant ministries of pastoral care that this is so. The practice of spiritual direction also has failed to mine the potential riches of providing spiritual direction for children. Ordinarily, spiritual direction is a ministry for persons who identify their readiness for it and who are in a position to claim its resources for their spiritual enrichment. Yet children normally do not ask for help in determining whether school is good for them, what food will provide the best nourishment, or what is appropriate to watch on television. Nor are they expected to pay for their own piano lessons or soccer club memberships. When it comes to any matter of emotional, physical, or spiritual health, young children are less likely to initiate and more prone to respond to guidance and structure. While there may be some exceptions to the norm, children usually have been excluded from the opportunity to form a regular relationship with a spiritual director. They are not considered eligible candidates for spiritual direction and they lack the awareness and means to initiate such relationships.

Our failure to welcome the little ones among us, our refusal to take seriously their spiritual potential, and our inability to listen for our children's souls has greatly diminished our spirituality, and it has cost the church a great deal in terms of its collective spirituality and vision. It may well be one of the many reasons children drift away from the church in later childhood. If young children are not affirmed in their real bond between themselves and God, and if they lack opportunities to bond with God and respond to that authentic encounter, then the older child's behavior and response may well reflect the lack of such loving reality.

Even though the church has underestimated and underutilized the young child's spiritual potential, it has faithfully attempted to express concern for children. The church's concern is embodied in three commonly used forms that can be summarized as (1) safeguarding our children by developing their sense of Christian identity and inclusion in Christian community; (2) concern for the emotional well-being and crises children have in their lives; and (3) ensuring that our little ones are sufficiently socialized in the spirit and doctrine of the Christian faith. It is helpful to examine each of these strategies more fully. While each has contributed positively in efforts to attend to the souls of our children, each also has serious limitations. The fact is that there remains a lingering and unsettling gap in our pastoral care, a gap that reveals our failure to take seriously the child's soul and the child's potential to develop a living, bonded relationship with God.

Three Common Forms of Concern for Children

Ensuring Christian Identity and the Inclusion of Children. The church has always claimed birth as a rite of passage that can establish the faith community's role in expressing concern for a child's religious life. In several mainline Protestant churches this takes the form of celebrating the sacrament of infant baptism. In other Protestant churches the form is also liturgical but identified as a service of *thanksgiving/celebration for the birth/gift of a child* or a service of *infant/parental dedication*. Common to these rituals is the church's desire to ensure the spiritual identity and well-being of the children among us. Although they are not usually identified as an expression of pastoral care, but rather as a liturgical or sacramental ministry, such rites have embodied an explicit and implicit concern for the child. In a *marker moment*, the child is affirmed as one who is loved by God, and these rites enable the parent(s) and the faith community to express publicly their concern for the child's future spiritual life and faith development.

In many ways, the promises made by the faith community at this time are explicit statements of caring concern. Promises to help support and nurture the child, as well as to help the child and the child's parent(s) to live up to their promises, are all indications of intent to care for the spiritual well-being of the child. This lifelong commitment of love toward the child aims to place the child's needs before our own. In some congregations, including *faith friends* or *godparents* provides a further level of commitment to the provision of ongoing care and involvement in the child's life. Through the church's liturgical or sacramental act, the child is bathed in the caring message: "You are not alone."

Unfortunately, some have mistakenly understood this ritual as a preventative act or a magical moment that will rust-proof (or even fire-proof) the child's soul for life! Such popular fiction usually expresses an underlying parental and spiritual concern for the child's very soul. This is understandable, since we know that life is unpredictable. Because we are neither immune to the vicissitudes of life nor the various *isms*, prejudices, and injustices that happen, we have legitimate concern for our children's future. No one wants a child's soul to experience unnecessary torment or anguish. By gathering around the child, we are stating our intention to view the child as central to our ministry and care. However short-lived the moment may be, we are professing a desire to help children learn how to turn away from the spell of abusive power and the human drive to dominate and control, and instead to claim the power of mutual love and service.

Over the years, concern for our children expressed in this early ritual has led the church to place its primary focus on the parents as a means toward realizing the spiritual identity of the child. This is certainly appropriate, and our educational and pastoral care support of parents needs both to continue and to be strengthened.[5] Within the church community as a whole, we must do our best to provide a healthy spiritual atmosphere in which all of us can live out the commitments we make and in which our young children can grow, learn, and bond in their relationship with God. If this kind of concern is left solely to the parents of the child, then we will simply be communicating that spirituality is an individual matter, rather than a dynamic and ongoing discovery and pilgrimage of the whole community.

The challenge that this common strategy places before us is how to take more seriously the child's own potential to develop a living and bonded relationship with God. Too often we assume that children will develop faith by osmosis and form their relationship with God simply by traipsing in and around the church! Our verbal promises to care for the child's spiritual development are presumed to be fulfilled through the church's various means of Christian education, nurture, confirmation or believer's baptism, and worship. We can no longer take this for granted. We need to create an environment specifically designed for young children and to provide opportunities of ritual, reflection, prayer, and story through which children can meet God—not just learn about God—and thereby form a relationship with God that is both real and wondrous. Children need to experience a loving God as present in their lives. Telling them about a loving God in the hope that in the future they will come to understand and experience God for themselves neglects their present potentiality for a lively and spontaneous spirituality.

Concern for Children's Crises. Since much of our pastoral care is about sharing and expressing God's love in ways that affirm that each person belongs
to God, then providing pastoral care to children who are in the Christian
community ought to be a natural and vital part of our commitment to be a
pastorally caring community. In general, Protestant churches have
responded insufficiently to this challenge. Within congregations, we continue to encounter attitudes and feelings that block people from offering
effective pastoral care to children. Authors Herbert Anderson and Susan
Johnson have asserted that "our children are in trouble partly because adults
disdain childhood"[6] and they further suggest that "we have fostered a culture
of indifference toward our children."[7] The reluctance of adults to accept
their own vulnerabilities leads them to define children as small, weak, and
needful. Disdain for children is further reflected in adult resistance to viewing children as fully human and embodying all human dimensions and
responses to life. Some adults, for example, have been conditioned to think
of childhood as the time of innocence, fun, play, and blissful ignorance of
the stresses and strains of life. When children express pain, it can be dismissed, ignored, or minimized because some adults truly do not believe that
children can have crises in their lives.

More recent public disclosures and research studies have shown us that
this is simply not true. Children suffer terribly from neglect, poverty, abuse,
violence in schools, depression, racism, gender inequities in the classroom,
advertising pressures, Internet and substance addictions, and eating disor-
ders, just to name a few terrors and problems. Children may have different
reactions to the stresses and conflicts of their lives, but they do feel them.
And if their feelings, losses, and fears are not expressed or dealt with in a
clear and sensitive manner, then these will continue to affect their relationships, their relationship with God, and their ability to cope with the world
later in life. Congregations are stewards of the mysteries of the children in
their midst. Caring adults will respond to all of the *stuff* of children's lives.

Pastoral care with children can also be severely compromised by the
prevailing belief that parents should be the primary caregivers. Many people
believe parents should be the only caregivers. Too often when children need
pastoral care, it is not offered because of a misguided fear of stepping onto
parental turf. We fear the accusation: "Mind your own business and stop
interfering." Such attitudes reflect the individualistic approach we have
taken with our children.[8] By keeping acts of care solely within the domain
of the family, we have relinquished the important role the entire church
community can play as nurturers, mentors, and wise elders. Children need
a variety of nurturing relationships in their lives in order to ensure that gaps

are addressed and to offer to them an image of God as Love that stretches beyond their immediate parental figures.

Another attitude that affects the church's potential to offer pastoral care to children is the discomfort or awkwardness many adults feel around children. The familiar adage "children are to be seen and not heard" comes to many minds too quickly. Children can make us feel ill at ease because they are too noisy, too curious, too restless, and too unlike adults. Their very *otherness* can lead many adults to ignore or avoid them, turning instead toward other adults for conversation and relationship. Such feelings serve to blind and block us from the needs of children for the support, friendship, and care of adults. By protecting ourselves from their energy and by protecting our own interests, we contribute to the marginalization of our children in the church. Our children, whom we identified as *somebodies* and called by name at the time we recognized their birth or celebrated their baptism, can too quickly become *nobodies* whose names we no longer know. When a pastoral crisis does occur in a household, we easily focus on adult grief, loss, and worry; yet it is not so automatic for us to place within our vision the children who are equally affected by the crisis. Making sure the adults cope assumes a higher pastoral priority than checking out how the children are doing.

Moving beyond these attitudes and learned behaviors is a challenge for the church in its responsiveness to the pastoral needs of children. It requires the community's conversion from thinking that pastoral care for children is incidental or that it is the special assignment of pastors, children's choir directors, church school teachers, and parents to recognizing that providing care for children is everyone's responsibility. Everyone has the responsibility to kneel to chat with children. If "it takes a village to raise a child" then the corollary is also true: "it takes a church to care for a child's soul." Everyone has a part to play in creating a community where children feel that they do belong to God, are valued, are taken seriously, and are loved beyond measure.

Some faith communities already have grasped the importance of including children in pastoral visits to people in the congregation and of making appropriate arrangements to visit just with children. We are beginning to learn that children are not helped when they are inappropriately protected from life's realities or excluded from what is going on. They are helped most when they are informed and when their questions are heard and dealt with sensitively and honestly. Obviously, it is important to be aware of the reality of child abuse in our society, and thus to secure the permission of the child's parent(s) or guardian if entering the home. If a child visits with us in the church building, then we can invite another adult to remain nearby. We can make sure that the door to the room remains open and that the child is positioned closest to the open door. A *child-friendly* environment is also important as part of letting children know that they are cared for. Keeping toys, stuffed animals, children's books, puppets, paper, and crayons at hand are relatively simple ways to make buildings and rooms places where children feel that they are cared about.

Visiting with a child can be especially meaningful when he or she is in crisis. We are also now much more aware of the impact upon children and their siblings when a family member dies.[9] We recognize also that children respond to various kinds of fears and losses, such as the death of a pet, a parent who moves out of the home, an older sibling who departs for college, a move to another city or country, a loss of a neighborhood friend, or the loss of health due to accident, cancer, or genetic disease. A child facing heart surgery, a child with a diagnosed learning disability, and a child being moved into foster care are but some of the situations that evoke crisis for a child.

Some pastoral care teams have discovered the value of sending notes or cards to children telling them they are being thought of and remembered in prayer during such times. Another way of caring for children is to develop a group of people whose sole commitment is to pray for church members, including the children in their midst. The names of children can be on this prayer list and this group can remember children who are particularly ill, troubled, or sad. Parents may even make a request to this group for prayer for their child. While this is not always a highly visible expression of concern for children, it provides significant support for our children who are experiencing difficult times.

What remains a challenge for us in developing a more comprehensive program of pastoral care for children is to take the next step to care for the soul of the child and to care for it in all of life's circumstances. This means continuing to address the child's grief, but also becoming intentional about paying attention to the child's soul during and after that time of grief. All too often our pastoral care with children is expressed by a reversion to using *baby-talk* with them, or by *talking to* them, *talking down* to them, or *talking once* with them about the crisis. Relating to a child's soul begins by taking its existence seriously and showing genuine interest, both when they speak and when they are silent.

Children do not always know how to put their feelings or longings into words. They frequently find it easier to express their relationship in non-verbal ways. Children's language is often composed of actions and interior attitudes more than words. Drawing, painting, making music, playing, or writing a letter or poem are but a few ways we can open up the child's inner world and listen for the soul of a child in crisis. It is also true that children will not always ask their questions the first time they are encouraged to express what is happening around them and inside of them. They will express them in their own time. Caring for children's souls involves befriending them and allowing them to share parts of their lives with us in a constant, evolving relationship of care. Adults providing care need to learn to be respectful of the child's pace, which will differ from their own. Sometimes it means learning how to wait, convinced that silence does not mean the soul is hiding, but simply pausing or processing.

Sometimes caring for children does mean asking them leading questions that draw out their souls' yearnings. Children do not need God presented to them in childish terms. They have a profound sense of the majesty of God and they easily speak of God. One of our tasks as adults is to get past our own reluctance to use God-language in a direct fashion with children. We need to be open to hear how the child is experiencing God during the unfolding crisis and to invite the child to give expression to his or her relationship with God. Sometimes this means listening closely for the questions about God that children themselves raise and then inviting them to speculate on their own answers.[10] At other times, it means asking some open-ended and leading questions:

* How do you find God?
* Are you waiting for God?
* Is God with you?
* What is God doing?
* Can you tell me what God is like?[11]
* What is God saying to you?
* What are you saying to God?

Another question that I like to keep in the back of my mind for my own reflection is: "What is the image of God that the child needs?" An old but marvelous anecdote illustrates the significance of this pastoral question. A little child is afraid of a fierce thunderstorm and runs to a parent, who says, "Don't be afraid. God is with you." The child replies: "I know, but I like people with skin on."

A comprehensive pastoral care will refuse to limit itself to times of crisis in children's lives. It will move beyond responsiveness to crisis and become proactive in expressing care for the child's soul in all of life's ordinariness. Are we constant in caring about how a child feels safe in God, waits for God, and finds God?

Concern for Children's Faith Knowledge. In addition to solidifying a child's identity as a child of God and caring for children in times of crisis, there is a third strategy that the church has traditionally employed to express its concern for children. The church has tried to make sure that children are familiar with biblical stories and the basic message of the gospel. We have generally assumed that if we share with children the religious tradition, especially the story of Jesus' birth, life, ministry, death, and resurrection, then we have given them resources for finding a purpose to life and for making and maintaining meaning in life. Among the reasons for this ministry, usually identified more as an educational task than a pastoral one, is the felt need to express concern for children's ongoing faith development. If we care enough to give them a religious tradition, then we are caring about their well-being, their future, and their spiritual lives. In essence, this is a preventative approach.

Sometimes it has worked, often because of the quality, character, and commitment of individual teachers who by their very nature make sure that faith is more *caught* than *taught*. Increasingly, however, the local church community is no longer being regarded as a place for the socialization of children into religious traditions. In many ways, the concept of a *Sunday school* has outlived its time. For various reasons, neither the Sunday time nor the structure of a school is sacred anymore. Learning about the content of the faith happens more often within the context of the entire faith community and perhaps less within structured and grade-defined classroom time. Where Sunday schools still exist, some parents simply drop off their children without coming to church themselves. This covertly gives the message to children that what they are doing is only marginally important and that it is not relevant to all of their lives, especially when they grow up.

We also know only too well that children drift away as they mature. While there are many contributing factors to this trend, it is clear that the provision of religious information is not adequate as a singular measure for ensuring that a child's soul needs are taken seriously. The content needs a lived context and experience that can be reflected upon and responded to according to the child's own rhythm. This requires an atmosphere that assures the child that there is a constancy, respect, and regularity to their relationships within the faith community.

Too often Christian religious education[12] is so goal-oriented, lectionary-focused, and curriculum-conscious that it loses sight of its opportunities to minister to the spiritual life of the child.[13] Concern for children's faith knowledge can easily degenerate into locked-in agendas, indoctrination, or vapid *sharing times* that disregard the mystery of God and the fruit of children's contemplation of and reverence for the mystery of God. We know, for example, how to teach about horses: provide videos about them for children to watch, encourage children to draw them, and learn what disciplines will take care of horses. It is only when children regularly mount and ride horses, however, that they internalize the experience and become connected to particular horses and horses in general.

This analogy is applicable to the content of the faith. Studying and learning about Jesus is essential, but if an experience of Jesus is lacking, then we have missed a vital step in our care for the child's soul. In many ways, "children apprehend more than they comprehend."[14] With regard to Jesus, we have generally tended to center upon the history of Jesus' life, following its development from birth to resurrection, to the exclusion of initiating children more directly into the mystery of the person of Jesus, his relationship with us, and our ability to respond to him, including through prayer, ritual, and times of silence.[15]

A major component of the church's educational ministry has been a special concern for the moral and ethical formation of our children. Church schoolteachers and parents alike want children to grow up with an awareness of right and wrong and knowledge of Christian values, especially the golden rule. Growing up in a framework that exposes children to Christianity seems to be a primary motivation these days for baby boomers. Boomers can be quite insistent that their little ones learn ways and means to inform their adulthood, the aim being the production of good kids and eventually a world of good neighbors and nice people. It is tempting for the church to be seduced by this agenda and to ignore developmental data that tell us that, in early years, the soul of the child is focused on yearnings for parental and divine protection. It is only in later childhood that children enter a period of moral sensitivity, moving eventually in adolescent years to seek models and heroes that reflect these laudable moral and ethical values.

There is a time for everything, and early childhood is not the time for intense moral effort. Early childhood is more a period of growth into the enjoyment of the persons and things that are freely given. For this reason, any faith content that is provided is not so much to direct the child in the immediate present to some moral realization, but for the completion of the child's being at home in and with God. In fact, what is Christian morality if not the response to God's love and our reaction to our encounter with God? The challenge for us in caring pastorally for our children is to refrain from any prompting to elicit a moral conclusion but instead to announce over and over again God's love and to help children to experience and enjoy it in his or her own reflection and prayer. The more deeply felt and enjoyed the young child's spiritual experience is, the more eager, autonomous, and authentic will be the response of the older child. Interestingly enough, the fact that, in later adulthood, the image of God as *Judge* often dominates may be due to our inappropriate proclivity to correlate early childhood Christian religious education with moral instruction. There simply is too much risk here in creating confusion for children about the friendlier face of God.

Each of these strategies that express concern for our children is significant, and together they constitute some important caring intentions that need to continue on behalf of young children. But taken alone—or even lumped together—each needs to go further to address the whole being and spiritual life of the child. Rituals soon after birth may be caring acts that signify or seal a child's identity as a child of God, but they do not guarantee that the child's soul will be heard and nourished in subsequent years. Nor do they guard the child from the soul's own deep questions or the turmoil and anguish that come from living life to its fullest. Caring for children in crisis is a vital aspect of our pastoral care with children, but responding to crisis can overlook the child's soul in the crisis as well as in more ordinary times and events in the child's life. Caring about children's faith knowledge is essential, but children are so much more than empty vessels needing to be filled with religious data to vaccinate them against life's slings and arrows of outrageous fortune, or lumps of clay needing to be molded with instructions and rules for right living. In coming to terms with these pastoral challenges in our ministries with children, it is important to challenge our thinking about the spiritual potential of the young child.

The spiritually alert soul of the child

Let me tell you about my pastoral encounter with six-year-old Susie. One day she flatly pronounced to me that Jesus had come with her today and was with us in the room. "Oh?" was all I could get out of my mouth before she went on to say, "He's wearing sandals just like yours." I replied, "I'm glad to know that, Susie. They're really comfortable shoes. Do either you or Jesus want to talk with me about anything today?" "Yeah," Susie answered. "Jesus wants me to tell you to tell all the other children only to listen to adults with soft eyes, soft eyes like his." This was a particularly striking comment since Susie had not grown up in a family that attended church. She had no religious instruction and had no formal relationship to the Christian church. Yet Jesus was a real person who walked and talked with her. Susie's Jesus was someone with whom she had a real relationship. She listened for his voice, and his "soft-eyed" presence in her life was clearly a source of protection and comfort for her soul.

In another encounter, a mother tells the story of her five-year-old son who one day blurted out the question: "Who do you love more, me or God?" The mother replied: "Of course I love you more." I wonder if it would surprise you to hear that the child then responded: "I think this is your big mistake."[16]

Both of these illustrations seem to suggest that these young children's words surpass a child's ordinary spiritual capacity, either by formulation or content. They raise the possibility that children have active souls that are acutely aware of the spiritual dimension of life prior to any serious promptings in life that are more cultural in character. Children seem to know things, including spiritual things, that no one has told them. They are spiritually alert and listen naturally for the voice of God. These moments may be like exclamation marks or elusive episodes that, like a flash bulb going off on a camera, shine vibrantly for a while and then fade away until another picture frame is advanced. What they do suggest, however, is that there is some mysterious reality and awareness of the holy present in the child, and we are able to glimpse it. The fact that we are dealing with elusive episodes "does not invalidate their importance, because it is proper to the child to live at first in a discontinuous way the riches (s)he possesses, which only gradually and through the aid of the environment later become a constant *habitus* in the child."[17]

It is my conviction that children possess an innate spiritual hunger and openness and that this is felt and deeply evident in children who are first and foremost in need of love and/or are rich in love. Since human beings are not satisfied with merely living, but yearn to live as people who are loved and loving, it follows that the child has this same existential need yearning to be satisfied. Even in cases where a child may be spiritually malnourished, and even preceding any formal religious instruction, there is potential for the existence of a mysterious bond between God and the child. There is a kind of natural bond between the child and God, who is first and foremost Love. The fact that a child seems capable of seeing the invisible, almost as if it were more tangible and real than the immediate reality, ought not to surprise us. Young children have wild and wonderful imaginations that can penetrate effortlessly beyond the veil of the visible. They see and bear with the utmost facility transcendent or truthful meaning. It is often as if there is no barrier between the worlds of the visible and invisible. That is why young children are often such good judges of human character. They know instinctively whom to trust and whom to fear. Children can recognize the intentions that lie behind *soft* or *hard* eyes.

This capacity of the young child to move with relative ease in the world of the transcendent, and who delights in contact with God, led one researcher to introduce the phrase "the metaphysical child."[18] The metaphysical child turns to God from a profound need within the child's nature. The child needs an infinite, global love beyond that which a human being is able to give. For the child, love is almost more necessary than food. Because it is in contact with God that a child experiences an unfailing love, the child is somewhat predisposed to a spiritual life. Far from imposing a spiritual life upon a child, we are reverencing the child's own soul that in an authentic exigence of life longs to come closer and closer to God. It is in contact with God that the child finds the nourishment the child needs to grow in stature, harmony, beauty, and strength.

The younger the child, the more capable the child is of receiving great things and of experiencing the satisfaction that comes with encountering great and essential things. In spite of our temptation to disbelieve, the young child is deeply serious, and the child's soul is capable of drawing closer to the core of things without getting lost in the superfluous trappings that often prevent adults from discovering what is essential. The implications for our pastoral care with children are striking. Too often in our pastoral care with children, we are not sufficiently serious, and we dumb down or succumb to using diminutives with children. As adults, because we often do not grasp theological knowledge ourselves or allow it to travel to the nucleus of our hearts and souls, we project that same struggle upon our little ones.

Yet the truth is otherwise. Children can deal with the greatest realities that we neglect to give them. The assumed incapacity of the young child becomes our way of rationalizing our own uncertainty, ignorance, and distress and serves to exempt us from the necessity of further spiritual exploration. We need to stop being afraid of approaching the great themes and signs with young children, and we must demonstrate a willingness to handle the profound questions raised by young ones. Children will ask questions that go to the heart of the matter and that arise out of the soul of the young questioner. These are questions like: Who made God? How big is God? Why do we have to die? How does God travel? Does God sleep? What does God wear? How we handle such spiritual matters as a way of listening to and enriching the soul of the child is the subject of the following section.

Becoming soul-Listeners for children

In suggesting that we err by being reductionist with young children, that we need not restrict our pastoral care to classroom situations or home visits, and that we need not include presentations of Christian moral principles, I am building upon my conviction that the most important thing we can do with

young children is to reverence, listen to, and provide their souls with opportunities to encounter the living God. It is important both to get a handle on
the role that we can have with young children and to explore ways and
means for attending to a child's soul and spiritual development.

As we contemplate our role in listening for and attending to the souls of
our children, the first step we can take is to relinquish past notions that have
shaped and influenced our ministries of caring for children. Some of these
past notions simply get in the way of listening for the child's soul. For example, we are often too obsessed with achieving successful children's programs
in the hopes that this will strengthen our adult membership. Boosting our
numbers in church school is far less important than ensuring that whatever
children are among us are able to "drink from the living streams." Counting
our children and being concerned about the appearance of success can
derail energies that are better placed in siding with these little ones and facilitating their relationship with God. Just as children have an eye for what is
essential, the challenge before us is to center our care for children in what
is essential.

Whether we admit it or not, we probably have functioned with and clung
to the assumption that children must become like us rather than the idea that
we must change and become like them. In our relationship with children,
this is one of the most important things for us to grasp. Jesus himself suggested this when he said to the disciples: "Unless you change and become
like little children, you will never enter the kingdom of heaven."[19] A common
interpretation of this is that we are to emulate those easily observed characteristics of children: readily excitable, basically trusting, easy to please, and
energetic. What if Jesus were calling us to something far more serious and
involved? To "become like little children" is about being on a constant journey of growth, transformation, and change.[20] One of the most important
changes we can make in our relationship with children is to transform the
way we look at them and treat them. In order to become more like them, we
must first come to know them and what their relationship with God is like.
Inevitably, if we listen, children will lead us to God. They will give us some
precious insights into what it means to have a relationship with God.

Yet another transformation is required. As stated earlier, we have tended
to intrude too readily upon our children, either with religious content that is
premature to their development, or by talking *to* them instead of *with* them.
It is important to know when to stop intruding, when to keep silent, and
when to withdraw and have faith that God is present in the mystery of what
is happening. This may require more self-control than child-control. If we
can do this, then we are beginning to embody an attitude of respect and

wonder, and we are beginning to see children as mystery in somewhat the same way as we see God as mystery. This attitude of respect and true hunger to know a child will open us up to a new and deeper level of absorption and appreciation in the things of God that we contemplate with them.

What I am proposing represents a major shift in the ways we relate to children. Rather than coming between a child and God, I am suggesting that we stand back to allow such contact to occur. This is not to say that we have nothing to contribute or to do. On the contrary, we have the clear task of initiating the child into certain realities. We do this by drawing upon several potential sources and resources that can help children to discover for themselves the presence of God. In this sense, our role as a pastorally caring faith community is perhaps most akin to the role Eli assumed with young Samuel. By reverencing the child, the child discovers reverence. We become soul-listeners who make sure the conditions are safe, the right means and resources are available, and the focus remains on the presence and mystery of God. This is so that the child's own discoveries, conversations, and contacts can be made. It implies the preparation of suitable physical and emotional environments in which children can feel secure, their imaginations can flourish, and the life of God can be encountered, received, and assimilated. The task of the caring community is to discern the optimum means to help young children listen for God.

Revealing children's soulfulness

I want to propose at least three means to help young children listen for God. These involve the creation of conditions in which children can meet, experience, contemplate, and respond to God. Whether or not they are truly *optimum* is best discerned by the individual faith community, its vision, and its commitments. Certainly they are not the only ways that children can meet God. I present them here as modest suggestions that can be expanded upon or modified according to particular needs and church contexts.

I refer to each of these three means as an *enticement*. If we are like Eli, then our role is to entice children into the habit of listening for the voice of God in their souls. We invite children to experience the fascination and attraction of God. The sole purpose of the enticements is to encourage children to receive and delight in the reality of a loving God. The enticements are opportunities for children to have personal spiritual experiences, to sense God's presence, and to understand, contemplate, and enjoy God's closeness.

The first enticement is the use of *rituals* designed for children that involve their participation and include signs and scripture, the second is through specifically chosen tangible objects that focus on *wonder* as a dynamic value, and the third is through *prayer* that takes the forms of praise, recollection, and silence.

Enticement to Ritual

"Humans are made for ritual," writes John Westerhoff, and "in turn our rituals make us."[21] Children especially are captivated by rituals and the visual and sensual majesty and pomp that often accompany them. Most of us can testify to seeing children's wide-eyed wonder when the candles are lit on a cake that somehow mysteriously appears year after year on a birthday. We have witnessed children gasp at the sight of sparkling brass instruments in an annual Christmas or Easter parade and take for granted that Santa Claus will finally appear on that sleigh with eight tiny reindeer. So, too, the church can care for its young ones by involving them in rituals that hold a similar kind of power to contribute to the growth of their spirituality. Rituals have the power to enchant and inspire the contemplation of our young children. Such rituals can be liturgical in nature or simply repetitive acts that provide a ritual context for communicating to children that what is presented is a word beyond all other words. Rituals can transmit meaning and make meaningful the experiences of children's daily lives. Children will be enticed to meet God through their own participation in visual and sensory ritualization. Ritual allows them to touch and feel for themselves the mystery and majesty of God.

A Place for Children's Ritual. In most of our churches, we have sequestered our children in instructional classrooms or learning centers in the church building. Many churches have done their best to make sure that these are child-friendly and conducive to the creative activities and minds of our young ones. What if we also considered creating, alongside educationally defined rooms, a place where holy ritual takes place—an *atrium* for children?[22] In ancient Christian basilicas, the atrium was the space that served as the anteroom of the church, both in the material and metaphorical sense of the word. The atrium is less a traditional place of classroom instruction than an environment that will be felt by children to be a holy place where they could expect to meet and have conversations with God.[23] It is the space that falls between the instructional classroom and the church sanctuary and the place where the child begins to live a spiritual life through meditation and prayer. In some ways, it is akin to ensuring that young children have their own retreat house within the church walls.

It can be clearly communicated to the congregation that the atrium is an area restricted to the children. There needs to be a soul-listener, one who functions as a spiritual guide and mentor for the children. Apart from this guiding adult, other adults enter only with the permission of the children. This is a place where the children can feel themselves held by God, and it is a space totally dedicated to their spiritual lives. It will be designed with their lives in mind. The children themselves may wish to give the room a name. It is helpful to have special furnishings such as a child's table, cushions, prayer rug, some rocks or pine branches, a flower in a vase, or other decorations appropriate for children. The table could be covered with a prayer cloth that can be changed by the children according to corresponding liturgical colors of the season. This area is not a substitute for the chapel or the sanctuary, since these are also important areas where the whole faith community gathers for prayer and worship, including the children. It is simply to be identified as the children's atrium, a quiet place where children go to hear the scriptures, light the candle, reflect, respond, and pray.

An Example of Children's Ritual. A ritual in the atrium provides children with an experience of being reverent. The focus is not to learn about God but to experience God.[24] During an atrium ritual, the children might first gather around the table while there is a symbolic placing of the Bible on the table by one of the children. It is important that the Bible be found not only in the hands of the adults but also in the hands of the children, whether they can read or not. Just as a child may not be able to count candles on a cake, they are still encouraged to blow them out. Then the guiding adult presents the content of the day's scripture text in his or her own words. This is a retelling of the story that is faithful to its essential form. The text, of course, is carefully chosen in light of the children's stages of development. It is usually not a passage in its entirety, but yet is complete in itself. It is preferably more than a single verse, but assembling several single verses from various texts is not recommended. During Advent, the focus may be an infancy narrative, or at another time of the year, perhaps a parable such as the Woman and the Lost Coin (Luke 15:8-10) or the parable of the Good Shepherd (John 10:3b-6, 11-16),[25] both of which express the personal love and protective presence of God.

The children may be prompted by open-ended questions that enable them to reflect on what they have heard. It is important not to answer the questions for the children or to provide explanations. Children need to make their own meaning in contemplation of the text. Taking the infancy narrative, for instance, we might say: "We too are at the crib. What shall we say?" Using the parable of the Good Shepherd, we might comment on the sheep as loved and protected, and then ask, "What sheep was Jesus talking about?"

"What names do the sheep have?" The children will grasp on their own and in their own time that the text hides something deep and precious to be discovered. What is discovered will be their enjoyment and recognition of God.

Next, the children can light the candle and hear the actual scripture text as it is read slowly and solemnly from the book. It may be read by a child or by the adult. After a few minutes of silence, during which the children ponder the Word they have heard, they may be invited to respond. The response may be in spoken form, drawing, or working with small figures (wooden, Lego, cloth, felt) that enable them to reenact the story in their own words and actions. Finally, the children can offer spontaneous expressions of prayer (this is described more fully in the third enticement—enticement to prayer), followed by the ritual extinguishing of the candle in order to return to the next event, which may be corporate worship, Sunday school, junior choir, or the trip home.

The Purpose of Children's Ritual. I want to emphasize that this kind of atrium experience is not the same as having children learn about the scriptures or study them with a didactic or moralizing purpose. Rather, it is a time for children to experience revelation, to linger with God, rest in God, hear the mystery of God, ponder the marvel of what they have heard, and come to know God better. It is a time for children to enter a more intuitive mode of consciousness and to engage their affections so that they develop a spirituality not only of mind, but also of heart and soul.

The experience of ritual in the atrium is not intended to subtract from the necessity of formal Christian education, but to supplement it with experiences that enable children to go beyond the words of scripture and to meet and spend time with God, who is signified in the words. As a supplemental experience, it need not happen weekly, although some sort of regular rhythm of entering the atrium is important to establish. Through this ritualization, we are enticing children to take a leap of faith beyond what can be seen in order to encounter the unseen. Children are capable of this leap. Through ritual, children grasp the invisible and move beyond what their eyes see and their hands touch. If children are immersed in the ritual, it will speak to them with its intrinsic richness.

One of the reasons the provision of ritual is so important is because ritual evokes memory. When the ritual is over, the child remembers the parts that comprised it. Young children have the ability to evoke an object in its absence by means of an image or memory. Ritual assists the evocation of children's memories of God. By providing ritualization at such a young age, children are enabled early on to read their everyday world as a life full of signs that point beyond the surface to the presence of God. In essence, by enticing children through ritual, we entice them toward a habit of listening to their own souls.

Liturgical Ritual and Children. The atrium experience can be carried over into the environment of the faith community's worship. Involving young children in the liturgical rituals of the worshipping community is important. Young children can serve as acolytes, ushers, pray-ers, candle lighters, readers, and carriers of bread and wine, and they can help pour water from a jug into the baptismal font or tank. When children are participating in liturgical rituals, it is important to give them opportunities to practice and rehearse their roles so that they gain familiarity with the ritual. Children no more want to fail or mess up in public functions than adults. Because worship holds such power and mystery for children, clear instructions about their role and our expectations of their participation will enhance the richness of their experience of the ritual.

Linking Rituals of Church and Home. Similarly, the environment of the family home can become an avenue for building upon the atrium experience. I have already suggested that this can be done through creating a personal area for the child within his or her room or a family room within the home.

Yet another way this experience can be translated into the home is by reviving the lost art of family devotions and developing a ritual framework for such daily devotions. Establishing a regular time and place and a routine will make household devotions into a ritual that is anticipated. It is important to have prior agreement that the time will not be violated by phone calls, sports, homework, or meetings. Household devotions can be a natural part of the day and can occur at a meal, before bath-time or teeth-brushing time, or even at bedtime. Candle lighting, a quiet moment, reading, reflection, and prayer are guiding parts of the family ritual. Congregations demonstrate pastoral care for children when they provide or encourage the use of family devotional material. This has the secondary benefit of helping parents learn to listen, contemplate, and pray. By helping children, we help parents. Many resources are available these days that are illustrated storybooks or compilations of daily readings, spiritual thoughts, and prayers. Some pastoral care committees include in their ministry the task of compiling a household devotional booklet comprising material compiled and written by church members. A book fair sponsored by a denominational or religious bookstore during coffee time following worship may be another way to help parents choose appropriate resource materials for their children.

Enticement to Wonder

Another way we can reverence the soul of a child and make a contribution toward its development is through creating an atmosphere where curiosity and wonder are aroused. We often refer to children's "wide-eyed wonder." Most things evoke wonder for children because most things are new to them. Wonder draws us forward with an almost irresistible force toward that which has astonished us. Wonder is a dynamic value that immerses us in the contemplation of something that exceeds our grasp.

Young children have a natural sense of wonder that includes not only the material but also the spiritual realm. They may not verbalize or give explanations for surprising kinds of events, but they have a spirit of expectation and sense the beauty that surrounds such events. They experience the joy of celebration, the compelling glow of the Advent wreath, and the stillness that comes in hushed form on Christmas Eve. They know the joy of Easter, the mysterious change of purple to white cloth on the life-size wooden cross, and have feelings in relation to the signs of Easter present in home, church, and society. Wonder is spontaneous to the child, and it is important not to extinguish this emotional and affective capacity, but to emphasize it as a way of entering into what is real. We can entice our children to wonder so that it becomes a habit of their souls, nourishing their adult spirituality. By providing young children with experiences of wonder, we find that, rather than merely repeating spiritual language we have given them, they discover their own spontaneous and candid expressions of the soul.

Too often, by the time we reach adulthood, we have had the capacity for wonder drained from us. Life's experiences, cynicism, and tribulations can temper our sense of amazement. We can lose our sense of surprise and are no longer astonished by anything. It is as if there is nothing we have not seen, and the posture of approaching something in the world as if for the very first time seems like an old piece of clothing that we threw away a long time ago. Wonder can be too easily squelched, and yet it is essential for linking our souls to the living God who is so amazing, so divine. The whole point of enticing children to wonder is to enable them to develop a relationship with God, who can be known, yet is always full of surprises.

To entice children to wonder, adults may want to open themselves once more to the *wow* in life. Can we feel awe over something strange, unexpected, or incredible that happens to us? Do we speak amazement over a redheaded woodpecker we have never seen before? Are we astonished by all the different kinds of drums, musical sounds, and rhythms of life? Can we gaze at a snapshot of the planet earth and wondrously imagine our world without borders and fences? If adults hope to arouse similar feelings of wonder in children, it helps for us to be in touch with them ourselves. If we feel a sense of wonderment about the nature of God or over something God has done, this sense of admiration and reverence can spill over into our words and actions and be captured by children. This means being willing to show that we are awed by the splendor and majesty of God and that we can still feel and express spontaneous awe over the unexplainable mysteries of life.

Children will be enticed to wonder when we provide stimuli that are worthy of their rapt attention. With young children, it is important to use concrete objects that they can see, hear, touch, taste, or smell. Children love child-friendly items that are very hands-on and that involve their whole selves. This is why children are fascinated by space or science museums where they can participate in exhibits or displays. The simple act of handling an actual piece of moon rock can lead a child to wonder about the immensity of the universe. Tangible objects provide a link to their own experiences, at the same time pointing to the intangible. The temporal objects that we use need to be capable of taking the child into deeper and further awareness of reality—divine mystery—the beauty of God that inspires and captivates us. They need to be able to capture children's deep desires, yearnings, and feelings, and give wings to their aspirations.

Soul-listeners for children need to choose these tangible objects carefully so that they are capable of giving the child an experience of God while simultaneously expanding the child's contemplative process and constantly exceeding the child's world. For a child's sense of wonder to flourish, the object must stimulate beyond the boundaries of the object itself and cause the child to wonder about the source of the limitlessness suggested by the object. Whatever tangible item is selected, it should enrich and beautify children's lives, stimulate both thought and feeling, and point to God.

If we offer young children too many stimuli and shift their attention too quickly, we may actually diminish their affective capacity for wonder. A child can develop a spirit of indifference toward the object of attention if the child's focus is shifted too quickly. The child may come to see the object only in terms of its surface characteristics and not its deeper, hidden beauty. "If the child does not have the time to dwell on anything, then everything will come to seem the same"[26] and the child will lose all interest in things. This presents a challenge to what has been our predominant thinking in working with young children. We have assumed that children will grow weary with anything continuous and be discontent with a single focus or something that requires concentrated effort. Reflecting the influence of television and its frequent commercial interruptions, we have generally accepted the theory that children have a limited attention span, eight minutes at most. Yet how many

of us have observed a child in rapt attention before a Disney video production, a puppet show, or a storyteller? The challenge for us is not to provide
multiple stimuli, but meaningful stimuli. Can we entice the child to wonder
what lies beyond the surface characteristics of the object? Given the opportunity, young children can sense a deeper and more mysterious reality. A sure
way for us to entice children to wonder is to select tangible objects worthy of
a fixed and undaunted gaze.

Obviously, there are many temporal objects that can inspire wonder in
the spiritual realm. Common objects are Christian symbols such as the
cross, nativity, Chrismon or Jesse tree, chalice, bread, fish, candles, baptismal font/tank, liturgical colors or symbols found in architectural carvings,
or stained glass windows. Other concrete stimuli include physical movement (gestures such as bowing, kneeling, raising hands with palms upward,
and dance), story, music, and song.

One of the most overlooked yet surprisingly familiar items for evoking
wonder is the parable. We are quick to use biblical stories such as creation,
Noah and the ark, Moses and the exodus, or David and Goliath, all of which
can offer the child majestic images that expand God in the child's eye. Yet
the parables can escape our glance as powerful stimuli for enticing young
children to wonder. This is because educators have often told us that even
children ages ten to twelve find it almost impossible to interpret and explain
the meaning of a parable.[27] We have been cautioned that children do not
readily make the transfer from these earthly stories to their heavenly meanings. We have heard and believed that only adults are able to hear parables
on their multiple levels and grasp their deeper meanings. According to
Mark's record of Jesus' interaction with the disciples (Mark 4:13), however,
it is important to remember that even adults do not always understand parables.[28] But this does not restrain us from exposing adults to the parables, nor
should we with children. Young children are quite capable of entering the
story of a parable, even if they are unable to grasp the full meaning of the
parable as it may have been originally intended. They will not respond to it
in the same way adults do, but it is evident that parables can exert an important hold on their feelings and make lasting impressions.

Parables can help children to recognize their own experiences while at
the same time pointing them to something or someone greater. Parables have
the capacity to initiate children into the mystery of life and into those things
that otherwise might escape a first glance. There is ample material for contemplation, amazement, and wonder in a parable, especially if the parable
chosen has natural connections to life experiences common to children. For
example, children may hear the parable of the lost sheep and feel intimately

connected to the experience of being lost, alone, or left out. Children (and this may be true for adults as well) often relate to parables best when they can relate to one of the characters in the parable.

Parables that have the particular capability of kindling wonder in children's eyes and souls are those that represent the realm of God as a small reality that becomes great. Children relate well to comparisons and respond easily to questions that invite them to draw comparisons.[29] The parables of the mustard seed (Matthew 13:31-32), the yeast in the dough (Matthew 13:33), and the sowing of the seed (Mark 4:26-29) are wonderful sources for children's contemplation of the mystery of life and the work of God. They contrast something very little with something very large, and evoke wonder. The gospel speaks to us of the mustard seed that is smallest of all seeds, yet it becomes a tree to which the birds of the air flock to make their nests. Similarly, the gospel speaks to us of a woman who mixes three measures of flour with yeast until all the dough is leavened, transforming itself from a little mound of flour into a large loaf of bread. No less amazing is the story of the seed of grain the farmer sows that produces a full crop.

All three of these parables present for children a contrast between the small and the great, and they emphasize that the growth of life is wondrous and inspiring. These parables do not speak explicitly about God, yet they initiate children into the mystery of life. They, too, were once small, and now they are growing. What extraordinary energy there must be to change a small seed into a tree, a small handful of flour into a full loaf, a seed into a full ear of corn, and a small baby into a grown-up! And this happens everywhere in the world! It is only natural that a child will wonder at the marvel of such creative energy that surpasses human capacity and that draws the child from a particular love of life to a global love of life.

A child's wonder can be further enhanced by physical activities that involve him or her in the experience of wonder. Children may plant seeds and watch them grow, or prepare and watch two different batches of dough, one with yeast and one without. The children may visit a farm at seeding time and again at the time of harvest. They can do a computer web search for "mustard bush" and look at pictures of what emerges from the little seed placed in their hands.

It cannot be denied that the story-form of a parable discloses a world where God is present with us in existential issues (life, death, and the need for meaning) and in the mystery of life itself. Parables both hide and reveal the mystery of God, and children will take the wonder of this mystery down to the deepest roots of their soul. It is our task to assist children to tap into these deep levels.

An important approach to our pastoral care with children is to entice them to wonder, to let the sense of wonder be reflected in our adult lives, and to introduce children to worthy tangible stimuli, including the parables, as means for evoking reverent awe in even the youngest of them. Enticing children to wonder and the total enjoyment of God may foster souls that, in later years, are more open than ever to hear the voice of God and experience the mystery of life.

Enticement to Prayer

Enticing children to pray is the third means for listening to and nourishing the soul of a child. Yet prayer has always had a confused role in the lives of young children. This is not so much because prayer has been absent, but because we have been less inclined to entice children into offering spontaneous expressions of their own unique relationship with God. More often than not, our primary concern has been to teach children how to pray and what to pray rather than to step aside and allow children really to express themselves. We have not listened to how children pray and instead have imposed our guidelines for prayer on our children. Sometimes this can be helpful, as evident in my own experience of receiving a book of children's prayers. What is at risk, however, is that we lead children too quickly along a road that is not theirs. Young children are disposed to prayer. They can, and do, pray with great spontaneity, facility, and sense of enchantment with God. In fact, we might be surprised at what we glean from the secret lives of their prayers.

Children's Prayers of Praise and Thanks. It is important for us to understand that praise and thanksgiving are the first and most precious responses that children can give to their wonder and enjoyment of the gift of God's presence. The prayers of young children are almost exclusively praise and thanksgiving. Attempts we make to lead children too hastily toward prayers of petition can distort or falsify the child's natural religious expression. Would we observe children offering petitionary prayers (sometimes dubbed *magical* or *Santa Claus* prayers, because they tend to bend the divine will to one's own advantage) if they had not first learned this habit by observation of adults? On rare occasions, examples of petitions will be heard, but these may be more the result of our teaching about prayer than a child's natural inclinations toward prayer. Or they may represent more of a deviation based on a presentation of God to a child that left the child unsatisfied.

It is important to note that children's prayers of thanksgiving are captured in more than verbal forms of expression. Sometimes children's movements, silence, or art reveal their true joy in God and speak their own praise and thanksgiving. Children also have a tremendous capacity, often overlooked, for visualizing their prayers. Thomas Williamsen tells the story of his five-year-old son, Erik, who visualized Jesus in his pancreas. Erik had developed diabetes. Shortly after the prognosis, he told his Dad that he pictured Jesus in his pancreas trying to get the insulin out by pricking it with a pin. After six months, Erik announced to his Dad, "Jesus didn't want me to have diabetes. My body just let me down."[30]

For the most part, however, children's prayer is expressed using short and essential phrases. Young children offer few words, and the phrases are often without formal structure. Frequently they are interspersed with long intervals of silence. Adults can often be tricked by the silence and think that the prayer is finished. This is not necessarily so. Many times the phrases will come in spurts, but the roughness of these could be described as having a beauty that transcends typical patterns of adult speech. Occasionally, I have witnessed young children praying naturally in a singsong voice. Children's prayers may not be eloquent, but they are sincere, and their words offer us the brilliance of prayer from the heart. Sometimes they pray to God and at other times they pray to Jesus.

Here are some examples of children's spontaneous and short-phrased prayers:

+ Thank you for the gift.
+ Thank you for looking after us.
+ Thank you for giving us food to eat.
+ Thank you for making soup. And crackers.
+ Jesus, joy.
+ Thank you for creating the whole world.
+ Jesus, I have fingers. You have fingers.
+ Because God said so. Everyone is good.
+ Goodness, light, Amen.
+ Thank you for giving us mothers and fathers.
+ Thank you for giving us legs for walking and playing.
+ Thank you, Jesus, for being with us. For doing things with us.

The Use of Prayer Formulae with Children. The key to helping children pray is to fret less about teaching structured prayers, and instead to establish conditions that will help prayer to arise. In saying this I am not proposing that we eliminate altogether introducing prayer formulae to young children. Formulae are useful for children, providing they are in short sentence form. Lengthy formulae are too severe a contrast to the child's way of praying, and they may be repeated by the child without any inner attachment to their meaning. If we are going to use prayer formulae, they need to be short and memorable. A few words enable the child to grow along with them.

A short scripture verse may be a suitable prayer that children can listen to, repeat, and begin to make their own. The scripture will be remembered on its own merits by children, especially if it is connected with something they are already discovering about God. For example, "The Lord is my Shepherd, I shall not want" (Psalm 23) may be a helpful formula if used as a response to the children's discoveries about the parable of the Shepherd who finds the lost sheep (Luke 15:4-6). Whenever we use a formula, it is also important to encourage children to add their own personal response of prayer: "Today, what will we say to God?"

Then there is the matter of the familiar prayer—The Lord's Prayer— and how to introduce it to young children. Since young children are not yet in the stage of moral interests, some of the prayer lines ("forgive us our tres- passes/debts . . . ") are simply not appropriate. At this early stage of child- hood, a few lines may be all that is needed: "Our Father, who art in heaven, Thy Kingdom come."

Since children are so impressionable, it is also important to present more than one or two names for God. Besides the examples I have given of Shepherd and Father, scripture texts that refer to God as Mother Hen might be used (Luke 13:34b): "Mother God, gather us together as a hen gathers her chicks." Prayers offered in this way may be spoken or sung. It is true that children love to hear the same words over and over again. It is comforting to hear familiar sounds, and it helps the meaning to adhere in their hearts. The simplicity of the words is what is important in using prayer formulae. We can furnish children with crayons, but ultimately we want them to create their own painting rather than one that is already drawn.

Having acknowledged that there is a role for prayer formulae in creating conditions for children to pray, a word of caution is in order. We ought not to move too quickly to use such prayers. It is better for us to withhold using prayer formulae until children have established their own interior agility for genuine and spontaneous expression in prayer. Also, it is important to say that I am not advocating that adults refrain from offering petitionary prayers on behalf of children beyond or within their hearing. This can model for children appropriate petitions and the importance of including the whole world in our prayers. But in thinking about how we can best entice children to pray, I am suggesting that we try to suspend our own words and prayers until children have been able to offer their own personal prayers. We aim to call forth children's own interior agility by which their hearts turn to God and respond to God with natural sensitivity and creativity.

Facilitating Children's Prayers: Space, Time, and Silence. As for conditions that help to facilitate children's prayers, these include such things as appropriate physical space, establishing regular times for prayer, and the creation of significant silence. By appropriate physical space, I am referring to a place in the church and home that can be identified as a child's prayer space. This should be distinct from a child's educational classroom environment or the church sanctuary or chapel. At home or in the church, it may be the atrium room, as described above. Wherever it is, it should be a location that is safe, bright, and accessible for children. This place is to be understood as an area for quiet solemnity. It is a place where children can assume that God will meet them and be with them. A sign such as "Shush!! Children Praying!" might be posted on the door.

With regard to the hours of prayer, a constant process of *recalling* throughout the child's day is a useful way to support a child's natural prayer agility. Before eating or going to bed, before leaving for school or after coming home from school, before leaving the church for home, before starting another activity, the child may shape a response to what already has happened or what is happening in the day. Children can be enticed to recollect by simple questions such as: "Where is God in my day? What do I want to say to God about my day?" Although we do not want to give the child the impression that prayer happens only in fixed times, the process of recalling the day, finding God in the day, and responding in thanksgiving to God is an important rhythm to establish from an early age. This suggests that part of our pastoral care for children includes spending time with parents to foster their sense of comfort and ease with daily prayer rhythms such as these.

Silence is another important element in enticing children to pray. Several North American public educators are beginning to realize what Eastern schools have known for some time. Silent meditation is a useful means in the classroom for sharpening the child's ability to concentrate and focus on the day's learning. It is this kind of silence that I am referring to. More than empty silence or the mere cessation of noise, it is about fostering an interior silence that helps the child's unspoken request for aid in focusing and listening to his or her own body and soul. This kind of silence arises slowly and extends to embrace the whole group of children in some way. It can become a ritual that young children anticipate and take delight in. At church, it can be a part of the atrium experience for the first three to five minutes that children enter the room. It should be long enough to be significant, true, and real.

The use of silence communicates the quality of listening that is so often disregarded by adults in their work with young children. We assume children need to be kept busy and active, moving from one activity to the next without a pause in between. Yet young children are not only capable of sustaining silence, they actually can feel totally at home in it. By incorporating silence into our ministries with children, we put in practice for them the message that our prayer is incomplete without a time of listening. The conclusion of the silence can be signaled in many ways, such as the ringing of a bell or an offering in a gentle voice of a familiar line of a psalm.

Being pastoral: Heeding children's souls

Enticing children to participate in ritual, experience wonder, and express themselves in spontaneous prayer and silence are but some of the ways we can express pastoral care for children, whose souls eagerly anticipate the love and company of God. Children, who perceive and relate to the world in ways that transcend adult logic and reason, long to be heard and responded to in the various events, circumstances, and crises of their lives.

There is nothing noble, nostalgic, silly, sentimental, or romantic about caring pastorally for our children. If we believe that God is revealed to us in the little ones that we have tended to sequester, then we have no option but to give effective pastoral care to our children. To provide meaningful pastoral care to our children is to give heed to the yearnings of their souls. To do so is to respond to the clear gaps in our current pastoral care strategies for children.

If we are able to listen to the world of children, its words, symbols, actions, prayers, wonders, and terrors, then we will all be blessed with glimpses of God that can only lead to a more complete spirituality and a transformed congregation. Ultimately, our children may be strengthened for life because they will have developed the habit of soul-listening. Creating conditions where children's souls are reverenced and they hear God's voice calling them by name is a pastoral care strategy that can entice us to wonder and pray.

·→═◉═←·

Reflection Questions

1. When and how did you first meet, hear, feel, or know God?

2. Who listened to your childhood soul?

3. In what ways have children altered your spirituality?

4. How does your congregation provide pastoral care for children? What can be affirmed? What gaps need to be addressed?

5. Three enticements were presented in this chapter as pastoral care strate-
    gies for attending to the souls of young children. Do these seem appli-
    cable to your context? What other strategies can you imagine?

⋯⇒◉⇐⋯

spiritual exercises

Meditate on the following text:

> When I was a child,
>   I spoke like a child,
>   I thought like a child,
>   I reasoned like a child;
> when I became an adult,
>   I gave up childish ways.
>
>   2 Corinthians 13:11

Offer the following prayer, repeating each line three times followed by a
minute of silence.

> Rise up, children of God.
> Let God's life rise up in you.
> Mud-stirred, first-clay, handiwork of God.
> Plaything of a potter who fell in love.
> Blessed be the work of God's hands.
> An offering of soul for the world.
> May the goodness of heaven be yours.

⋯⇒◉⇐⋯

A new pastoral care ritual

Here is a blessing ritual for children going to school for the first time. It can
be included in a worship service or may be a special ritual for the children's
atrium experience. Children are invited to gather around the speaker(s) and
to participate as instructed.

Speaker: We bless these children with the elements common to our lives.
They are gifts of God for the people of God—rock, wind, flame, and
water.

(The speaker gives a small rock to each child and encourages the children
to touch the rock.) Hold, feel, and stroke this rock. This rock is a piece
of our earth. We can stand on rock. It is as solid as you are. May you
always stand on solid ground. We pray God's blessing upon you, for you
are gift for the world.

The Children Respond: We walk with God.

(The speaker blows gently on each head.) We are surrounded by air. It can blow softly and strongly. May it stir your soul to run, fly, hide, sing, and breathe. We pray God's blessing upon you, for you are gift for the world.

The Children Respond: We walk with God.

(The speaker lights a candle and holds it aloft before each child's eyes.) The light from this flame shines before you. In its light we see how precious you are. May you be given light to guide you and show you what is right. We pray God's blessing upon you, for you are gift for the world.

The Children Respond: We walk with God.

(The speaker dips fingers into a bowl of warm water and touches each child's eyes.) This water is cool and cleansing. As a deer pants for water, so your souls long for God. May God alone be your heart's delight and may you see the things God sees. We pray God's blessing upon you, for you are gift for the world.

The Children Respond: We walk with God.

Speaker: May our God who made rock, air, flame, and water bless us all as we grow in spirit and truth. Amen.

7
Toward complementarity: pastoral care and spiritual direction

⋅→≣●⊜≡←⋅

My soul is satisfied as with a rich feast,
and my mouth praises you with joyful lips.

Psalm 63:5

THE RELATIONSHIP BETWEEN pastoral care and spiritual direction continues to be a matter of lively conversation in several circles. The current
and compelling attraction of Protestants to spiritual direction suggests two
possible trajectories. One is the eventual substitution of spiritual direction
for pastoral care. The other is the amalgamation of the two practices so that
distinctive features are absorbed and no longer observable in practice. Both
of these trajectories would have tragic consequences for the practices. Too
many valuable and distinctive dimensions would be lost.

If, in essence, Protestant churches substituted spiritual direction for pastoral care, then spiritual direction would be in danger of being both misappropriated as a specialized ministry and misrepresented in its purposes. In
turn, Protestant churches would severely limit pastoral care to a narrow set
of particulars—particular people, particular means, and particular methods.
This represents a reductionist approach to pastoral care inasmuch as it
squeezes pastoral care into a form that is focused primarily on individuals.
Amalgamation also would lead to several significant losses for Protestant
congregations, not the least of which would be the opportunity for untrained
laypersons to reclaim their rightful heritage of being soul companions and
offering spiritual guidance to one another.

What is needed is for each of these practices to retain their autonomy.
At the same time, Protestant churches can take intentional steps to address
soul matters in an integrated and comprehensive manner within a congregational practice of pastoral care. If Protestant churches can recover the central purpose of pastoral care—which is to listen for the soul—and begin to
practice soulful pastoral care, then we will preserve the best of our communally focused Protestant pastoral care legacy while leaning into the potential

for complementarity between the autonomous practices of spiritual direction and pastoral care.

Complementarity is most effectively achieved if there is first a discernible regard for the depth of each practice and a clear understanding of how each practice is autonomous.

pastoral care and spiritual direction: autonomous practices

Pastoral care and spiritual direction must retain their distinct identities and legitimately autonomous practices. At the same time, however, they can take steps to move toward a more complementary relationship that supports common objectives and cooperative opportunities. In proposing a relationship based upon complementarity, the purposes and scope of each practice can be clarified, strengthened, and affirmed as distinct.

Once practitioners recognize the autonomous nature of each practice, they can pursue ways and means for the practices to complement each other. One possible outcome of complementarity is that Protestant clergy and laity may be far less inclined to turn toward spiritual direction as a way to fill a gap, and spiritual directors may find their services to be less in demand by Protestants. There may be fresh ways and means, however, for Protestants to avail themselves of the distinct resources that spiritual direction has to offer, and spiritual directors themselves may discover a whole new set of resources in Protestant congregations for their particularized work and clientele.

Before taking a closer look at how these two practices can move toward complementarity, it is important to compare the practices and to recollect their distinctive identities and contributions. Please see the chart on the next page.

Different Opportunities, Parameters, and Responses. Unlike any other caregiving ministries or professions, pastoral care has the distinct privilege of crossing all thresholds, be they spiritual, social, personal, or political. We find ourselves listening for the soul when we are in a conversation, in a social situation, at a church service, group meeting, hockey game, political protest, or funeral, engaging in an act of systemic advocacy, or even when we are at home reading the paper or praying. Pastoral care can be informal or formal, highly confidential or entirely public. It can be personal — expressing concern for individuals — or contextual — expressing concern for the communities and systems that influence our broad vision of what it

A Comparative Summary

Pastoral Care	Spiritual Direction
❖ a mutual ministry	❖ a shared spiritual journey
❖ deals with life cycle and has sustained involvement	❖ time-restricted and disciplined involvement
❖ crosses all worlds and elements	❖ deals primarily with the spiritual world
❖ both initiated and responsive care	❖ responsive or by referral
❖ includes all persons and ages	❖ attends to particular persons, usually adults
❖ impulse is often crisis driven, both situational and maturational	❖ impulse is personal spiritual need
❖ no contract or fee	❖ contractual and fee/donation for service
❖ central agenda is overall conditions for growth and fulfillment of life centered in God	❖ central agenda is attending to the presence/action of God in the life of the individual
❖ focus is on greater self-understanding, agency, and formation of healthy ego	❖ focus is on developing a relationship with God and reduction of ego-dependence
❖ begins with presenting concern and behavior	❖ begins with experience and prayer life
❖ explores the why, what, and how	❖ explores the who and where questions
❖ raises to consciousness the conversation between life experience, faith, and culture	❖ raises to consciousness the conversation between self-will and the will of God
❖ both public and private/confidential encounters	❖ a confidential and private encounter
❖ methods include listening, confession, diagnosis, analysis, interpretation, feedback, guidance	❖ methods include listening, storytelling, feedback, discernment, direction
❖ exploration of options, provision of reality-based hope, and discerning God "in the midst of all of life"	❖ exploration of what is happening to faith in the midst and affirming life experience as revelation of the divine
❖ requires training in pastoral care and ethics	❖ requires training in spiritual direction and ethical guidelines for directors

means to be essentially human and interdependent. Although in practice, pastoral care has notoriously neglected children and is only more recently beginning to attend more fully to the pastoral concerns of men, in principle, pastoral care makes no gender restrictions or age distinctions. Men and women, both adults and children, are all recipients of pastoral care.

In contrast, spiritual direction is much more limited in its opportunities and range of responses. Although spiritual direction can be given in groups, it is most often given to individuals. Spiritual direction generally excludes children, and without apology, responds to particular persons. These are usually adults (primarily women)[1] who have made a deliberate choice to enter spiritual direction or who have been referred to a spiritual director. In contrast to persons seeking pastoral care, who are at varying stages in their human, psychological, and faith development, those seeking spiritual direction usually have a certain level of emotional maturity that aids their capacity to make use of spiritual direction. In other words, one must have an ego before one can surrender it to God. This method of *surrender*, or supporting the *letting go* of whatever is in God's Way, is essential to spiritual direction. This contrasts with many acts of pastoral care that can happen with persons whose egos are fragile (or still under construction) and thus find themselves unable to surrender what they do not yet possess.

Spiritual direction is also time-bound and normally limited in practice to the private sphere. The spiritual director generally does not socialize with or enter the public arenas of those being directed. Most spiritual directors have fees or recommended donations, thereby establishing a contractual, disciplined, confidential relationship for a negotiated period of time. This stands in contrast to those who view pastoral care as absorbed within the fabric of the church's ministry and service for its members and wider community. Whenever or however pastoral care happens, it is without the attachment of a fee. Pastoral caregivers freely offer pastoral care because it is a dimension of the church's ministry and "the priesthood of all believers."

Although all human experience can be said to be spiritual, the spiritual director is most concerned with those qualities, events, and prayerful practices that seem clearly and specifically *spiritual* and that are brought forward in a time-bound session. The spiritual director is listening in that hour for how the presence or leading of God, or the grace of God, is evident and working most directly in the lives of individual persons. Pastoral care, however, listens for the soul in the full range of human experiences that happen at any time, and aims to help individuals, couples, and faith communities discover and discern the spiritual meaning in those experiences. Pastoral care that practices listening for the soul will hear it speaking in diverse moments that are both ordinary and extraordinary, such as arranging a wedding with a couple, rocking a child to sleep, discussing the purchase of new choir gowns, planning an agenda for a church committee meeting, responding to a local community tragedy, or in the struggle of deciding whether or not to blow the whistle on harassing behavior. Attending to all moments of life by listening for the soul within those moments is the comprehensive agenda for soulful pastoral care.

Different Practitioners, Structures, and Competencies. One can argue that spiritual direction, especially within the Roman Catholic tradition, still operates predominantly within a hierarchical framework. While more and more Protestant clergy and laypersons from various denominations are exercising the ministry of spiritual direction, it remains true that the largest proportion of those trained to be spiritual directors are immersed in specific religious communities in which they have received extensive training for the specific vocation of spiritual direction. Over the years, there has been a great deal of experimentation with the terminology with the aim of lessening the authoritarian strains in the tradition and emphasizing more clearly the role of God as the true director. Various terms such as *spiritual companion, spiritual friend, soul friend, spiritual guide,* and *prayer guide* have all been used. Still, the most commonly used term—*spiritual director*—reflects an understanding that one voluntarily seeks direction from another who is perceived to have more experience, authority, training, and wisdom in matters pertaining to the soul and its relationship with God.

It is true that Protestants have not always achieved congruence between their theology of the priesthood of all believers and their pastoral practice. The professionalization of the clergy contributed to the expectations held by many laypersons that the clergy are the trained and accountable providers of pastoral care. More recently, however, Protestant congregations are beginning to rediscover the mutuality involved in giving and receiving pastoral care. Laypersons gifted with skills for pastoral care either are providing it instinctively, or because they have participated in training programs that lead to increased understanding, skill, ability, and (in some cases) even certification. Also, ethical guidelines and codes of conduct now rightly inform and frame our pastoral care, and pastoral caregivers, both lay and clergy, are becoming appropriately versed in the legal and ethical requirements of ministry as they pertain to pastoral care. They are more cognizant of the need to function in systems of accountability and peer supervision.

Although spiritual directors have been less subject to court cases and allegations of religious/clerical abuse, they are just beginning to address publicly the matter of accountability systems. With the infusion of layper-sons and Protestant clergy into the practice of spiritual direction, there is an increasing recognition of the need for spiritual directors to develop an accountability system. Matters yet to be resolved include defining mini-mum acceptable standards for formation in the ministry of spiritual direc-tion, and defining what gifts, attitudes, and competencies are required for spiritual directors. Spiritual directors are now coming together to provide support and enrichment for each other, as well as to establish more formal associations, networks, and professional forums, but mechanisms for evalu-ating and licensing spiritual directors are yet to be determined.[2]

Pastoral care can be enhanced by spiritual direction, but since there are significant differences in the range and scope of opportunity presented to pastoral caregivers and spiritual directors, pastoral care ought not to become spiritual direction. It needs to remain autonomous. What we can say is that some of the principles and techniques of spiritual direction can shine through our pastoral care when it has recovered its central purpose of lis-tening for the soul. When our pastoral care is soulful, then it will once again be the core form and primary mode in our society for offering spiritual guid-ance. The same, however, cannot be said in reverse, and this is why the two practices must retain autonomy.

Spiritual direction is not the core from which pastoral care takes place; neither must it assume the posture of being the sole tradition from which spiritual guidance emerges. Spiritual direction obviously includes some of the same skills associated with pastoral sensitivity and wisdom. But the chief aim of spiritual direction differs radically from pastoral care. The primary purpose of spiritual direction remains that of addressing *particular persons* who are searching at a *particular time* for a deeper awareness of God. But because people yearn to experience a community that cares for them on all levels of mind, body, and soul, and that cares about seeing God in all situa-tions of their lives, pastoral care remains a more wholesome, encompassing, and essential form for nourishing all ages, conditions, and sorts of people in their lives of faith in God.

Moving Toward Complementarity

Affirming Common Aims

While there are many challenges facing the movement toward comple-mentarity, perhaps none is more pressing than the question of how both practices can further an objective they hold in common—deepening human interconnectedness and communal identity. How to assist the faith community's own real struggle to present an alternative to an individualistic and consumptive orientation to life is, indeed, a pressing matter of concern to both Protestant and Catholic faith communities. Paying attention to the primacy of community is essential to the development of a healthy soul and to shattering the illusion that we can remain separate and disconnected from one another. Helping people to understand the real limitations and human nature of faith communities, and to encourage the reentry into the faith community (including becoming an active participant in its transformation) is a responsibility pastoral caregivers and spiritual directors have in common.

For example, the Protestant laity and clergy who enter formal spiritual direction include many living on the edge or periphery of their own denomination and/or congregation. For whatever reasons, they have felt marginalized from their denominational roots, and they seek through spiritual direction to find a home away from home. Spiritual direction can complement pastoral care by responding in ways that do not inadvertently reinforce a posture of isolation or independence from faith community. Spiritual direction can enhance pastoral practice by refusing to reinforce the age-old schisms that exist between the practices themselves and between public and private spirituality.

Presently, spiritual directors within local, national, and international networks are responding in a variety of ways to denominations and local churches. These range from those who wish to strengthen their stance with local and broader faith communities to those who see no need to have any relationship, so long as some form of peer accountability and supervision is in place. Spiritual direction disconnected from the reality of local faith communities undermines our common objective of strengthening our connections to God and neighbor. To move toward greater complementarity, individuals must develop relationships of trust between local faith communities and centers for spiritual direction.

Developing Cooperative Ventures

The possibilities are endless for pilot projects and cooperative ventures. As is outlined in the Appendix, Christ Church Cathedral in Vancouver is experimenting with a cooperative arrangement between their congregation and The Cathedral Centre for Spiritual Direction. As we consider cooperative ventures, here are some provisional clues for working toward complementarity.

Cooperative Agreements. At a minimal level, we can open up forums for discussion and for the development of cooperative agreements between congregations and spiritual directors or centers for spiritual direction. Such agreements might make public commitments and covenants (1) to respect one another by not disparaging one another or one another's work; (2) to remain open to processes of corporate discernment, accountability, and support within our respective faith communities; (3) to draw upon the teachings and practices of one another's communities of faith and to respect the relationship of individuals to their faith communities (however healthy or in need of healing that relationship may be); (4) to discuss guidelines for congregations to make referrals to spiritual directors (and vice versa); and (5) to represent accurately and in all forms of public communication our qualifications, affiliations, limitations, and ethical guidelines.

Sharing Resources. Protestant congregations and centers for spiritual direction might offer human, monetary, or physical resources to one another to ensure a wide set of opportunities for laity and clergy. It is possible to build stronger links between neighborhood churches and places of spiritual renewal and leadership. Since it is likely that retreat centers, convents, monasteries, and spiritual direction centers will continue to exist in some form well into the future, the reasons they are valued need to be explored by congregations and mined for clues that might assist their own spiritual renewal.

For example, it may well be that we need to place more emphasis on the physical environment of our church buildings and the ways these can become more hospitable for soul journeys. Our churches may need to consider redesigning physical spaces so that men and women are either less distracted or more attracted toward an encounter with the holy. How do our sanctuaries, rooms, and outside properties respond to the natural work and rest rhythms of shift-working, leisure-denied, and stressed people, including children? For many people, a relationship with a place felt to be sacred space is central for nourishing the soul. We need to revisit how our church facilities can become less environmentally chaotic and more consecrated, simplified, symbolic, or creation-centered.

Other possible ways to share resources include making arrangements for intensive, weeklong, or ten-to-thirty-day experiences of directed retreats within the congregational setting. Or it may be possible to budget for and give oversight to the development of a congregationally based and defined ministry of spiritual direction.

Creating Networks. We can create informal and formal networks between centers for spiritual direction, congregations, regional church bodies, lay education centers, and theological schools. Local clergy and laity can serve as pastoral and educational resources for congregations or for spiritual directors or their clientele. Similarly, spiritual directors might find themselves on loan to or in-residence with congregations or theological schools, encouraging by their presence "a very high priority indeed on training in prayer, on the practice of silence and reflection, on deepening the awareness of the presence of God, on helping people to understand the principles of spiritual growth, and on placing all theological work within a framework of worship and prayer."[3] Spiritual practices of the Christian life, though vehicles and not ends in themselves, are yet an undervalued arena of healing and transformation for individuals and faith communities. Discovering soulful practices not only will bind us to a deeper relationship with God, but will also free us to love one another, the stranger, and even the world more deeply.

Appropriate cautions

In moving toward complementarity, Protestants must be careful to present themselves neither falsely as spiritual directors (presenting credentials, competencies, titles, or skills we do not possess) nor as having more experience or familiarity with spiritual disciplines or aspects of the spiritual life than is true to our own pilgrimage. It is also important for us to resist the temptation to allow spiritual direction to become simply another pastoral care program to be managed within the congregational context. If our attempts to move toward complementarity result in a mere increase in flurried activity, then our attempts become self-defeating. The invitation before us is not to decentralize ourselves even further, but radically to reorient attention to the soul so that it becomes central within our pastoral care.

If we are to give serious consideration to the Protestant impetus to attend to the soul, Protestant churches will need to be prepared for a radical shift in our present distributions of time and energy. How ministry personnel understand their role and use their time is of vital importance to this radical refocusing of our energies. The development of complementarity requires denominations and congregations to be intentional about releasing their ministry personnel to be less administrators, managers, or development officers, and more resource persons, spiritual interpreters, *pray-ers*, and stewards of the Mystery. Complementarity means reframing our use of human and physical resources as well as our priorities in pastoral care.

Moving Toward Soulfulness

The relationship between pastoral care and spiritual direction will likely be in progress for some time. But if complementarity is to happen, and listening for the soul is to become once more the central pastoral agenda for Protestant churches, then we will be witnesses to several major changes in our churches. When souls become our core agenda, we are about far more than techniques for doing the work of the church better or providing an opium to boost church growth to the heights. The movement toward complementarity will keep us accountable, faithful, and in solidarity with our common quest to deepen our connection with God that manifests in a spirit-filled life and compassionate commitment to others. Without listening to souls, hearing them into speech, and rooting them in a deep connection with God, we all perish. With such listening, we dare to risk seeing anorexic souls and communities find nourishment for life.

EPILOGUE
signs of soulful pastoral care

✦═◉═✦

P RACTICING SOULFUL PASTORAL CARE is both simple and complex. It is simple because it is more about listening for the soul than fixing the soul. It is complex because it is never clear what models and methods best suit a local congregation. Yet the invitation is still before us to "keep on keeping on" and to experiment with the various dimensions of soulful pastoral care described in this book.

Soulful pastoral care will assume different shapes, reflecting diverse contexts and congregations. Moving toward soulful pastoral care requires long-term commitments, sustainable inclinations, and the will to experiment with varying means for attending to the soul's relationship with God and the world God loves. Soulful pastoral care requires a congregation to make its primary agenda to listen intentionally and evocatively for the soul in ways that attend to deepening individual connections with God and to the realization of deeper connectedness in community.

In the end, how do we discern whether soulful pastoral care is happening? Although it is the nature of things in the spiritual realm to be always unfolding and never entirely fathomable, there are some definite signs that point toward a soulful pastoral care. Taken in isolation, no one of these signs can evoke a soulful pastoral care. Woven together, they form a soulful pastoral care that can embrace people in every circumstance.

Soulful pastoral care becomes visible as ordinary people seek together to be in full companionship with God. Soulful pastoral care will:

✦ make soul-listening the primary agenda and initiating action of pastoral care
✦ attend to children as fully as adults and respect everyone's innate spiritual potential
✦ listen skillfully, evocatively, and hospitably for the soul in all sorts and conditions of people and in all circumstances of life
✦ foster the spirituality of the faith community as well as individual spiritual development

✦ understand life as a mystery to be lived and continually discerned rather than solved

✦ assist people to see reality more clearly and to discern the presence, voice, and activity of God

✦ encourage contemplative living as a means toward restoration of self, others, and the world

✦ attend to communal means for listening to the soul's rhythm of death and resurrection

✦ present diverse tools and means for developing the spiritual life to respond to differences in personalities and learning styles

✦ affirm and share methods for developing a spirituality that integrates body, mind, and soul

✦ be exercised by laity and clergy who have participated in appropriate training and sought feedback

✦ establish peer support and accountability mechanisms and engage regularly in individual and communal spiritual practices

✦ demonstrate the faith community's connectedness to the wider world through a communally discerned ministry that is experiential and countercultural

These signs could be described as embryonic. A soulful pastoral care will, no doubt, go beyond them in order to respond to an ever-beckoning future. As long as we are listening for the soul of pastoral care itself and are open to hearing God into speech, our pastoral care will always be on the move toward increased effectiveness and a restored and spirited community. If God is the basis for the journey of life, then the journey is one from which we cannot turn back. Moving toward a soulful pastoral care will fill us and imbue the world with a vigor for life, a respect for its sacredness, and a desire for its interconnectedness and union with a loving God. If the love that God offers us is the most important reality that can be seen and known by any of us, then together we have all that it takes, through any and all pastoral circumstances of life, to move toward a soulful pastoral care.

APPENDIX
A case study: Listening for the soul

꧁

This case study can be used for group discussion, as reality-practice (by role playing pastoral care with the survivor), or as part of a personal reflection on soulful pastoral care.

context

Two loyal church women, both in their later years, decided (with the approval of the church session) to reestablish a Sunday school program. They began in September, but by Christmas, one of the women was unable to continue because her health was declining rapidly from bowel cancer. Almost a year to the day later, the other woman also had to stop teaching since she, too, was diagnosed with bowel cancer. Later, her cancer progressed to include the areas of her stomach and pancreas. Both women initially survived rigorous rounds of chemotherapy treatments.

Eventually, one of the women was declared cancer-free while the other continued to fight for health until she died just before Christmas, almost a full three years from the time of her original diagnosis. The funeral was held within the church and was conducted by the pastor. Prior to this death, the woman had shared with her female friend and fellow-journeyer that she truly celebrated the recovery to health that her friend had achieved.

Not surprisingly, the surviving woman had a very difficult time with her friend's death and felt the entire situation was unfair and incomprehensible. Shortly after the funeral, besides giving individual pastoral attention to the survivor, the pastor of the church worked with the congregation to develop a public presentation to the children of the Sunday school that honored the joint founders, recognized their accomplishments, and affirmed their labors, especially noting the vision of the woman who had died.

Listening for the soul
Grief

The whole congregation is grieving the loss of this woman and her contribution to the church, including the children and teachers in the Sunday

199

school. For the woman who survived, there is a profound sense of loss of friendship, companionship in walking the difficult road of cancer, and in their working partnership on behalf of a church vision.

Guilt

The woman who survived the battle with cancer is dealing with *survivor guilt* and likely has several existential questions. Why did she survive and her friend die? Why was she healed while cancer led to death for another? Why had one set of prayers for healing apparently been answered and not the other? How is it possible to be thankful to God for healing when another died?

Anger and Fear

The surviving woman is angry with her friend for dying and leaving her alone. She probably has an unacknowledged fear that she too might relapse and cancer might claim her life. Perhaps she is angry with God. Surely if God were fair, both would have lived or both would have died.

Thanksgiving

The congregation, the pastor, and the surviving friend all have memories of this woman that are wrapped up in gratitude for her life, her contribution, her faithfulness, and her courage in the face of adversity. She provided them with hope and a sense of accomplishment.

pastoral analysis

How might we enable a faithful "letting go into the arms of death"? What prayers and actions will enable the congregation, the Sunday school children, and in particular, the surviving friend to begin to let go and receive healing? How can the pastoral caregivers in this situation pay attention to their own dynamics of grief? Can we hear the survivor into speech? Can we encourage and participate in her spiritual healing so that she might be able to face her own death and "let go into the paths of life"? What prayers and spiritual guidance will extend her capacity to receive the grace offered to her by God?

soulful pastoral actions

Even though I walk through the darkest valley, I fear no evil; for you are with me; your rod and your staff—they comfort me. (Psalm 23:4)

Ritual

The congregational ritualization of grief already has begun in the recognition and affirmation given within the Sunday school, and it can be continued in ways that will prevent further isolation from the reality of this death within the flow of daily life. Since the church is a community of memory in a way that the workplace, neighborhood, and the funeral home are not, Sunday school teachers and church members can be invited to come together to tell their stories, share memories, and express concerns for the children they teach who may have experienced this woman's influence. They can pray for themselves, the Sunday school, the deceased woman, the children, and all those who continue to suffer from cancer and grief. The knowledge that one woman's life will continue to matter to a community, even after death, can be a powerful source of comfort for others, including the surviving friend. In the context of worship, pastoral prayers and preaching can address grief, loss, healing, change, and hope. Facing the inevitability of death prepares the community for the deaths that yet will come to them and makes it possible to accept death with the hope that it does not destroy life, since God's love is stronger than death.

Visitation

The survivor herself requires follow-up visitation. It is important to assess whether she has people and resources to support her in her ongoing grief journey and to challenge her to draw upon these now and in the future. Of no less importance will be the simple act of providing her with opportunities to give voice to the many feelings and thoughts at work in her, and offering feedback on what is heard and not heard. Building upon the awareness that death can be a healing reality, she can be encouraged to explore how her own physical healing and survival, and the gifts of grace given to her by her deceased friend, are now opportunities for spiritual wholeness and "choosing life." One of the ways we can choose life is through allowing ourselves to be drawn into an ongoing *death* in which we die to everything that thwarts God's intentions for life, peace, and joy. Inviting this woman to explore what thwarts God's intentions may lead to an awareness that sets her free to begin to live in God. Praying with her in ways that capture her feelings, questions, and needs, and inviting her to share her own struggles, pain, and gratitude with God, or to pray her sighs too deep for words, will enable a connection with the resources of the faith.

Spiritual Guidance

It is also important for the whole people of God, including the survivor, the pastor, and the lay caregivers, to reflect upon their respective images of God as healer, source of life, and death. This includes looking at the normalcy of our human anger toward God. Some spiritually guiding questions for soul-centered pastoral conversation, worship, or educational contexts might include the following: What image of God was present in death? Does something need to be affirmed or discarded? How was God present as comfort and strength throughout? When was God absent in this experience? What is God's response to guilt? How is grief a strange gift or prism through which to see God? Who is God for us now? As a result of this experience, who is God calling us (and who is God calling the survivor) to be? What might God be saying to us through this experience? Can we see God at work in our ministry?

There may be some scriptural passages that can serve as meditative resources for the survivor, the congregation, lay caregivers, and the pastor. For example, the story of Naomi and Ruth, two women who parted company and made different choices for their well-being, may be helpful. Or the story of Job and his trials and tribulations (especially in the context of his anger at false comforters) may provide some resonance with broken-hearted souls in this situation. Jesus' own weeping in the company of Martha and Mary (who wept over the death of their brother Lazarus) may provide consolation for those who have not yet imagined God's own brokenness and promise of life made vividly present in the company of Jesus. If death is part of the old order, it may be helpful to meditate upon Romans 8:18-39, which speaks of the groaning of all of creation. Envisioning how God is actively working against the powers of death in all of creation may move us to protest unjust and brutal forms of death.

In ongoing acts of pastoral care, it is important to listen for clues and to pray that God will reveal what has been missed, unheard, or avoided. The pastor and others can uphold the surviving woman in contemplative prayer, perhaps by visualizing a radiant woman healed and set free from anger, fear, and guilt. The whole community can pray repeatedly: "Help us/me to choose life, so that we/I and your descendants may live" (Deuteronomy 30:19).

NOTES

Introduction

1. Usually the term *soulful* is used to describe something that is full of deep feeling or emotion. For example, we may call a piece of music soulful. Throughout this book, I use *soulful* as an adjective to describe pastoral care so that it means attending fully (with deep intention, feeling, and commitment) to the soul as the essential self in relationship to God.

2. Marjorie Thompson, *Soul Feast* (Louisville: Westminster John Knox, 1995), 6.

3. For a helpful exploration of the historic development of the confluence and confusion between spirituality and psychology, see the first chapter of Gerald May's work, *Care of Mind Care of Spirit: A Psychiatrist Explores Spiritual Direction* (New York: HarperCollins, 1992), 2–20.

4. During these same decades, charismatic renewal groups began to emerge, coming to birth both within and beyond Protestant church circles. Evangelical and Pentecostal movements flourished, largely due to the appeal held by the promise of a vibrant, spirit-filled life. Many people were likewise attracted to Eastern religions and the meditative practices of Asian cultures as a way of trying to foster a deeper connectedness with the ultimate source of life.

5. Several classics present the care of souls as the essential model of pastoral care. *A History of the Cure of Souls*, by John T. McNeill (New York: Harper & Row, 1951), remains a definitive historical survey of all that has contributed to the understanding of and care for the human soul. See also E. Brooks Holifield, *A History of Pastoral Care in America* (Nashville: Abingdon, 1983), Daniel Day Williams, *The Minister and the Care of Souls* (New York: Harper & Brothers, 1961), and Dietrich Bonhoeffer, *Spiritual Care*, translated by Jay Rochelle (Minneapolis: Fortress Press, 1985).

6. Henri Nouwen, *The Living Reminder: Service and Prayer in Memory of Jesus Christ* (New York: Seabury, 1977), 74.

7. The Association of Theological Schools revised its accreditation standards in 1996. Within *Basic Programs Oriented toward Ministerial Leadership* is a new section under "Program Content" that addresses matters of personal and spiritual formation. See Section A.3.1.3 in Bulletin 42, Part 3, "Procedures, Standards and Criteria for Membership" (Pittsburgh's The Association of Theological Schools), 94.

8. The "Project in Congregational Spirituality" was funded by a Lilly endowment to determine ways to help strengthen congregational spirituality. Austin and Princeton Theological Seminaries and officers from the Presbyterian Church U.S.A. worked with teams from eight Presbyterian congregations over a two-year period from January 1997 to September 1999. The project sought to contribute to the renewal and building up of congregations as seedbeds for growth in faith and discipleship. The congregational teams met six times in a retreat or conference center near their homes and lived a shared life marked by personal and corporate disciplines of the faith such as prayer, keeping the sabbath, attention to Scripture, discernment, and disciplined reflection upon the life of the world in which they live. For more information about the project, contact E. Dixon Junkin,

Educational Director, Project in Congregational Spirituality, 222 Woodcastle Drive, Florence, AL 35630.

9. Literature on congregational development and church growth has mushroomed in the last decade. Common examples include William Easum's works: *The Church Growth Handbook* (Nashville: Abingdon, 1990), *How to Reach Baby Boomers* (Nashville: Abingdon, 1991), and *Dancing with Dinosaurs* (Nashville: Abingdon, 1993). See also Thomas Bandy's *Kicking Habits: Welcome Relief for Addicted Churches* (Nashville: Abingdon, 1997), Kenneth Callahan's *Twelve Keys to an Effective Church* (San Francisco: Harper & Row, 1983), and numerous publications by the Alban Institute, Bethesda, Maryland, including but not limited to Loren Mead's *The Once and Future Church* (1993), *More Than Numbers: The Ways Churches Grow* (1993), *Transforming Congregations for the Future* (1994), and James Newby's *Gathering the Seekers* (1995).

10. Pertinent personal, theological, and anthropological assumptions undergird my understanding of soulful pastoral care as being committed to nurturing persons toward a deeper relationship with God. Whether we consciously recognize, acknowledge, or name God as existent, I believe that mystery/divinity/the holy other has entered the process of human history. Believing this means that God's self-communicating grace and ongoing creative spirit are accessible, abundantly present, and visibly at work as a loving, integrative, interconnecting force in the world. This is recognizable in the life of every man, woman, and child, and within the mystery of creation itself. The graciousness and goodness of God come to meet us, seek our freedom, and cooperate with our human desires to live abundantly and authentically. We seek to respond to this mystery by creating conditions where others can flourish in their full humanity and grow freely in responsiveness toward the God who dwells within and beyond.

11. Select phrases from the hymn "God Be in My Head." *The Book of Hours*, 1514. Hymn #430 in *Voices United* (Toronto: United Church, 1996).

chapter 1

1. Simone Weil, *Waiting for God* (San Francisco: Harper & Row, 1951), 105.

2. James Ashbrook recently proposed the phrase "minding the soul" and defined it as "remembering and attending to the way life is in the universe in which we find ourselves." James Ashbrook, *Minding the Soul* (Minneapolis: Fortress Press, 1996), 210.

3. Nelle Morton, *The Journey Is Home* (Boston: Beacon, 1987).

4. Sam Keen and Anne Valley Fox, *Telling Your Story* (New York: Doubleday, 1973, Signet Book edition, 1974), 8.

5. James Ashbrook, although speaking particularly of those in the more specialized ministry of pastoral counseling, makes a point that is analogous for those who listen for the soul. He wisely reminds us that we contaminate the spirit of mutuality when the listener's needs get in the way of serving the well-being of the other. Ashbrook, *Minding the Soul*, 136–37.

6. Jean Vanier, Canadian, born in 1928 and son of the late Governor General of Canada, Georges Vanier, founded L'Arche. In 1964, with the support of his spiritual director, Father Thomas Philippe, Jean Vanier invited two men with a developmental disability, Raphael Simi and Philippe Seux, to live with him in an old house in the French village of Trosly-Breuil. He named the house L'Arche after Noah's Ark and gradually welcomed not only more men and women with developmental disabilities but also the assistants who would work and live with them. Since then, L'Arche has grown into an international federation of more than 100 communities in nearly 30 countries. For more information about L'Arche, contact: www.larchecanada.org.

7. Margaret Guenther explores various metaphors as windows for viewing the ministry of spiritual direction. In addition to the first chapter, in which she explores the metaphor of hospitality, she devotes chapters to listening itself, the teacher, and the midwife. Margaret Guenther, *Holy Listening* (Cambridge, Mass.: Cowley, 1992).

8. Alan Jones, *Journey into Christ* (New York: Seabury, 1977), 13.

9. Thomas Moore, *Care of the Soul* (New York: HarperCollins, 1994), 220.

10. Macrina Wiederkehr, *A Tree Full of Angels* (San Francisco: HarperCollins, 1988), 26.

11. These questions are found in chapter 1, "Human Faith," in James Fowler, *Stages of Faith* (San Francisco: Harper & Row, 1981), 3.

12. Carolyn Gratton, *The Art of Spiritual Guidance* (New York: Crossroad, 1995), 18.

13. These two spiritual prayer exercises were adapted from prayers that can be found in Kent Ira Groff's book *Active Spirituality* (Bethesda, Md.: Alban, 1993), 141-42.

chapter 2

1. Thomas Ryan, *Disciplines for Christian Living* (New York: Paulist, 1993), 136.

2. Wilkie Au and Noreen Cannon, *Urgings of the Heart: A Spirituality of Integration* (New York: Paulist, 1995), 144.

3. Brita L. Gill-Austern, "Responding to a Culture Ravenous for Soul Food," *Journal of Pastoral Theology* 7 (Summer 1997), 71.

4. John Miller, citing Michael Murphy's work on the evolution of human nature in *The Contemplative Practitioner* (Westport, Conn.: Bergin and Garvey, 1994), 4.

5. Wayne Oates, *Nurturing Silence in a Noisy Heart* (New York: Doubleday, 1979), 5.

6. Alan Jones, *Journey into Christ* (New York: Seabury, 1977), 120.

7. Henri Nouwen, "Contemplation and Ministry," *Sojourners* (June 1978), 9.

8. Nouwen, "Contemplation and Ministry," 12.

9. Jones, *Journey into Christ*, 120.

10. Jones citing George Eliot, *Journey into Christ*, 120.

11. Nelson Thayer, *Spirituality and Pastoral Care* (Philadelphia: Fortress Press, 1985), 93.

12. John of the Cross, *Dark Night* 1.10.6, about 1582.

13. See Tilden Edwards, *Spiritual Friend* (New York: Paulist, 1980), 69–89, and Nelson Thayer, *Spirituality and Pastoral Care* (Philadelphia: Fortress Press, 1985), 82.

14. Marcus Borg, *Meeting Jesus for the First Time* (New York: HarperSanFrancisco, 1994), 32–3.

15. Ryan, *Disciplines for Christian Living*, 138.

16. Ryan, *Disciplines for Christian Living*, 136.

17. Thomas Merton, *The Inner Experience*, unpublished manuscript, 1959. The draft manuscript can be studied at the Thomas Merton Studies Center in Louisville, Kentucky.

18. Marjorie Thompson, *Soul Feast* (Louisville: Westminster John Knox, 1995), 44.

19. John Miller, citing the philosopher Wilber, who drew upon the thought of St. Bonaventure, in *The Contemplative Practitioner*, 23.

20. Edwards, *Spiritual Friend*, 115–16.

21. Earle and Elspeth Williams, *Spiritually Aware Pastoral Care* (New York: Paulist, 1992), 11.

22. Macrina Wiederkehr, *A Tree Full of Angels* (San Francisco: HarperCollins, 1990), 60.

23. T. S. Eliot, *Burnt Norton* V, line 158.

24. Douglas Steere, *Dimensions of Prayer* (New York: Harper & Row, 1978), 40.

25. Dag Hammorskjold, *Markings* (London: Faber & Faber, 1964), 35.

26. Kent Ira Groff, *Active Spirituality* (Washington, D.C.: Alban, 1993), 174–75.

27. Howard Clinebell, *Basic Types of Pastoral Care and Counseling* (Nashville: Abingdon, ninth printing, 1991), 129.

28. Ryan, *Disciplines for Christian Living*, 145–49.

29. Segundo Galilea, "Politics and Contemplation: The Mystical and Political Dimensions of the Christian Faith," in *The Mystical and Political Dimensions of the Christian Faith*, ed. Claude Geffre and Gustavo Gutierrz (New York: Herder and Herder, 1974), 28.

30. Adapted from a hymn by a Swiss Anabaptist, written shortly before martyrdom, and cited by Thomas Williamsen in *Attending Parishioners' Spiritual Growth* (Washington, D.C.: Alban, 1997), 17.

31. Williams, *Spiritually Aware Pastoral Care*, 34.

chapter 3

1. Cited by Alan Jones, *Journey into Christ* (New York: Seabury, 1977), 54.

2. Scott Peck, *The Road Less Traveled* (New York: Simon and Schuster, 1978), 15.

3. Rita Nakashima Brock, *Journeys by Heart: A Christology of Erotic Power* (New York: Crossroad, 1995), 56.

4. Rosemary Radford Ruether, *Women and Redemption: A Theological Vision* (Minneapolis: Fortress Press, 1998), 276.

5. Dietrich Bonhoeffer, *The Cost of Discipleship* (New York: Macmillan, 1963).

6. A general exception has been when churches have sought to determine specific mission and ministry matters (an individual's call to ministry, church mission projects, and so forth). In spite of this, Protestant churches have been less inclined to initiate discernment processes that help individuals to live the rhythm of death and resurrection on a daily basis.

7. Howard Clinebell notes that "the same is true of much alcoholism and other addictive illnesses," including food addiction. See *Basic Types of Pastoral Care and Counseling* (Nashville: Abingdon, 1991), 219.

8. Douglas Hall, *Christian Mission: The Stewardship of Life in the Kingdom of Death* (New York: Friendship, 1985), 34–5.

9. Such participatory affirmations of faith may be in the form of creedal statements. The United Church of Canada has a contemporary affirmation of faith that includes the sentences: "In life, in death, in life beyond death, God is with us. We are not alone. Thanks be to God."

10. Many popular and easily accessible books describe the grief process based on contemporary clinical research. For a clinical discussion of the various manifestations of grief, see William Worden, *Grief Counseling and Grief Therapy: A Handbook for the Mental Health Practitioner* (New York: Springer, 1982). Other helpful resources include Edgar Jackson's *The Many Faces of Grief* (Nashville: Abingdon, 1977), and *When Someone Dies* (Philadelphia: Fortress Press, 1980). See also Therese Rando, *Grief, Dying and Death* (Champaign, Ill.: Research, 1986).

11. Anthropologist Victor Turner, in his work on the role of ritual in the process of human development, introduced the concept of *liminality* as a way of describing what happens in the "in-between time" as we move "out of the structure where order and predictability provide a sense of security" and into liminal time and the anti-structure, where "we face awareness of the chaos that surrounds us." Liminal time is the middle phase, when our old categories no longer work, but new ones are not yet in hand. Still other

theorists speak of a process of disintegration or disorientation that leads into a middle phase of sifting and sorting, eventually bringing one to the threshold where reintegration or reorientation can take place. Common to all these descriptions of the middle phase is the movement of letting go of someone or something (a previous role, status, or world-view), entering a transition time of contradiction and preparation for transformation, and then eventually restoring equilibrium by reintegrating into life with a new status, role, identity, or worldview. It should be noted that an obvious reluctance to describe liminal-ity as part of the dying process has been equally common. For a helpful synopsis of Victor Turner's extensive work on the role of ritual in liminal process, see Urban Holmes, III, *A History of Christian Spirituality* (New York: Seabury, 1980), 7.

12. Maria Harris, *Proclaim Jubilee: A Spirituality for the Twenty-First Century* (Louisville: Westminster John Knox, 1996), 90.

13. Darkness is too often viewed as a spiritual enemy rather than an intimate com-panion and means for soul-awakening. St. John of the Cross is most known for his metaphor of "the dark night of the soul." The human soul is not able to look at the whole light of God any more than the naked eye can safely gaze into the bright sun. If we were to see the whole truth at once, it might kill us. In this sense, it is important to realize that darkness is more of a protective adaptation of our finiteness to God's infinite glory. The darkness allows and permits the inflowing of God into the soul. For a good discussion on the pastoral implications of metaphors used by St. John of the Cross, see Wayne Oates, chapter 7, "The Presence of God in the Darkness," *The Presence of God in Pastoral Counseling* (Waco, Tex.: Word, 1986), 103–16.

14. William Barry is citing Gerald May's thinking about the psychodynamics of spiri-tuality. William Barry, *Spiritual Direction and the Encounter with God* (New York: Paulist, 1992), 70.

15. Walter Brueggemann, in the foreword to Ann Weems' book *Psalms of Lament* (Louisville: Westminster John Knox, 1995), xii.

16. An interesting example of a resource that enables a faith community to respond in ritual and prayer to violence or disaster is Frank Henderson's *Liturgies of Lament* (Chicago: Liturgy Training, 1994). Sample services are provided along with lists of scrip-tures, prayers, and other texts. The appendix treats interchurch and interfaith opportuni-ties for using lament as a way to deal with life's tragedies.

17. Permission of the publisher should be obtained before using a psalm such as this in printed form within a public context of worship. Weems, *Psalms of Lament*, 3.

18. Timothy Carson, "Liminal Reality and Transformational Power: Pastoral Interpretation and Method," *Journal of Pastoral Theology* 7 (Summer 1997), 107.

19. Juan Luis Segundo, a Jesuit from Uruguay, suggested this as a basis of a spiritual-ity of liberation. The phrase was recollected by Robert McAfee Brown in *Spirituality and Liberation* (Louisville: Westminster, 1988), 125.

20. Walter Brueggemann, *Cadences of Home* (Louisville: Westminster John Knox, 1997), 13.

21. Jones, *Journey into Christ*, 51.

22. M. Shawn Copeland, "Saying Yes and Saying No," *Practicing our Faith*, ed. Dorothy Bass (San Francisco: Jossey-Bass, 1997), 60.

23. From an article entitled "Covenanting as Human Vocation," in *Interpretation* 33 (No. 2), 115–29.

24. Frederick Buechner on "Vocation" in *Wishful Thinking* (San Francisco: Harper & Row, 1973), 95.

25. See Saint Ignatius of Loyola, *The Spiritual Exercises of St. Ignatius*, ed. Robert Gleason (New York: Doubleday, 1964); Pierre Wolf, *Discernment: The Art of Choosing Well* (Liguori, Mo.: Triumph, 1993); Thomas H. Green, S.J., *Weeds among the Wheat, Discernment: Where Prayer and Action Meet* (Notre Dame, Ind.: Ave Maria, 1994); Danny Morris and Charles Olsen, *Discerning God's Will Together* (Bethesda, Md.: Alban, 1997); Dietrich Bonhoeffer, *Life Together* (New York: Harper & Row, 1954); Suzanne Farnham et al., *Listening Hearts: Discerning Call in Community* (Ridgefield, Conn.: Morehouse, 1993).

26. See David L. Fleming, S.J., *The Spiritual Exercises of St. Ignatius (A Literal Translation and a Contemporary Reading)* (St. Louis, Mo.: The Institute of Jesuit Sources, 1978). In particular, the second week includes discernment of choices, and the fourth week covers discernment of spirits (consolation and desolation).

27. For a fuller presentation of the Quaker Committee of Clearness, see Morris and Olsen, *Discerning God's Will Together*, 58–9.

28. This is a phrase from the first verse of Hymn #581, "When We Are Living," from *Voices United* (Toronto: United Church, 1996), hymn words translated from the Spanish by George Lockwood, 1987.

chapter 4

1. Cited by Elaine Smith in her article "Integrating Psychology with Spirituality: A Paradigm for Clergy Support Groups," *Congregations: The Alban Journal* 23, No. 6 (Bethesda, Md.: Alban, 1999), 9.

2. For example, see David Schuller et al., *Readiness for Ministry, Volume II: Assessment* (Ohio: Association of Theological Schools, 1976), 9.

3. Dorothy Bass, ed., *Practicing our Faith* (San Francisco: Jossey-Bass, 1997), xiii.

4. Morton Kelsey, *The Other Side of Silence* (New York: Paulist, 1976), 207.

5. Howard Rice, *Reformed Spirituality* (Louisville: Westminster John Knox, 1991), 197.

6. Thompson, *Soul Feast* (Louisville: Westminster John Knox, 1995), 134.

7. Thompson, *Soul Feast*, 128.

8. Margaret Guenther, *Holy Listening* (Cambridge, Mass.: Cowley, 1992), 11.

9. John Ackerman, *Spiritual Awakening* (Washington, D.C.: Alban, 1994), 92.

10. Tilden Edwards, *Sabbath Time* (Nashville: Upper Room, 1992), 91.

11. Bass, ed., *Practicing our Faith*, 79.

12. Rice, *Reformed Spirituality*, 195–96.

13. Edwards, *Sabbath Time*, 13.

14. Edwards, *Sabbath Time*, 71.

15. Thomas Ryan, *Disciplines for Christian Living* (New York: Paulist, 1993), 92.

16. Ryan, *Disciplines for Christian Living*, 126.

17. François Fenelon, cited by Richard Foster in *Celebration of Discipline* (San Francisco: Harper & Row, 1978), 69.

18. Martin Luther, cited by Richard Foster, *Celebration of Discipline*, 78.

chapter 5

1. Howard Clinebell, *Basic Types of Pastoral Care and Counseling*, revised and enlarged edition (Nashville: Abingdon, ninth printing, 1991), 395.

2. See chapter 16, "Training Laypersons for their Caring Ministries" in Clinebell's *Basic Types of Pastoral Care and Counseling*, 394–415. Other helpful resources include Hendrik Kraemer's classic work *A Theology of the Laity* (Philadelphia: Westminster,

1959), Howard Stone's *The Caring Church: A Guide for Lay Pastoral Care* (San Francisco: Harper & Row, 1983), George Peck and John Hoffman's *The Laity in Ministry* (Valley Forge, Pa.: Judson, 1984), and Paul Stevens and Phil Collins's *The Equipping Pastor* (Washington, D.C.: Alban, 1993).

3. Steve Jacobsen, *Hearts to God Hands to Work: Connecting Spirituality and Work* (Washington, D.C.: Alban, 1997), x.

4. As cited by Howard Rice in *Reformed Spirituality* (Louisville: Westminster John Knox, 1991), 138.

5. Kenneth Leech, *Soul Friend: The Practice of Christian Spirituality* (San Francisco: Harper & Row, 1977).

6. Corinne Ware, *Connecting to God* (Washington, D.C.: Alban, 1997), 9.

7. Martin Marty, *Friendship* (Allen, Tex.: Argus, 1980), 8.

8. See Marty, *Friendship*, chapter 3.

9. 1 John 4:20 (adapted).

10. Marty, *Friendship*, 108.

11. Brother Lawrence, *The Practice of the Presence of God* (Old Trappan, N.J.: Fleming H. Revell, Spire, 1977).

12. Ware, *Connecting to God*, 78–9.

13. Rather than list all of the possibilities, readers are simply referred to Corinne Ware's helpful book *Connecting to God*, in which she lists all kinds of excellent resources, both classical and contemporary. Also, church members are encouraged to consult their resident clergy and to contact denominational offices, bookstores, theological schools, lay education centers, and public libraries. One of my favorite study books for soul companionship groups is *Practicing our Faith*, edited by Dorothy Bass and available in paperback (San Francisco: Jossey-Bass, 1997). Each chapter is conducive for an evening's gathering and evokes lively discussion about a particular spiritual practice that can enrich our connection with God. Also, an extensive list of additional resources is provided for each chapter and for persons interested in delving further into the particular practice identified.

14. James Fenhagen, *Mutual Ministry* (New York: Seabury, 1977), 86.

15. This biblical reflection is adapted from a spiritual renewal exercise contained in the doctoral dissertation of W. Wayne Soble, "Readiness for 'The Way': A Design for Renewal" (1984, Knox College and the University of Toronto), appendix J-1, 188.

chapter 6

1. This prayer could be described as a dangerous petitionary prayer for a young child because it contains a reference to death. In effect, it presents God as a fearsome entity who is ready to grab your soul. Teaching this prayer runs the risk of placing God at a disadvantage. If the fear remains, God could be understood to have failed. In spite of this potential risk, the prayer itself, as well as the familiar ritual of saying the prayer each evening, provided me with great comfort and a diminishment of fear.

2. Iris Cully, *Education for Spiritual Growth* (San Francisco: Harper & Row, 1984), 123.

3. Ages three to eleven cover a wide range and considerable variation in development, yet there are generally accepted characteristics of these ages that can inform our understanding of what it means to listen for the souls of our young children. Drawing upon Swiss psychologist Jean Piaget's understanding of how children grow, between the ages of three and seven, most children will lack inductive or deductive logic and be unaware of contradictions in thoughts or images. Toward the end of this phase, children will move

into a more intuitive phase in which their intuitions about their experiences are the main source for understanding the relationship between things. Prior to the age of twelve, most children will not be capable of abstract thought. Psychoanalyst Erik Erikson's schema for describing how individuals work through various life concerns at various chronological periods suggests that it will be important for us in our work with children between three and eleven years to affirm curiosity, imagination, and the need for affection and physical activity. Most developmental theories suggest that repetition that aids memory and participatory activities that involve seeing, touching, and imitating will be extremely important. The faith development work of James Fowler (in reference to this age range, Intuitive-Projective faith, ages three to six, and Mythic-Literal Faith, ages seven to eleven) and John Westerhoff (Affiliative Faith in childhood) help us to think about the implications of childhood development for the growth of spirituality. A helpful secondary source that summarizes the impact of developmental and faith theories on work with young children can be found in chapters 4, 5, and 6 of Sara Juengst's book *Sharing Faith with Children* (Louisville: Westminster John Knox, 1994).

4. Groome states quite clearly that, for children in this age range, the function of symbols is only representative and that reasoned mental operations are not possible. Preschool children lack the vocabulary and are not able to form a concept. Young school-aged children can form concepts, but these are based more on intuition than on reason. Thomas Groome, *Christian Religious Education* (San Francisco: Harper & Row, 1980), 244.

5. One of the ways the church can strengthen its role with parents is by helping parents understand that the church's ritual of inclusion is simultaneously a paradoxical invitation to begin to let go of the child. In effect, parents have an interim role with children, who need to create their own life stories. A major element of the parental vocation is to encourage the child's own spiritual formation and formation of a self before God. When parents recognize that ultimately the child belongs not to them but to God, then they are set free to care for their children without being overly protective or anxious.

6. Herbert Anderson and Susan B. W. Johnson, *Regarding Children* (Louisville: Westminster John Knox, 1994), 1.

7. Anderson and Johnson, *Regarding Children*, 2.

8. Although I am presenting a case for the entire church community to be actively involved in the spiritual formation of children, it is equally important to consider the role of the wider community and cultural environment. For a helpful exploration of what it means to link family and society, see Anderson and Johnson, *Regarding Children*. They devote their fifth chapter to the necessity of fostering an interdependent relationship between family and society to raise children in respectful ways. In calling for a greater partnership between family and society, they point out our need to "diminish the privatization of family and other consequences of individualism" (104) and claim that "where there is no village, the family will fail" (108).

9. The first wave of grief literature that referenced children gave primary emphasis to how parent(s) handle the loss or death of a child. In more recent decades, a wealth of books, articles, and video resources that are formulated for caregivers of children and for children themselves has emerged. These cover a multitude of issues, including grief, illness, separation, divorce, and abuse. By no means an exhaustive list, the following resources are examples of what may be helpful to pastoral caregivers or to children themselves: Leo Buscaglia, *Fall of Freddie the Leaf* (Thorofare, N.J.: Charles B. Slack, 1982), Juliet Rothman, *A Birthday Present for Daniel: A Child's Story of Loss* (Buffalo: Promethus Books, 1996), Earl Grollman, *Talking About Death—A Dialogue Between*

Parent and Child (Boston: Beacon, 1976), William Van Ornum and John B. Murdock, *Crisis Counseling with Children and Adults* (New York: Continuum, 1983), Donna Gaffney, *The Seasons of Grief: Helping Children Grow through Loss* (New York: Plume, 1988), Joanne E. Bernstein, *Books to Help Children Cope with Separation and Loss* (New York: R. R. Bowker, 1983), Christine Adamec, *When Your Pet Dies* (Berkley Publishers, 1996), Barbara Hazen, *Why Did Grampa Die?* (New York: Golden Books, 1985), B. Mellonie and R. Ingpen, *Lifetimes: The Beautiful Way to Explain Death to Children* (New York: Bantam Books, 1983), and Erin Linn Levy, *Children Are not Paper Dolls* (Springfield, Ill.: Human Services Press, 1987).

10. If children do not have answers to their own questions, usually they will just say so. When we attempt to draw out the child's own thinking and imagining, not only is the child affirmed, but the adult is guided toward offering a more perceptive response that is less likely to project the adult's meaning onto the child.

11. As a result of his extensive research on the inner lives of children, psychiatrist and Harvard University professor Robert Coles rightly cautions us about our habitual tendency to encourage children to depict God in graphic terms. Because children have such a great sense of mystery, our reliance upon graphic or visual depictions can be too limiting. For this reason, I have avoided the wording often used by clergy and Christian religious educators, namely: "What does God look like?" For an in-depth study of Christian, Jewish, and Muslim children's views on a variety of spiritual matters, see Robert Cole's *The Spiritual Life of Children* (Boston: Houghton Mifflin, 1990).

12. I realize that *Christian religious education* is a highly debated term in Christian literature. Some favor *Christian education, religious education,* or *Christian religious education.* Since I am referring to religious education done by and from within Christian community, I choose to use the term *Christian religious education.* This term simply identifies the Christian church's ministry of educating children in matters of the Christian faith. Since it is a cumbersome phrase, however, I will also refer simply to the church's *educational ministry.* For a fuller discussion on terminology, see Thomas Groome, *Christian Religious Education,* chapter 2.

13. In fact, Susan Johnson has proposed that the church's educational task should be understood primarily in terms of spiritual formation. See Susan Johnson, *Christian Spiritual Formation in the Church and Classroom* (Nashville: Abingdon, 1989). In contrast to Johnson's approach, it is not my intention to replace the church's educational ministry with spiritual formation. Rather than substituting formation for education, I wish to supplement educational ministries by creating distinct conditions that can reveal the existing soulfulness of children. To use the term *spiritual formation* is problematic. It can presume a condescending approach to children inasmuch as adults then seek to *form* children rather than position themselves *alongside* children as children find and create spiritual meaning themselves. This is not to suggest that formative processes should be absent, but that they be suspended sufficiently to allow for children's own inner lives to be manifested. Although children are not fully realized beings, we can approach our pastoral care with the presumption that children already bear within them the fullness and truth of God.

14. This phrase was coined by Iris Cully in her work *Christian Child Development* (San Francisco: Harper & Row, 1979), 69.

15. Young children are often confused by the difference between God and Jesus. God is usually anthropomorphic, but children can accept that God can be both far away (in heaven or up in the sky) and close at hand (able to protect as a parent). God is seen as one who cares in watchful fashion for the child, everything, and everyone. Jesus is also

identified as someone loving and concerned to help children. Generally, Jesus is understood by children to be a human person and is often thought of as a friend, companion, and someone to imitate. Many children pray to Jesus as well as to God. Unless helped to make the connection, they do not often grasp that the baby Jesus in the manger is the same grown-up Jesus who died on a cross. There also can be confusion in children's minds about how Jesus lives both on earth and in heaven.

16. This illustration is given by Sofia Cavalletti in her book *The Religious Potential of the Child* (Chicago: Liturgy Training, 1992), 36.

17. Cavalletti, *The Religious Potential of the Child*, 37.

18. Cavalletti citing A. Frossard's work, in which it was said, "There are none so truly metaphysical as children," *The Religious Potential of the Child*, 46.

19. Matthew 18:1-4.

20. Anderson and Johnson use the metaphor *childness* to capture the difference between being *childlike* and retaining qualities of *being* a child in adult life. They suggest that vulnerability, openness, immediacy, and neediness are qualities of *childness* that must endure in the adult struggle toward childhood. *Regarding Children*, 10.

21. John Westerhoff, *Will Our Children Have Faith?* (New York: Seabury, 1976), 55.

22. I am borrowing Sofia Cavelletti's use of the term *atrium* that is based on her extensive research with catechetical methods with young children. In fact, Cavelletti borrows Maria Montessori's earlier use of the term, which was assigned to the physical environment dedicated to the child's religious life. Cavelletti, *The Religious Potential of the Child*, 56.

23. A recent article in a Canadian newspaper described a new Jewish museum in Toronto that was created for young children. It has similarities to the atrium experience that I am recommending, and it is interesting to note that such an experience is being emphasized in a religious tradition other than the Christian tradition. In this Jewish museum, young children tour several rooms that give them real, participatory experiences of prayer, Jewish holidays, customs, the Hebrew language, and the sacred presence of God. Children stand before a miniature Wailing Wall that bears the wishes of today's children and to which they may add their own prayers. They can unroll a flannel Torah and place felt pieces on it to depict stories contained within the five books of Moses. They can hear an adult's explanation of a particular story from the Hebrew Scriptures, or climb on Noah's ark and curl up to listen to the recorded story. In a play kitchen called Shabbat Table, children can set up a proper sabbath meal, braid a challah loaf, set up the special candlesticks and kiddush cup, and practice saying the blessings with the help of a grown-up. *Belleville Intelligencer*, 15 February 1999, 9.

24. In giving this example of an atrium ritual, I am drawing upon the earlier approach of Sofia Cavelletti and the later work of Sonja Stewart and Jerome Berryman, *Young Children and Worship* (Louisville: Westminster John Knox, 1989), which they dedicated to Cavelletti. More recently, a program called "Children in Worship" (developed by Stewart and Berryman for children ages four to seven in the Christian Reformed Church in North America, The Reformed Church in America, and the Presbyterian Church in Canada) presents biblical stories in such a way as to help young children experience as well as learn about God. In contrast to Cavelletti, Stewart, and Berryman, I am not proposing an educational curriculum, but a methodology for caring pastorally for the souls of young children.

25. This is an example of what I mean by selecting a passage that will not necessarily present the text in its entirety but will still retain a sense of the passage as complete. Verses

1-3a and 7-10a may best be left until dealing with older children, since it is not advisable to mention the wolf or the hireling when engaging young children.

26. Cavalletti, *The Religious Potential of the Child*, 140.

27. Sara Juengst, *Sharing Faith with Children* (Louisville: Westminster John Knox, 1994), 71–3.

28. It can be argued that parables are more world-shattering and world-making events than about rational meaning. For adults to inquire about their meaning may be to ask the wrong questions of the parable.

29. In describing communication patterns that help children talk, William Van Ornum and John Mordock claim that "asking children to describe how two people or two events differ from each other is more productive than asking a general question." *Crisis Counseling with Children and Adolescents* (New York: Continuum, 1983), 35.

30. Thomas Williamsen, *Attending Parishioner's Spiritual Growth* (Washington, D.C.: Alban, 1997), 8–9.

chapter 7

1. If men entering the priesthood are removed from the statistics, it is clear that the primary clientele for spiritual direction are women.

2. Spiritual Directors International is a prominent and growing ecumenical network committed to fostering the ministry of spiritual direction and the ongoing development of spiritual directors—men and women, lay and ordained—in the Christian community. In March 1996, it produced a *working document* for a three-year period and in 1999 published in booklet form a code of ethics for Spiritual Directors. The "Guidelines for Ethical Conduct" are intended to be given to directees and to inspire spiritual directors toward integrity, responsibility, and faithfulness in the practice of spiritual direction. More information about Spiritual Directors International and their guidelines for ethical conduct can be obtained by contacting their web site at www.sdiworld.org. For an interesting discussion on malpractice considerations for spiritual directors, see Timothy Brown and Harriet Learson's article "Should Spiritual Directors be Licensed?" in *Review for Religious* (Sept.–Oct. 1990), 653–63.

3. Kenneth Leech, *Spirituality and Pastoral Care* (Cambridge, Mass.: Cowley, 1989), 79.